W9-DEX-169

WOODROW WILSON CENTER SERIES

The politics of elections in Southeast Asia

Though most governments in Southeast Asia are widely described as authoritarian, elections have been a feature of politics in the region for many decades. This volume, bringing together ten separate case studies by leading authorities, examines the countries that have conducted multiparty elections since the 1940s—Indonesia, Malaysia, the Philippines, Thailand, Cambodia, Burma/Myanmar, and Singapore. It identifies the common and distinguishing features of electoral politics in the region. The contributors to this volume, unlike most earlier students of politics in Southeast Asia, conclude that it is not something peculiar to the political culture of the region that shapes its political behavior. It is, rather, the same forces and structures that shape politics in North America and Europe.

Other books in the series

Continued on page following index

The politics of elections in Southeast Asia

Edited by
R. H. Taylor

WOODROW WILSON CENTER PRESS

AND

CAMBRIDGE
UNIVERSITY PRESS

Published by the Woodrow Wilson Center Press and
the Press Syndicate of the University of Cambridge
The Pitt Building, Trumpington Street, Cambridge CB2 1RP
40 West 20th Street, New York, NY 10011-4211, USA
10 Stamford Road, Oakleigh, Melbourne 3166, Australia

© The Woodrow Wilson International Center for Scholars 1996

First published 1996

Printed in the United States of America

Library of Congress Cataloging-in-Publication Data
The politics of elections in Southeast Asia
edited by R.H. Taylor.
p.   cm.—(Woodrow Wilson Center series)
Includes index.
ISBN 0-521-56404-2 (hc).—ISBN 0-521-56443-3 (pbk.)
1. Asia, Southeastern—Politics and government—1945–
2. Elections—Asia, Southeastern.   I. Taylor, Robert H., 1943–
II. Series.
DS526.7.P654   1966
324.959'053—dc20   95-53038
                                                    CIP

A catalog record for this book is available from the British Library.

ISBN 0-521-56404-2 hardback
ISBN 0-521-56443-3 paperback

WOODROW WILSON INTERNATIONAL CENTER FOR SCHOLARS

BOARD OF TRUSTEES

Joseph H. Flom, Chairman; Dwayne O. Andreas, Vice Chairman.
Ex Officio Members: Secretary of State, Secretary of Health and Human Services, Secretary of Education, Chairman of the National Endowment for the Humanities, Secretary of the Smithsonian Institution, Librarian of Congress, Director of the U.S. Information Agency, Archivist of the United States.
Private-Citizen Members: James A. Baker III, Joseph A. Cari, Jean L. Hennessey, Gertrude Himmelfarb, Carol Iannone, Eli Jacobs, Paul Hae Park, S. Dillon Ripley.
Designated Appointee of the President: Anthony Lake.

The Center is the living memorial of the United States of America to the nation's twenty-eighth president, Woodrow Wilson. Congress established the Woodrow Wilson Center in 1968 as an international institute for advanced study, "symbolizing and strenghening the fruitful relationship between the world of learning and the world of public affairs." The Center opened in 1970 under its own board of trustees, which includes citizens appointed by the president of the United States, federal government officials who serve ex officio, and an additional representative named by the president from within the federal government.

In all its activities the Woodrow Wilson Center is a nonprofit, nonpartisan organization, supported financially by annual appropriations from Congress and by the contributions of foundations, corporations, and individuals.

WOODROW WILSON CENTER PRESS

The Woodrow Wilson Center Press publishes books written in substantial part at the Center or otherwise prepared under its sponsorship by fellows, guest scholars, staff members, and other program participants. Conclusions or opinions expressed in Center publications and programs are those of the authors and speakers and do not necessarily reflect the views of the Center staff, fellows, trustees, advisory groups, or any individuals or organizations that provide financial support to the Center.

Woodrow Wilson Center Press
Editorial Offices
370 L'Enfant Promenade, S.W., Suite 704
Washington, D.C. 20024-2518
telephone: (202) 287-3000, ext. 218

Contents

Tables

Contributors

BENEDICT R. ANDERSON is Aaron L. Binenkorb Professor of International Studies in the Department of Government at Cornell University.

SUCHIT BUNBONGKARN is professor and dean of the Faculty of Political Science at Chulalongkorn University.

HAROLD CROUCH is senior fellow in politics in the Department of Political and Social Change in the Research School of Pacific and Asian Studies of the Australian National University.

KATE G. FRIESON is a member of the Department of Pacific and Asian Studies of the University of Victoria.

JOMO K. S. is professor of economics in the Faculty of Economics and Administration at the University of Malaya.

BENEDICT J. TRIA KERKVLIET is professor in the Department of Political and Social Change in the Research School of Pacific and Asian Studies of the Australian National University.

ANEK LAOTHAMATAS is professor in the Faculty of Political Science of Thammasat University.

DANIEL S. LEV is professor in the Department of Political Science at the University of Washington.

R. WILLIAM LIDDLE is professor in the Department of Political Science at Ohio State University.

GARRY RODAN is senior research fellow at the Asia Research Centre of Murdoch University.

R. H. TAYLOR is professor of politics and pro-director of the School of Oriental and African Studies of the University of London.

Acknowledgments

In addition to the contributors to this volume, I owe a debt of thanks to many individuals who assisted in one way or another in its production. John Dunn, Sudipta Kaviraj, and Alexander Magno contributed papers and comments of critical importance to the development of all our ideas. Our thinking and the revising of the papers after the September 1993 conference were enriched by their comparative perceptions.

Toby Alice Volkman, then on the staff of the Social Science Research Council (SSRC), as well as the members of the Southeast Asia Committee of the SSRC and the American Council of Learned Societies, was most helpful in shaping and developing the original idea for the book. I learned a great deal from their advice.

Mary Brown Bullock, former director of the Asia Program, and the staff of the Asia Program of the Woodrow Wilson Center in Washington, D.C., where the original conference was held, were extraordinarily helpful in arranging the conference and seeing the book through to completion. Among others at the Woodrow Wilson Center, Joseph Brinley and Carolee Belkin Walker of the Woodrow Wilson Center Press were most helpful.

Financial support for the project was provided by both the Social Science Research Council and the Woodrow Wilson Center. Thanks are owed to these farsighted providers of support for social science research and publication.

Introduction

Elections and politics in Southeast Asia

R. H. TAYLOR

"General elections," wrote Sir Lewis Namier, "are the locks on the stream of British democracy, controlling the flow of the river and its traffic." His point can be generalized to the histories of all Western democratic nations. In each country's elections those who seek to direct its public affairs must defend their records and convince the voters that the policies they propose for the future are feasible, desirable, and best carried out by those who propose them. The office seekers try to show that their opponents' policies are ill conceived and that their past failures in office make them poor bets for managing the government in the future. The voters consider the competing cases and make their decisions. Their votes are cast and counted, the candidates elected take office, and a new government is formed or an existing one renewed.[1]

The moment the election was called it was every man for himself. The by-election had been a spectacle, a sort of one-day cricket match where the nation watched from the pavilion. Now the match was everywhere, and in that action-stations mood anything went. The Election Commission, that genteel cricket board, watched helplessly as government vehicles were used for campaigning, vats of election hooch were brewed, and rival goonda gangs fought pitched battles. In this electoral match it was the sponsors who won, whatever the scoreboard might read at the end of the day. The winners strode the field, but afterwards they championed their paymasters. We who queued at the ticket booths simply went home to our lives. In the end I found that politics *was* a game—a party game—but business was in earnest. Who paid the piper called the tune. The general election was a mass forgetting of this simple law, a willing suspension of healthy disbelief.[2]

---

[1] David Butler, Howard R. Penniman, and Austin Ranney, "Introduction: Democratic and Nondemocratic Elections" in David Butler et al., eds., *Democracy at the Polls: A Comparative Study of Competitive National Elections* (Washington: American Enterprise Institute for Public Policy Research, 1981), 1. The quotation comes from Sir Lewis Namier, *Avenue of History* (London: Hamish Hamilton, 1952), 183.
[2] I. Allan Sealy, *Hero* (London: Secker and Warburg, 1990), 231–2.

1

These two quotations provide us with starkly contrasting views of the same modern and now nearly universal phenomenon: "national" or general elections. The first, in the language of political science, states what an election is, as conceived in formal democratic theory as developed from British historical experience.[3] The second, in the language of an Indian novelist, provides an alternative description of the same phenomenon: one that points to a range of electoral purposes that have nothing to do with the rational choice of the individual citizen implicit in the first. How can we account for the difference? Neither statement fully matches what little we know of elections in Southeast Asia. What does the historical experience of politics in that region show about the nature of elections when examined against these alternatives?

FUNCTIONS OF ELECTIONS

The issues raised by the role and functions of elections in society are of interest not only for theoretical reasons but also because policymakers, Western governments, and much world opinion currently hold that democratic elections are the sine qua non of good government. This perception is often based on contradictory assumptions and rarely on empirical observation. More often it is premised on theoretical or ideologically based preconceptions or expectations and desires.[4]

The current debates in Southeast Asian studies, similar to arguments advanced in relation to Latin America, Eastern Europe, and the former Soviet Union, as to whether economic development and changing class structures in Thailand, Malaysia, Indonesia, Singapore, and the Philippines, centering on the rise of both independent capital and an emerging business- and consumer-oriented middle class, must lead to the development of less authoritarian polities rarely, if ever, consider the role of

---

[3]Curiously, though the volume from which this quotation comes is a study of elections in 28 countries including India, Israel, Japan, Sri Lanka, and Turkey, the authors refer to democracy as only part of the "histories of all *Western* democratic nations." Emphasis added.

[4]Murray Edelman is instructive on this point: "The conspicuous scheduling of an election in a third world country known for its despotic rule is accepted as evidence of a turn toward democracy. Political maneuver thrives upon publicized actions that mean less than meets the eye. A closely related gesture entails the presentation of a development that benefits a particular group as one that serves everyone." Murray Edelman, *Constructing the Political Spectacle* (Chicago: University of Chicago Press, 1988), 24–5.

the central formal institution of democratic government, namely, elections.[5] Conversely, the largely unquestioned thesis of most Western observers of the struggle for economic reform in Vietnam and Burma/Myanmar inevitably links the holding of "free and fair elections" and the creation of a pluralist democratic system of government as a necessary, if not a prerequisite, condition for successful and lasting economic reform.

These contradictory analyses of the relative importance of formal elections in relation to the formation of liberal polities and economic development fail to acknowledge how, in practice, elections have been a regular feature of Southeast Asian politics since the 1940s and, in some cases, earlier. But here another paradox arises. With the partial exception of the Philippines prior to Marcos's declaration of martial law in 1972, and the 1975 and 1995 parliamentary elections in Thailand, elections for presidents or legislatures have never directly caused a change of government. Nor has any incumbent party ever lost a referendum or plebiscite. So why do Southeast Asian governments bother to hold elections? What functions and whose interests do they serve?

UNEXAMINED ASSUMPTIONS ABOUT THE ROLE OF ELECTIONS

The conventional answers to these questions usually take one of the following forms: (1) Elections are essential legitimizing acts in the eyes of capitalist democracies with aid to dispense, which for reasons of their own domestic politics and personal ideals wish to be seen assisting fellow, or at least struggling, democracies. (2) Elections were accepted by the Westernized nationalist leaders of postindependence states as modern and were often required by the withdrawing colonial power. (3) Popular doctrine and opinion in nationalist movements explicitly articulated a view that independence meant government by the people, or democracy, and elites shared this view. (4) Elections were seen, as in democratic theory, as a way of allowing the expression of diverse, but not ultimately destructive or confrontational, interests and cultures in pluralistic societies, preserving the rights of minorities while championing the power of the majority. These points, all derived from formal theories of democracy, seem irrele-

---

[5]See, for example, the discussion in Richard Tanter and Kenneth Young, eds., *The Politics of Middle Class Indonesia* (Clayton, Victoria: Monash Papers on Southeast Asia No. 19, 1990).

vant to the actual practice of domestic politics when occasionally mentioned in most of the literature on politics in Southeast Asia.[6]

Despite the ineluctably authoritarian caste to Indonesian, Thai, Burmese, Vietnamese, Malaysian, Singaporean, and Filipino politics now
and during most of the past four decades and longer, no governing elite
has ever abandoned the idea of elections. Elections have been held regularly, and few leaders have attempted to adopt the fascist pose of the
people's leader through undetermined will. Not only are elections held,
but they are taken seriously. Massive amounts of money are spent mobilizing voters and organizing polls. The loss of one or two seats to the
opposition, where an opposition exists, results in pages of analysis and
predictions of doom by the ruling group, when it is obvious to all that
the election outcome has not shaken the formal position of the ruling
authorities one iota.[7]

[6]Herbert Feith makes clear in *The Decline of Constitutional Democracy in Indonesia* (Ithaca: Cornell University Press, 1962), 38–45, how central but inchoate the idea of democracy was in Indonesian nationalist thought. A recent American college text, Clark D.
Neher, *Southeast Asia in the New International Era* (Boulder: Westview, 1991), omits
"elections" from its index, though "democratization" gets a mention. A recent volume in
the growing literature on democracy in Asia, Africa, and Latin America, Larry Diamond,
Juan J. Linz, and Seymour Martin Lipset, eds., *Democracy in Developing Countries: Asia*
(Boulder: Lynne Rienner; London: Adamantine, 1989), contains two excellent accounts
of the ways in which theory and practice diverge in the region. See Chai-Anan Samudavanija, "Thailand: A Stable Semi-Democracy," 305–46, and Zakaria Haji Ahmad, "Malaysia: Quasi Democracy in a Divided Society," 347–82.
[7]Examples of these points are plentiful. Observe the behavior of Lee Kuan Yew after losing
one or two seats to the opposition in Singapore. Or of his successor following the August
31, 1991, Singapore elections. The stage-managed campaigning and near certainty of
result of Indonesian elections have often been commented on. Like De Gaulle, former
Thai Prime Minister Prem used to threaten an election if he did not get his way in parliament, curious behavior for a man who respected the will of the people as expressed by
their democratically elected representatives. The consequences of the February 23, 1991,
coup in Thailand, with the coup group's initial promise of elections in six months, indicates that Prem is not the only Thai who views elections as not the central institution of
politics but still insists upon them. Mahathir and the United Malays National Organization almost seem to dare the electorate to vote for the opposition. And in Burma, the
army in 1990 held an election widely seen as the "free-est and fairest" in the country's
history, declared it a success, and spent the next five years making certain that the elected
representatives did not meet to form a government—in the name of democracy.
    Edelman's observations about electoral practices and the generation of an opposition are
instructive. "The effective gesture of creating difference is the constitution of opposition for
an incumbent or aspiring leader. There is always a rival who represents a choice, an alternative course for the polity. Even in one-party states and totalitarian states where opposition is prohibited, the leader keeps constantly before the public an evocation of an
alternative that has allegedly brought disaster in the past or promises to do so in the future.
Political oppositions create each other by invoking the differences between them. Construction of symbols of that difference inevitably follows and helps reify the alternative. "A
somewhat similar contradiction holds where there are deep ideological differences, as in

If elections in Southeast Asia have not fulfilled the functions required of them in formal democratic theory, why have electorates turned out in large numbers on polling days to cast their ballots after following the campaigns and their personalities with apparent interest?[8] Being involved in the process of governance, even if vicariously, might be one explanation. The prospect of reward for backing the winner might be another. Also, patron-client relationships, administrative pressures, corporatist-like desires for organizational solidarity and control, and similar inducements may be present.[9]

Related to the question of what elections do are issues arising from other formal democratic institutions, such as parliaments and constitutions. If constitutions are not documents revered and adhered to despite the consequences for the rulers but, rather, formally or, more often informally, altered and amended to fit their momentary requirements, why bother to have them? Similarly, the legislature is, after all, from the point of view of the ruler, largely an expensive nuisance that must be kept in check to forestall any political threat to his or her power. Since few legislatures in Southeast Asia, again with the exception of the Philippines, have actually ever proposed, let alone passed, any program or policy contrary to the wishes of the head of government or state, why bother?

RELATIONSHIP BETWEEN ELECTIONS AND DEMOCRACY

Clearly, elections are important but perhaps for reasons different from those asserted in formal democratic theory. It may be that Namier's *"locks* on the stream of democracy" might have a different meaning in the context of contemporary political practice. The legitimacy that the

---

the case of leaders of democracies who define themselves in terms of their differences from leaders of dictatorships or from their radical critics. Here the very intensity of the focus upon opposition induces antagonists to act in ways that emulate the other. Democratic leaders become so preoccupied with talk of subversion or invasion that they place a higher priority upon security and regimentation than upon civil rights and public participation. By the same token, despotic leaders worry about the attraction of foreign ideologies and so claim they are building 'true' democracies and may establish a facade of democratic procedures." Edelman, *Constructing the Political Spectacle,* 49–50.

[8]See the discussion of one such campaign in John Pemberton, "Notes on the 1982 General Election in Solo," *Indonesia* 41 (April 1986): 1–22.

[9]These explanations are similar to those given in the second quotation from the Indian novelist: the involvement of money, the joy of participation, and the suspension of belief, none of which is accounted for in formal theory.

electoral process, as well as electoral victory, provides ruling elites would seem to be obvious. But when electorates are aware of manipulated campaign procedures, when law and practice do not provide a level playing field but, rather, distort the process strongly in favor of the incumbents, what kind of legitimacy is created?[10] The electoral process does carry within it the promise of popular control of the state. Will the continued practice of elections eventually change a state's nature and make it genuinely open to contests of the kind postulated by formal theory? If this is too much to hope for, might they not at least lead to the emergence of regimes more attentive to the rights and views of citizens? Or to the emergence of citizens who will demand their democratic rights against authoritarian rulers?

Questions such as these obviously arise when we begin to think about the role of elections in Southeast Asian polities. Others also become apparent, such as those of the relation between elections and the types of authoritarian regimes that exist, the nature of party systems, and the relative levels of economic development that exist among the region's polities. It is often postulated that a high level of economic development is a prerequisite for the holding of democratic elections. That proposition needs to be tested by examining whether there is any correlation between economic structure or wealth and electoral behavior in the region. But these questions may obscure the possibility that elections are held to ensure a sense of powerlessness on the part of the electorate.[11]

The generalized nature of patron-client relations throughout Southeast Asia poses a comparative point of departure for electoral studies and

---

[10]James C. Scott notes the call for election boycott as a means of denying the legitimacy of the electoral process and of a regime when an opposition believes an election to be fraudulent or meaningless. (*Domination and the Arts of Resistance: Hidden Transcripts* [New Haven and London: Yale University Press, 1990], 46.) Though election boycott was frequently advocated in colonial Burma, it does not seem to have been advocated successfully in postcolonial Southeast Asia.

[11]"Audience interpretations of the spectacle are manifestly constrained in some measure by what is reported, what is omitted and, perhaps more fundamentally, by the implications in news reports respecting limits upon the ability of citizens to influence policy. In subtle ways the public is constantly reminded that its role is minor, largely passive, and at most reactive. The intense publicity given to voting and elections is itself a potent signal of the essential powerlessness of political spectators because elections are implicitly a message about the *limits* of power. Everyone who grows up in our society is bound to become aware, at some level of consciousness, that an individual vote is more nearly a form of self-expression and of legitimation than of influence and that the link between elections and value allocations is tenuous. The reiteration in patriotic oratory and grade school civics lessons that people control the government comes to be recognized as a way of insuring support for government actions people dislike and over which they exercise no effective control." Edelman, *Constructing the Political Spectacle*, 97.

democratic theory based on the experience of North American and European industrial democracies. Although elections may be exercises in creating national solidarity and social inclusion, as well as opportunities for civic education, the liberal sociological assumptions of such contentions stand in contrast to the historically postulated, organic nature of patron-clientalist Southeast Asian societies. Although the electoral act holds up the principle of atomized individual free choice in politics, as the market does in economics, this might actually destabilize, rather than reinforce, the existing social order, at least from the perspectives of dominant elites.

THE COMPARATIVE STUDY OF
ELECTIONS IN SOUTHEAST ASIA

The questions one can ask about elections are universal, not specific to Southeast Asia. The regional cases included in this volume are part of a global phenomenon, now nearly universal, and integral to the nature of the modern secular constitutional republic. Much of what we say about elections in Southeast Asia must therefore apply to what we say about elections in Europe, America, and the remainder of the globe. The essays brought together here are attempts to answer some of the questions raised about the role of elections in modern politics.[12] A number of conclusions emerge from these analyses.

First, and perhaps most important, given the contingent nature of electoral politics in any society, is the fact that the nature of the first election of a prolonged series establishes the ground rules for the conduct of subsequent "national-level" politics. All of the authors, but particularly Benedict R. Anderson in his opening comparative essay, make clear that having access to government and being acceptable to those already in power is essential not only for believing in the legitimacy of electoral

[12]The essays were originally presented as papers at a conference organized at the Woodrow Wilson Center in conjunction with the Southeast Asia Committee of the Social Science Research Council and the American Council of Learned Societies in September 1993. In addition to the papers reprinted here, contributions were also received from Alexander R. Magno, University of the Philippines; Sudipta Kaviraj, School of Oriental and African Studies, University of London; and John Dunn, University of Cambridge. Their contributions were especially important in broadening the discussion in order to understand more fully the role of elections historically and analytically. Since the conference was held, elections have taken place in Thailand, the Philippines, and Malaysia. The results of those exercises further confirm the conclusions reached in the papers.

politics but also for having any chance of gaining power through the ballot box.

This fact leads to a corollary: Elections are double-edged weapons in the rise of democracy and in the formation of a dominant, stable, and permanent political order. On the one hand, they are pacifying instruments. They are often means of depoliticizing populations, limiting the politically possible to formalized campaigns and episodic voting opportunities. This usually follows the elimination of the left or other groups unwilling to accept a secular republican definition of the modern political world. On the other hand, in circumstances where narrow, aging, ineffectual regimes have effectively lost touch with, or alienated, the bulk of the population, elections can provide a lever for prying open and widening the sphere of legitimate political activity by demonstrating the illegitimacy of the old regime. The essay on Burma illustrates this point. It remains to be demonstrated, however, whether such elections provide an opportunity for genuinely new groups to enter politics or are merely the means by which a faction that previously lost influence within the regime can regain influence or control.

This difference in perspective is related in part to how one views an election. As political phenomena, elections can look different from the perspective of those in power at the top and those with little or no power at the bottom of a polity. Elections hold out a threat and an opportunity to both these groups; their effectiveness in the eyes of both is a function of whether they succeed in pacifying or not. The degree to which the electoral process is perceived to be fair and honest has a bearing here. How fraudulent does an electoral process have to be before it denies legitimacy? Garry Rodan's discussion of electoral politics in Singapore, as well as R. William Liddle's analysis of the bases of electoral legitimacy in Indonesia and Jomo K. S.'s of the role of money in Malaysia, is instructive on this point.

In order to understand the meaning and role of elections in any society, one needs to contextualize the election process. Elections have meaning only within a particular historical space and time, and to see them outside their context is to deny them any significant meaning. Discovering the meaning of elections is a genuine comparative project. Suchit Bunbongkarn's and Anek Laothamatas's essays on contemporary interpretations of democracy and elections in Thailand illustrate dramatically how the meaning and role of elections can be interpreted differently by different social groups in the same political structures—with potentially disastrous implications for the stability of elected regimes. But, as Harold Crouch argues about Malaysia, elections can also ensure that regimes remain responsive to the changing perceptions of significant social groups.

Elections in Southeast Asia, as in most of the Asian and African world, have accompanied, rather than been a consequence of, the rise of the modern bureaucratic state, the idea of the nation, capitalism, and industrialization as happened historically in Europe and North America. Therefore, the "burden" elections are expected to carry in Southeast Asian history is much greater than in European and American history. This is an essential point about the context of elections in the region. Elections in Southeast Asia also developed when several models of electoral life were available—American two-party presidential, Soviet one-party communist, European multiparty parliamentary.

All the studies in this volume concentrate on real or state-managed two- or multiparty electoral processes, like those we think we are familiar with in North America and Europe. Excluded from consideration here is the study of the role and meaning of elections in Vietnam, where the Communist Party has held up an alternative model of electoral politics that fundamentally denies the legitimacy of multiparty politics. This reminds us that the acceptance of the concept of electoral competition carries with it a large number of assumptions about the nature of society and how it should be organized for life, production, and consumption.

The concept of an election is essentially an individualizing notion. It assumes that various class, status, and other social identities and forms of action are less real and significant in political life than many people believe. Elections require people to think of themselves as momentarily atomized, if only during the time they are in the voting booth. The concept of individual choice in the ballot box, however, often flies in the face of political realities outside it, where job, family, security, socialized beliefs, or other factors impinge on perceptions of political choice.

There is what can be described as a "teleological pull" to elections and all that goes with them. It is difficult to imagine the present world without elections, because they combine so many aspects of modern notions of political life, even in the face of many other political, social, and economic realities. We all read about elections in other countries in our daily papers. As Kate G. Frieson writes in her essay on Cambodia, when the United Nations sought to establish peace in that war-torn and fractured society, the primary vehicle it could imagine to use for that purpose was an election. But as she shows, to many Cambodians that process carried a number of meanings other than, and perhaps contrary to, those intended in New York.

Elections in Southeast Asia and the rest of Asia and Africa are not indigenous. Although there may be some historical evidence of lots cast three thousand years ago in Asia Minor, this hardly measures in any-one's memory. How are elections indigenized? Or are they? Is the indi-genization process part of the defanging of the potential empowerment of people held out by the notion of elections? "We do this thing this way here and always have, so shut up" is the answer often given to those who raise doubts about the appropriateness of prevailing political patterns.

In their ideal form, elections are means of resolving political conflicts without resorting to physical force. But they may be merely masks for coercion that is occurring or has taken place in a different context or a different time. In societies with intense levels of conflict, elections are probably meaningless because the fundamental conflict will be over what the election is about or who it is for, not who will win a particular race. Those able to participate hold out elections as acts of legitimacy; those who are denied or reject participation argue for their illegitimacy. But that is a political choice in itself, as Benedict J. Tria Kerkvliet notes in his discussion of the long history of electoral politics in the Philippines.

The current advocacy of elections as the sine qua non of democratic politics and good government needs to be examined in terms of who is expected to be the victors in these contests and which contests will be recognized as genuine. Elections are institutions that can encourage change in social attitudes by destroying patterns of deference and forcing elites to recognize the legitimacy of a "loyal" opposition. Both these processes individualize society while leveling political forces as they are brought into the legitimate, permitted sphere of political action. In the same way, elections cause affirmation of an identity people may not feel. The contest defines the players themselves and in relation to the other participants in the election.

Studied systemically in their specific and their universal circumstances, elections in Southeast Asia clarify important aspects of political, eco-nomic, and social change in the region. No longer able to legitimate themselves through claims of birth or right through might, ruling elites have found they must concede the importance of elections. New social groups and classes, new and old interests can attempt to use the opportunities elections offer for organization and discussion, even if greatly constrained by law and practice, to try to open further opportunities and rights for themselves. Successful elites have been able to manage this process through incorporation as well as coercion. Elections are indeed Janus-faced, both granting and constraining liberty, depending on the circumstances.

Elections should no longer be ignored in Southeast Asian studies. They provide a means for understanding the rise of new social classes and the fixed or changing locus of power in any society. The alleged uniqueness of various Southeast Asian cultures, however defined, can no longer be relied on as an explanation of the politics of the region. Students of the region need to study its politics on its own terms, but without ignoring the universal features to be found there.

Might it be that our recognition of the importance, but limited and constrained position, of elections in contemporary politics points to the possibility that elections may be in the process of being superseded in modern politics? If elections no longer provide a means for the circulation and renewal of elites, maybe something else is happening. Can we think of what it may be that allows elections to continue but as an even less effective vehicle of their democratic promise than was previously thought? Or is this going too far and merely an expression of our own discontents?

However we may wish to answer these questions for ourselves, the essays in this volume point in directions requiring further study and reflection, not only in Southeast Asia but throughout the world. For the future of Southeast Asian studies, Dan S. Lev's concluding comments are particularly significant. As he notes, what is striking about all of these studies is the fact that culture as an explanatory variable is not relied on to "save" the theses advanced. Any attempt to argue that one can understand Southeast Asian politics through analytical lenses different from those we would apply to our own societies is abandoned for a recognition that the same modern political forms and forces—but in their particular and specific contexts—shape, constrict, or expand all of our political lives.

1

Elections and participation in
three Southeast Asian countries

BENEDICT R. ANDERSON

GENERAL CONSIDERATIONS

"National"-level elections—that is, those designed to produce a legislative body with a status and jurisdiction formally nearly equal to that of the preexisting executive—are a quite recent innovation in Southeast Asia.[1] For the three countries under discussion in this essay, the relevant dates are 1907 for the Philippines, 1918 for the Netherlands East Indies (now Indonesia), and 1933 for Siam (now Thailand). In each case, the innovation came on the heels of, and was a clear response to, political crisis: in the Philippines to the anti-Spanish revolution of 1896–98, and a brutal, costly American "pacification" of the insurrectionary movement; in the Netherlands East Indies to a brief post–World War I revolutionary upsurge in the Netherlands itself, as well as the spectacular expansion of the Sarekat Islam on Java; and in Siam to the overthrow of the absolutist monarchy via the coup of June 24, 1932.

This pattern followed closely the one that can be observed in the historical evolution of the electoral mechanism in the areas from which it was imported to Southeast Asia, that is, Western Europe and the United States: In other words, the development of national-level legislatures and the expansion of the suffrage followed a certain democratization of political life rather than brought it into being. In the United States, we have

---

[1]In the colonized territories, there was, of course, no question of the colonial executive being elected or substantially answerable to the new legislatures. In uncolonized Siam, the monarch, after 1932, was supposed to be merely the head of state. Accountability began to develop, hesitantly, only as the executive branches were nationalized.

only to think of the woman suffrage and civil rights movements, with their elaborate repertoires of extraelectoral political activities, culminating in the passage of the Nineteenth Amendment in 1920 and the Civil Rights Act of 1965. In Europe, we remember the agitations that led to the summoning of the Estates-General and the Duma, as well as the political emancipation of Catholics in the early nineteenth century United Kingdom.

These precedents demonstrate rather clearly the Janus-face of electoralism. On the positive side, the right to vote in elections, even when they were scarcely free or competitive, was understood as the most signal emblem of full citizenhood in the modern age: It conveyed legal *status* and entitlement. Hence the irresistible push toward adult suffrage in polities moving toward self-definition as nation-states. (How important this aspect of things is can be seen from the reaction one could expect to a law that would deprive people of the vote if they did not exercise it over, say, a ten-year period.) The second key positive side of electoralism was the promise it held out, to the socially disadvantaged above all, of the enactment, in brief, decisive historical moments, of laws enforceable on every relevant site of struggle within the state's geographical stretch. Legislation would do at a sweep what a myriad of strikes, demonstrations, absenteeisms, featherbeddings, sit-ins, marches, assassinations, and prayer meetings could not, precisely because the latter were inevitably local or regional, episodic, and without legal force. If one thinks of the series of laws passed between 1850 and 1950 in the United Kingdom forbidding child labor, protecting female workers, guaranteeing minimum wages, developing social security, legalizing trade unions and certain kinds of strikes—laws that had their parallels in most of Western Europe—the attraction of electoral politics is completely understandable. Furthermore, not only were such laws in place, but also, because they emerged from the electoral process rather than as boons granted by a paternalistic executive, they were understood as largely irreversible.

At the same time, confidence in the electoral process in Western Europe was also based on the general assumption that laws, once enacted by legislatures, would be nationally enforced and with reasonable impartiality. This assumption in turn derived from the preexistence of powerful, centralized bureaucracies, inherited from the age of absolutism and to varying degrees modernized as civil services in the aftermath of the

French Revolution. (The United States formed a striking exception to the pattern, with consequences for the Philippines to be discussed in that section.)

On the other side of the coin, one has only to remind oneself that the Civil Rights Act of 1965 was designed not merely to enfranchise millions of Southern Blacks, but also to put an end to, or to make obsolete, sit-ins, freedom marches, riots, and so forth. "After all, now you have the vote," Congress appeared to be saying. But normal voting is in many ways a peculiar activity. On a particular day, determined either by law or by government decision, between hours regulated by the same, at places settled on usually by local authorities, one joins a queue of people whom one does not typically know, to take a turn to enter a solitary space, where one pulls levers or marks pieces of paper, and then leaves the site with the same calm discretion with which one enters it—without questions being asked. It is almost the only political act imaginable in perfect solitude, and it is completely symbolic: It is thus almost the polar opposite of all other forms of personal political participation. Insofar as it has general meaning, it acquires this meaning only by mathematical aggregation. From this perspective, one can readily conclude that, under normal circumstances, the logic of electoralism is in the direction of domestication: distancing, punctuating, isolating. If one asks in whose interests this domestication occurs, one comes immediately to the question of "representation."

It is, of course, notorious that the socioeconomic and gender profiles of elected legislatures differ enormously from those of their electorates: For example, legislators are almost invariably much richer and much better educated, as well as far more likely to be male, than their constituents. The reasons for this wide discrepancy are well known and need not detain us here. The point to be underscored is rather that one effect of electoralism is in the direction of confining active and regular political participation to specialists—professional politicians—who not only have a strong interest in their institutionalized oligopoly, but who are largely drawn from particular social strata, most often the middle and upper-middle classes. If one therefore considers that electoral systems open to those groups that accept its terms are as characteristic of bourgeois political dominance as absolutist monarchies are characteristic of aristocratic hegemony, then one is probably well positioned to reflect comparatively on electoralism in modern Southeast Asia.

SIAM

Elections were inaugurated in Siam in the wake of the overthrow of the absolutist monarchy in a bloodless coup organized by a small conspiratorial group of military and civilian commoners. Most of these commoners were government officials, and the prime animus for the conspiracy was the near monopoly of top bureaucratic positions, especially in the armed services, by mediocre members of the royal family and related aristocratic lineages.[2] But the coup group's formal claims to legitimacy rested on both its nationalism and its inauguration of constitutional democracy.

At the same time, the economic and social structure of Siam in the 1930s made the second of these claims largely nugatory. The country's good fortune in not being directly colonized and the conservative policies pursued by Rama V (r. 1868–1910), which together helped to shelter much of the Thai agricultural population from the direct impact of capitalism, meant that what nonbureaucratic bourgeoisie existed in the 1930s was substantially of immigrant-Chinese origins, like the still very small working class. Furthermore, literacy was then very little advanced. It was only in the 1920s that a law on compulsory primary education was promulgated; and it was so casually enforced that in only one-fifth of the country's provinces had more than half the population completed primary schooling by the end of the 1950s.[3] In effect the social basis for serious electoralism did not yet exist. Hence, the suffrage was restricted, and a large proportion of the early legislators were appointed. Under these circumstances it is not surprising that the army, the most powerful arm of the state, quickly became dominant, and the rule in Thai politics up until the 1970s was military dictatorship, more or less thinly disguised.

This situation did not begin to change until the era of Marshal Sarit Thanarat's dictatorship (1958–63) and the onset of the Vietnam War. At the prodding of the World Bank, the Thai government dismantled many inefficient state corporations and opened the country far more extensively than before to foreign capital. Bangkok's close relationship

---

[2]See Benjamin A. Batson, *The End of the Absolute Monarchy in Siam* (Singapore: Oxford University Press, 1984); and Thawatt Mokarapong, *History of the Thai Revolution* (Bangkok: Thai Watana Panich, 1972).
[3]Harvey H. Smith, et al., *Area Handbook for Thailand* (Washington, D.C.: U.S. Government Printing Office, 1968), 161.

with Washington meant a huge infusion of funds for—aside from expanding and equipping the armed forces and the police—infrastructural and communications development. At the same time, an enormous increase in institutions of higher education quintupled the student population within one decade. As a result, a new nongovernmental middle class was created, which encompassed both the assimilated children of the old Chinese bourgeoisie as well as ethnic Thai, while the working class essentially became Thai rather than Chinese. By the early 1970s Japanese capital investment was overtaking American, and an extraordinary economic boom began that has continued with only minor interruptions to the present day.[4]

While the social and economic bases for bourgeois democracy were thus quietly being established, the political structure began to show signs of unraveling in the later 1960s. The ironfisted Sarit had drunk himself to death in 1963, and his two lieutenants, Marshals Thanom Kittikajon and Praphat Jarusathian, did not have his decisive ruthlessness. Increasingly close ties with the United States as the Vietnam War deepened led to the stationing of almost 50,000 American military personnel on Thai soil by 1968. Their presence—inevitably bringing with it ostentatious prostitution, births of Amerasian children, the spread of modernized drug trafficking—aroused a growing nationalist reaction. The American presence also provoked Peking and Hanoi to encourage a hitherto rather tame Thai Communist Party to begin a rural guerrilla movement with which the Thai military found it increasingly difficult to deal. Thai youngsters sent to the United States for advanced study came substantially under the influence of the anti–Vietnam War movement, with its bitter criticism of Washington's mercenary, authoritarian satellite regimes in East and Southeast Asia.

In the palmy days of the late 1950s Sarit found it quite easy to abolish both the existing constitution and the legislature, and not to make even the pretense of holding elections. But in the late 1960s, with the demise of this *esprit fort*, the Thanom-Praphat government responded to growing internal and external pressures by writing itself a conservative constitution and by reestablishing elections. It was a sign of the times that while the dictators patched together an election machine that, backed by the territorial military, the police, and the ministry of the interior,

[4]The processes sketched out in this paragraph are elaborated on and documented in my "Withdrawal Symptoms: Social and Cultural Aspects of the October 6 Coup," *Bulletin of Concerned Asian Scholars* 9, no. 3 (July–September 1977): 13–30.

won them a large majority in the rural areas, they were overwhelmingly defeated in Bangkok, the capital of the new Thai and Sino-Thai bourgeoisie, as well as of the bulk of the working class. When rivalries among military and bureaucratic cliques threatened the cohesion of the dictators' parliamentary majority, they responded in November 1971 by a seriocomic "self-coup" against their own creations—immediately after Kissinger's secret visit to Peking, and on the eve of Nixon's official visit there to rub noses with Chairman Mao. That Washington could deal so with so-called Red China—whose menace Thai military leaders had for a generation insisted on to the public—and moreover without notifying its "close ally" Siam, demoralized the regime and encouraged those who detested it. In the autumn of 1973 demands for a constitution and for elections, initiated by a small group of liberal students and university lecturers, quite suddenly snowballed into an extraordinary uprising that brought 500,000 persons out on the streets of Bangkok—militant political participation on a scale without even close precedents in Thai history.[5]

Although most student leaders insisted that the aims of the demonstrations that brought about the dictatorship's abrupt collapse and the ignominious flight of Thanom and Praphat were the restoration of constitutionalism and electoral democracy, there is no reason to suppose that these were the primary aims of most of the protesters. Under the interim regime of Professor Sanya, which lasted from mid-October 1973 to February 1975, the country experienced more, and more various, political participation than in any period before or since: Press censorship virtually disappeared to the delight of bourgeois editors, newsmen, and readerships; genuine trade unions were rapidly formed, pressing a host of demands by means of strikes and marches; peasant leagues were created to urge land reforms of various kinds; high school children demanded the expulsion of hated principals; all kinds of people insisted on the removal of the American military presence, and so on.

The elections finally held at the beginning of 1975 were certainly the most competitive that Siam has ever experienced and produced a parliament in which for the first time three moderately left-wing parties won a significant minority of seats. Probably as important, if not more so in

---

[5]The best sources for the activities described in this and the following three paragraphs are David Morell and Chai-anan Samudavanija, *Political Conflict in Thailand: Reform, Reaction, Revolution* (Cambridge, Mass.: Oelgeschlager, Gunn and Hain, 1981); and John L. S. Girling, *Thailand: Society and Politics* (Ithaca: Cornell University Press, 1981).

the longer run, was the fact that there was no government party managing the elections from within the Supreme Command and the Ministry
of the Interior. Hence there emerged a proliferation of conservative and
centrist parties, coalitions among which formed the bases of the two
politician-led cabinets holding power before the bloody events of October 6, 1976. These conditions permitted a very new horizontal
dispersion of power outside Bangkok, just as the "Great Boom" was
producing a new class of provincial entrepreneurs in many parts of the
country. For these people, bourgeois electoral democracy offered substantial benefits. A parliamentary seat opened direct access to governmental decisionmaking outside the centralized bureaucratic structures
before which these people had earlier always had to appear as clients.
One did not have to be well educated, or well connected in the capital,
or male in gender, to gain a seat: one simply had to have strong local
roots and plenty of money. (The vast expansion into the provinces of
powerful Bangkok banks in this period also opened up important new
credit opportunities.) By playing one's cards right, one could parlay all
this into a cabinet position (something unimaginable before) and then
use that cabinet position to enlarge one's financial resources and build
up further one's provincial power-base.[6]

The parliamentary regime of 1975–76 was not without its successes,
which included negotiating the withdrawal of American military personnel and creating a large fund for rural development (a response to the
new influence of provincial legislators), but it failed in its central pacificatory function. Strikes and demonstrations continued and gradually
became more violent because the cabinets were able neither to enact
serious labor or land-reform legislation nor to suppress the agitations.
In the spring of 1975 the anciens régimes in Indochina abruptly collapsed,
panicking the monarchy, the military, and the new bourgeoisie. Out of
this came the right-wing extraparliamentary mobilizations of 1976 and
a rising number of assassinations by hired professional gunmen of student activists, left-wing politicians, and labor and farm leaders.

The political polarization climaxed in the bloody events of October
6, 1976, which drove most of the legal left underground, or into the
jungle arms of the Communist Party (CPT), or into exile abroad. The
dictatorial regime installed after October 6 was, however, very unlike

[6]The argument in this and the following paragraphs is drawn from my longer article,
"Murder and Progress in Modern Siam," *New Left Review* 181 (May–June 1990): 33–
48.

those of 1958–73. The fragile outcome of complex bargaining between the military factions, the royal family, and right-wing professional politicians, it was headed by an extremist civilian judge who so angered the military that they deposed him within a year. For the first time in Thai history, an army coup was presented to the public as a blow for moderation and accommodation, as well as for the restoration by stages of a parliamentary regime.

At this juncture, the government of Siam had a remarkable stroke of luck. The Vietnamese invasion of Cambodia in December 1978 and the subsequent Sino-Vietnamese war encouraged Peking to ally itself with Bangkok in support of Pol Pot. Bangkok's price was the withdrawal of Chinese Communist Party support for the CPT (which, furthermore, by supporting Peking's anti-Hanoi policy, immediately lost its safe bases in Vietnam-dominated Laos and Cambodia). A hopelessly divided Thai left became demoralized and collapsed, and General Kriangsak Chomanan's government was shrewd enough to offer a general amnesty and to abide strictly by its terms. Hence by 1980, the crisis atmosphere of the later 1970s had fully dissipated. There was no longer a left to fear, and Bangkok had solid support in Washington, Peking, and Tokyo.

It was now the moment for a relieved Thai bourgeoisie to resume its struggle for political hegemony, primarily through sustained pressure for the restoration of regular elections and a parliamentary-controlled national executive. Elections were held quite regularly during the 1980s, producing parliaments with no representation of the Left and heavily dominated by provincial entrepreneurs.[7] While General Prem Tinsulanonda was Prime Minister for much of the decade, his cabinets were always based on coalitions of political parties. How solidly this new electoral system was coming to be entrenched is best demonstrated by three political novelties: (1) Powerful generals became eager to stand for election and serve in parliament (Kriangsak himself, Athit Kamlangek, Chaowalit Yongchaiyut, and others); (2) A new style of political assassination appeared, targeting not students, trade unionists, and farmer-association leaders, but parliamentarians and would-be parliamentarians. These murders were typically carried out by gunmen hired by other parliamentarians and would-be parliamentarians—proving that in the 1980s the market value of futures in parliamentary seats had

---

[7]The best overall account of Thai politics in the 1980s is James Soren Ockey, "Business Leaders, Gangsters, and the Middle Class: Societal Groups and Civilian Rule in Thailand," (Ph.D. thesis, Cornell University, 1992).

soared astronomically; (3) The huge uprising of May 1991 against the regime of General Suchinda Kraprayoon was led by cellular-telephone–wielding capitalists and parliamentary politicians (including former senior military officers)—but not student activists or trade unionists.[8] Their aim was quite clear: the full restoration of an electorally based parliamentary regime, which they know suits their interests best, and which they can be confident of dominating. They are also fairly sure that in the present constellation of international and national forces, elections can finally fulfill their pacificatory promise.

At the same time, because the full emergence of bourgeois electoralism came historically well after the development (from the end of the last century) of a centralized bureaucracy, capable, more or less, of executing national policy, there is the possibility of the other side of Janus coming to the fore: that is, that meaningful legislation in the sphere of labor, social welfare, land law, and so forth, could some day be administratively implemented into irreversible social gains. In this sense, electoral democracy holds out some genuine prospects in the longer run.

THE PHILIPPINES

National-level elections were introduced in the Philippines by its American conquerors in 1907. The immediate background for this innovation was Asia's first modern revolution, the successful insurrectionary movement launched in 1896 against Spanish rule, which began in the environs of Manila and later spread through much of Luzon and tangentially into parts of the Visayas. While the movement was led largely by small-town notables and provincial gentry, it also involved widespread participation of the popular classes and by women and adolescents, as well as by adult males. Hence the Americans' counterrevolutionary intervention required a ruthless military campaign that may have cost up to a quarter of a million Filipino lives. But colonial policymakers recognized from the start that stable colonial rule required the creation of a class of Filipino

[8]In February 1991, ambitious leaders of Class 5 of the Thai military exploited anger within the armed forces at various policies of the civilian Chatchai Chunhawan government to stage a successful coup. Coup leader Suchinda installed a well-respected businessman and former diplomat as prime minister, promising not to assume this role himself. When he broke this promise in the spring of 1992, a bloody political crisis began that led to his fall and disgrace toward the end of May. Civilian government was then restored and confirmed by elections in the fall of 1992.

political leaders with a strong interest in collaboration with the conquerors and in the demobilization of the mass of the population.[9] They quickly decided that the first necessary step was the creation of a national legislature representing at least those areas of the colony where the revolutionary Republic of 1898 had drawn a following. (The Muslim far south was initially excluded.)

Naturally enough, the form of electoralism introduced was modeled, even if parodically, on America's own. It is useful to recall that in the first decade of the 20th century, the United States had arguably the most corrupt form of electoralism among all the industrial powers. Not only were women excluded from the vote, but so were millions of adult nonwhite males. Poll taxes and gerrymandering were widespread, to the benefit of courthouse cliques and urban machines. Violence, in the South and the West, was far more a part of electoral politics than in advanced Western Europe. Furthermore, the United States of that era was quite peculiar in the general absence of a national-level professional bureaucracy, such as had emerged in Britain, Sweden, Germany, or France.

Out of this background came the strange malignities of colonial-era electoralism (which in significant ways recall V. O. Key's classic study of politics in the American South during much the same era).[10] First of all, linguistic, property, and literacy qualifications were set so high in the Philippines that as late as the eve of World War II only about 14 percent of the adult population of the colony was entitled to vote. This mechanism effectively confined legitimate participation to the small stratum that commanded English or Spanish, and/or had substantial property. Second, the American system of single-member districts, with legal residence in those districts required of candidates, took on a peculiarly oligarchic hue from its linkage with the colony's ethnolinguistic heterogeneity. (Spanish had never become a lingua franca there, as it had in Latin America, and English was only just beginning to make inroads.) Hence cacique politicians could hunker down behind walls not only of local money-power and patron-client relations, but also of language.

---

[9]See especially the splendid essays by Ruby Paredes, Michael Cullinane, and Alfred McCoy, in Ruby B. Paredes, ed., *Philippine Colonial Democracy* (Quezon City: Ateneo de Manila Press, 1989); Peter Stanley's shrewd *A Nation in the Making: The Philippines and the United States, 1899–1921* (Cambridge, Mass.: Harvard University Press, 1974); and Glenn A. May, *Social Engineering in the Philippines* (Westport, Conn.: Greenwood Press, 1980).

[10]V. O. Key, Jr., *Southern Politics in State and Nation* (New York: Vintage, 1949).

(One recalls colonial master politician Manuel Quezon's frustration at having to have his public speeches translated only 100 miles north of Manila.)[11] This system had one further stabilizing advantage, which reminds us indirectly of Thai electoralism in the 1980s. It dispersed power horizontally across the archipelago, while concentrating it vertically: The provincial caciques were assured of more or less equal representation in Manila. A final malignity was the development of this decentralized system of oligarchy in tandem with the failure to create a professional central bureaucracy. Pre–Hatch Act American practice,[12] translated to the Philippines, produced a quickly Filipinized state machinery subordinate to congressional oligarchs, both more corrupt and less unitary than anywhere else in colonial Southeast Asia.

But political mechanisms in themselves were not enough to stabilize the colonial regime. The real cement to the emerging system was free economic access to the highest-tariff state of the advanced industrial world. The key crop was sugar, which could be sold in the United States at prices well above those on the world market, and which could be produced by a serf-like, miserably exploited work force at very small cost. Hence the rapid rise, in the American era, of hugely wealthy provincial sugar magnates. Other caciques profited by Washington's selling off of 400,000 acres of rich agricultural land confiscated from Spanish friars. Furthermore, their control of the colonial legislature enabled them to plunder the state treasury via such institutions as a quickly bankrupted Central Bank of the Philippines. Thus, thirty-five years of colonial elections to a national-level legislature failed to produce a single significant piece of legislation for the benefit of the Filipino population as a whole. All this made the American stabilization project exceptionally successful. Backward Malaya aside, the Philippines was the one important colony in Southeast Asia that, in the 1930s, had no serious nationalist movement.

[11]See Andrew B. Gonzalez, *Language and Nationalism: The Philippine Experience Thus Far* (Quezon City: Ateneo de Manila Press, 1980), 58, with documentary citations.
[12]Enacted in 1939, the Hatch Act was an unprecedentedly far-reaching law designed to establish a coherent merit-based national civil service by protecting it from being abused by powerful and unscrupulous politicians. To see how far American practice was from Northern European, and how close to Filipino, one might note that provisions of the Act prohibited threatening, intimidating, or coercing voters in national elections; forbade the current practices of promising and withholding certain kinds of employment and unemployment relief as a reward or punishment for political activity; and outlawed interference with the nomination and election of candidates to federal office by administrative servants of the United States.

During and immediately after World War II the Philippines plunged into a new participatory crisis. Under the Japanese Occupation, the American market for Philippine hacienda agriculture collapsed, electoral mechanisms were frozen, and a variety of armed guerrilla groups came into being, the most powerful of which (in Luzon) was led by a mix of communist and socialist activists. Furthermore, the independence that the American Congress, for its own reasons, had insisted on promising for 1946 could no longer be avoided. In the new world of the United Nations, a state becoming independent in 1946 could not bar women from voting, and the exclusionary suffrage of the colonial years was no longer respectable or tolerable.

The resolution of this crisis had two fundamental features, in both of which electoralism was a central element. First, the cacique oligarchy saw no other way to restore its old position except in close collaboration with the United States. On the one hand, this meant the activation of the Tydings Act on war-damage compensation, which was made contingent on passage of the so-called parity amendment.[13] Passage of this amendment to the Philippine constitution required a three-fourths vote in a Congress that, as a result of elections under unsettled postindependence conditions, for the first time contained representatives of the wartime insurgent Left (the only time that the Left in the Philippines has had significant congressional representation). President Manuel Roxas therefore arranged the unseating of these representatives on trumped-up charges of electoral fraud, thereby starting the polarization process that led to the Hukbalahap insurrection of 1948–54. This move was followed by utilization of the constabulary and various private armies to restore order on haciendas largely abandoned by their owners during the Japanese period. The violent crushing of the Huks, with substantial American help, ended in the political incapacitation of the popular sector for a generation.[14]

Second was the adaptation of electoralism to conditions of independence in a state without a coherent bureaucracy, or a serious profes-

[13]This Rehabilitation Act, sponsored by Senator Millard F. Tydings, offered $620,000,000 for distribution to those Americans and Filipinos who could prove that they had lost a minimum of $500 as a result of the war. (The average *annual* per capita income of Filipinos was then a quarter of this sum, making it quite clear whom the act was meant to reward.) The so-called parity amendment was composed to give Americans access to business opportunities on a basis of equality with Filipinos after the transfer of sovereignty and was, of course, a brazen infringement on that sovereignty.
[14]The classic account of the rise and fall of the Hukbalahap is Benedict J. Kerkvliet, *The Huk Rebellion* (Berkeley: University of California Press, 1977).

sionalized military,[15] and with control of police and privately armed goons fragmented between provincial oligarchs. The huge disruption of the war, a steady increase in the population along with growing urbanization, as well as normalization of the suffrage, meant that old-style cacique power was no long sufficient in itself. Sustaining the system of oligarchic control required far greater use of money and guns than had been true before the war, leading to further pillaging of the state's finances. On the other hand, an extension of American electoral practice turned out to have unexpected advantages; there was an astonishing proliferation of electoral offices at every level of government, to the point that by the mid-1980s one elective post was available for every 1,400 voters—something completely unimaginable in contemporary Siam. This development made possible not any real democratization but the channeling of electoral participation into a complex network of patronage-based local machines. The joke went that everyone in the Philippines was connected to *someone* who held some electoral office or other.

The peculiarity of this very expensive and malignant system was that it was designed to secure cacique hegemony and was not in any way the expression of new political power accruing to the rather small urban bourgeoisie that started to expand in the 1950s. In the early 1960s the latter did make some efforts to reform the electoral system along lines reminiscent of the Progressive Movement in the United States half a century earlier. But these efforts came to little, and meantime, changes in American immigration laws encouraged more and more urban, middle-class Filipinos to pack their bags for California. When a new generation of activists emerged in the later 1960s, it devoted itself mostly to extraparliamentary politics, culminating in the formation, and later rapid expansion, of the armed, illegal, insurrectionary CPP-NPA (Communist Party of the Philippines–New People's Army). In the meantime, the enormous costs (in money and violence) of cacique democracy led to ever greater pillaging of the state and hence to the institution of the Marcos dictatorship in 1972.[16]

---

[15]In 1947, Washington arranged for a continuation for a further ninety-nine years of its twenty-three land, sea, and air bases in the Philippines. Manila was effectively told that the United States would handle its defense for the indefinite future and that the Philippines had no need of real armed forces. Even today, almost half a century after independence, the Philippine military is worse trained, more poorly equipped, and more disorganized than the military of any other major country in Southeast Asia. Furthermore, imposition of the American practice of having all senior military promotions and appointments subject to congressional approval encourages factionalism and political favor-seeking among the officer corps.

[16]See the elegant, data-backed analysis in Thomas Nowak and Kay Snyder, "Clientelist

There is here an instructive comparison with the Sarit-Thanom-Praphat dictatorship in Siam a decade earlier. That these three military men were, like Marcos, thieves is indubitable. But they were thieves on a far smaller scale, and the money they stole remained in-country. Their power was based on the long-established hierarchy of a national army (something the Philippines has never had, for the reasons already mentioned) and a centralized bureaucracy. Hence they did not in the least feel threatened by the expansion of a successful Sino-Thai entrepreneurial class (from whom most made their private fortunes, rather than from the state). Marcos, on the other hand, to the end of his days, remained a cacique, a politician who built his power—"by hand," as it were—on patronage and a military and police establishment that he treated as his private security forces. Hence the paradox that the regime of civilian Marcos was far more brutal and murderous than that of the Thai field marshals; and that through his system of crony-monopolies, "businessman" Marcos ruined the Philippine economy just as the Thai military regime was presiding over the onset of the Great Boom.

Marcos's cacique dictatorship was finally brought down in 1986 by a rather bizarre convergence of forces. The first and foremost factor, ironically, was the illegal CPP-NPA that operated entirely outside any electoral process but built a huge nationwide network of participatory political organizations down to the barrio level. The rapid growth of the CPP-NPA so alarmed the United States that it finally turned against Marcos and eventually hauled him into golden imprisonment in Hawaii.[17] Most direct, of course, was electoralism itself. Bastard political son of Quezon that he was, Marcos was incapable of Sarit's absolutism. Hence, in the end, he went down in electoral flames.[18] By then he had alienated the noncrony big entrepreneurs, the Catholic Church, the fragmented residual middle class, the intelligentsia, many younger military officers, substantial parts of the popular sector, and, above all, many still-powerful caciques who longed for a restoration of the old horizontal dispersion of oligarchic power. The irony is that Marcos may actually have won (in technical terms) the elections of 1986, by the usual brutish

Politics in the Philippines: Integration or Instability?" *American Political Science Review* 68 (September 1974): 1147–70.
[17]See the very entertaining, detailed account in Raymond Bonner, *Waltzing with a Dictator* (New York: Times Books, 1987), especially the last three chapters.
[18]It will be recalled that late in 1985 he decided to "prove" his domestic legitimacy to the United States by calling for a "snap" presidential election. He assumed that the "guns, goons, and gold" methods by which he had been winning elections for three decades would do the trick again. But now the Americans had turned against him, and as Bonner shows (ibid.), the CIA went into action on behalf of Corazon Aquino.

methods, but that this victory, precisely because it was electoral, ended his reign. The response was a military mutiny followed immediately by a massive popular uprising in Manila in which tens of thousands of fed up citizens suddenly participated: People Power.

As in Bangkok after October 14, 1973, Philippine politics was for a brief time more open and participatory than it had been since the end of the nineteenth century. But the interregnum did not lead to a renewed polarization of political life, nor to a successful October 6, 1976–style right-wing military coup (though not for want of trying). The army was too weak, too divided, and too incompetent. There was no powerful civil bureaucracy to lend its support. The feeble Filipino bourgeoisie had been hemorrhaging for years through emigration and a downward-spiraling economy. The CPP-NPA, wracked with internal problems, failed to take any decisive steps; and besides, the 1986 of Teng Hsiao-ping and Mikhail Gorbachev was not the 1976 of the Gang of Four, Leonid Brezhnev, and the triumphs in Indochina. World communism was by then in rapid, irreversible decline. Hence the ultimate benefici-aries of 1986 were the caciques, who, under the leadership of Corazon Aquino and her brother Peping Cojuangco, largely restored the old elec-torally based, pacificatory congressional system of the pre-Marcos era.[19] Nothing is more striking than the contrast between the restorationism of Philippine electoralism in the post–1986 years and the transformatory character of Thai electoralism in the same period. Nor is it easy to imag-ine in the future an evolution of the system such that broad electoral participation would produce positive legislation seriously enforceable on a nationwide basis.

INDONESIA

During the last two decades of conservative Dutch colonial rule a "na-tional-level" legislature of sorts did exist—the so-called Volksraad, or People's Council. Like the Philippine Congress, it was established by the colonial regime with cautious cooptation in mind. But its electoral basis was even scantier: It included substantial representation of Dutch offi-cials and planters; many of its members were appointees; and it had no real power at all. Hence the popular nationalist and Islamic movements

---

[19] For a more detailed discussion of the Bourbon character of the Aquino regime, see my "Cacique Democracy in the Philippines: Origins and Dreams," *New Left Review* 169 (May–June 1988): 3–31.

largely ignored it, and it never effectively fulfilled the purpose for which it was established. The version of the Volksraad established by the Japanese Occupation authorities had even less power and was entirely appointative, but it did include a considerable number of leaders of the popular movement in Dutch times.[20]

In the last year of the Pacific war, the Americans were already fighting their way back through the Philippines, so that when the Japanese Empire collapsed in mid-August 1945, there was no vacuum of power. Such was not the case in the Indies, where the Dutch, themselves not liberated from Nazi occupation until the late winter of 1945, were for a long time in no position to reimpose themselves by military means. The result was the spontaneous outbreak of what everyone in Indonesia at the time speedily named "The Revolution."

But it was a revolution of a special kind. It was, for example, neither planned nor led by a single disciplined party; its legal armed forces were only one segment of a mass of *badan perjuangan* (paramilitary organizations) of various political persuasions and varying levels of military training and equipment. It was so highly decentralized that a weak national leadership had no means to prevent the social-revolutionary movements that wiped out the hated collaborator ruling classes in, for example, Aceh and East Sumatra, in 1945–46. The sufferings endured by much of the population during the Great Depression, and especially the Japanese Occupation, shattered the prestige of the once all-powerful colonial bureaucracy, which by the 1930s was manned 90 percent by "natives." The experience of fighting what by 1948–49 was effectively a guerrilla war against the Dutch further politicized the population in the contested areas of Western Indonesia, and invited a still wider popular participation. No country-wide elections were held during the revolutionary years, but President Sukarno and Vice-President Hatta were wisely careful enough to appoint to the revolutionary parliament, the so-called Komité Nasional Indonesia Pusat (Central Indonesian National Committee), representatives of all the major political groups and *badan perjuangan*, not least because of the absence of a single powerful party, a united military, and a cohesive, authoritative bureaucracy. The Republic, to survive, required this participation.[21]

---

[20] The Japanese divided the Indies into three separate terrains: Sumatra under the 25th Army, Java under the 16th Army, and the "Great East" under the Navy. Each terrain had its own distinct quasi-Volksraad.

[21] See George McT. Kahin's classic *Nationalism and Revolution in Indonesia* (Ithaca: Cor-

If one inspects the political photographs of the period—which include
cabinet ministers in shorts and sandals—one is struck by how little the
KNIP members were distinct in dress and housing from the ordinary
townspeople around them. The contrast with congressional opulence in
the Philippines is at first startling, until one recalls that in the colonial
period the Dutch and Indonesian Chinese had completely dominated
economic life; there was no substantial group of native or mestizo agrarian magnates, and an independent indigenous bourgeoisie was in its del-
icate infancy. Hence in the revolutionary period, leadership was in the
hands of youthful former political activists and military men who were
not at all sharply distinguished from one another in social origins or
economic resources. (Ex-political prisoner Sutan Sjahrir became prime
minister at age thirty-six; former private high school teacher Sudirman
became supreme commander at thirty.)

The final political settlement (1949) with the Dutch left the vast ar-
chipelagic country sovereign but flat on its back in terms of its finances,
material infrastructure, and modern-sector economy. It had neither an
air force nor a navy, and the eastern part of the nation had been largely
cut off from the western since 1942. Even had important politicians or
colonels been so inclined, a dictatorial, authoritarian political system
was out of the question for these practical reasons. Moreover, the agreement with The Hague had stipulated that members of various local pup-
pet mini-parliaments set up by the colonial authorities after 1946 in
areas they controlled militarily would merge with the KNIP into a larger
independent parliament. Because many of these members believed that
they might not be returned if free elections were held, passage of the
necessary legislation was repeatedly delayed, and the elections—the only
free national-level elections Indonesia has ever had—did not take place
until 1955.

In the meantime, the participatory traditions of the nationalist movement and of the revolution, combined with the difficulties of demobilizing
the huge, disorganized congeries of armed groups, and various disap-
pointments with the immediate fruits of the independence agreement
(such as Dutch retention of West Irian, the immunity of Dutch corporate
capital from nationalization, and so on), led in some provinces to armed
rebellions and in others to militant extraparliamentary political activities.
The elections were thus quite consciously set up to channel and con-

nell University Press, 1952); and for a more detailed discussion of the early stages of the
revolution, my *Java in a Time of Revolution* (Ithaca: Cornell University Press, 1972).

tain these forces and dissatisfactions. It could indeed be argued that they ended up being the most open and participatory elections held anywhere in Southeast Asia since World War II: full adult suffrage, a competitive press, very little violence or gerrymandering, remarkably little emphasis on money, and so on. Dozens of parties participated, though the final tally was dominated by the Big Four (Masyumi, the Nahdatul Ulama [NU], the Indonesian Nationalist Party [PNI], and the Partai Komunis Indonesia [PKI]), each supported by millions of voters.[22] Of particular importance was the success of the PKI—the only Southeast Asian Communist Party both eager to participate electorally and permitted by the system to do so. (It gained almost the same percentage of the popular vote as did Fidel Ramos in narrowly winning the recent Philippine presidential elections.)

Yet this electoral success was to have ironic outcomes. The Communists, like the others of the Big Four, had discovered quite quickly that in vast, backward, heavily illiterate rural Indonesia, where the bulk of the voters resided, the most efficient way to do well electorally was to attract to its ranks village headmen and other local notables. Once attached, these people could often be counted on to bring in their villagers' votes, without the Party itself having to make substantial and expensive efforts lower down. (After all, voting is a very simple act usually involving very little personal cost.) But since village headmen typically owned or controlled the most land in the villages, recruiting them required electoral programs that did not threaten their interests. Furthermore, the Party's success in these elections, and the provincial elections in Java that followed in 1957, began to give Party members a personal stake in electoral offices at all levels. Hence it is not surprising that quite early on Donald Hindley was speaking of the "domestication" of the PKI, a domestication in which electoralism played a central role.[23] The same logic pushed the Party's leaders to disband leftover communist guerrilla bands in Central Java, and to control leaders of trade unions and farmers' organizations whose militancy threatened the accommodations on which parliamentary success depended. On the other hand, the Party's electoral successes deeply alarmed its competitors, as well as the army leadership. In part, out of this fear came the end of electoral

[22]The key study of Indonesian electoral democracy is Herbert Feith's *The Decline of Constitutional Democracy in Indonesia* (Ithaca: Cornell University Press, 1962); an excellent detailed study of the 1955 elections is the same author's *The Indonesian Elections of 1955* (Ithaca: Cornell Modern Indonesia Project, 1957).
[23]Donald Hindley, "President Sukarno and the Communists: The Politics of Domestication," *American Political Science Review* 56 (December 1962): 915–26.

politics with the Declaration of Martial Law in 1957, the big regional rebellions of 1958 (also the banning of the Masyumi for its involvement), and the institution of Guided Democracy by Sukarno and the army leaders in 1959.[24]

Although for his own reasons Sukarno cooperated with the military in destroying the parliamentary regime, he was not eager to become the military's prisoner. Recognizing the importance of a political counterweight to his generals, he succeeded in protecting and encouraging the (now) Big Three to continue building their political bases in return for their solid backing of his personal authority and especially of his foreign policy, *but without elections*. The largely unanticipated consequence of intense party competition without elections was the extraordinary mass politicization and mobilization of the Guided Democracy era, particularly after Sukarno revoked martial law in May 1963. Within each of the Big Three, influence and activity tended to shift away from party parliamentarians (though Sukarno's appointive Gotong-Royong parliament continued to meet throughout) toward their mass affiliates— unions, youth and women's groups, peasant organizations, intellectuals' associations, and so on—who carried the burden of the round-the-clock struggle for Sukarno's favor and for the organized popular support that guaranteed that favor.

This mass mobilization was accompanied and exacerbated by the collapse of the economy and the rise of hyperinflation especially after 1963, as a consequence mainly of the rash nationalization of Dutch corporations in 1957, and their takeover and mismanagement by the military thereafter, to say nothing of the hostility with which the capitalist powers regarded Sukarno's active foreign policy and alleged coddling of the Communists. Hence a growing political hysteria prepared the way, after the so-called coup of October 1, 1965, for the vast army-steered pogrom against the Left, in which half a million people were murdered and hundreds of thousands imprisoned under brutal conditions for many years.

There is no need here to spend any time on the series of elections held regularly since 1971 by Suharto's New Order military regime. They are

---

[24]The classic text on all this is Daniel S. Lev, *The Transition to Guided Democracy: Indonesian Politics, 1957–1959* (Ithaca: Cornell Modern Indonesia Project, 1966). For his most recent evaluation, see the trenchant remarks in his "On the Fall of the Parliamentary System," in David Bourchier and John Legge, eds., *Democracy in Indonesia, 1950s and 1990s* (Clayton, Victoria: Monash University, Centre of Southeast Asian Studies, 1994), 38–42.

carefully managed to produce externally plausible two-thirds majorities for Golkar, the government's electoral machine, and a passive parliament without any genuine representative character. One of the more effective propaganda devices used by the regime to justify its highly authoritarian and centralized character has been that the former political system encouraged intense social conflict and unstable, fractured government. But it is important to observe the elisions here involved between the electoral regime of the 1950s and the nonelectoral Guided Democracy system of the early 1960s. There is not much evidence that the electoral regime created, in itself, intense social conflict, but the evidence abounds that an electionless Guided Democracy did so. Nor was liberal democracy brought down by the Communists or even the parties as a whole; the cabinets of the period were less unstable in themselves than they were destabilized by the military and military factions, as well as (to a lesser extent) by Sukarno—who between them controlled the regime of Guided Democracy.[25]

At the same time, the peculiar experience of Guided Democracy allows us to think about the faces of electoralism in an unexpected way. The intense, competitive political mobilizations it encouraged were precisely the consequence of no elections. No mechanisms existed for temporary, punctuated adjudications of who were winners and losers, and thus ultimately the struggle for power and influence could be decided only by violently coercive means. Seen from this angle, the pacificatory aspect of electoralism appears in a warmer light—for one could then pose the question of whether free elections in 1964 might not have prevented the bloodbath of 1965–66.

Because of the economic successes of the New Order regime, to which oil and massive foreign aid and investment have been essential, Indonesia's social structure has substantially changed over the past twenty-five years. For the first time a substantial Indonesian bourgeoisie has been created, alongside the Sino-Indonesian one inherited from the colonial era—even if it is still politically weak and very much concentrated in the capital and a few other large cities. Should one thus cast Suharto as Indonesia's Sarit? Should one thus expect in the longer run a middle-class struggle for a demilitarized, genuinely electoral regime, now that any political threat from the Left has long since been violently elimi-

[25]For lively, up-to-date discussions of this whole question, see especially the essays by Ruth McVey, Herbert Feith, Jamie Mackie, Daniel Lev, Adnan Buyung Nasution, Greg Fealy, and Anton Lucas, in ibid.

nated? This prospect is by no means implausible, but the obvious incomparabilities should be noted. Sarit presided over a small country, largely homogeneous in ethnic and religious terms, which did not suffer the ravages of colonial capitalism, Japanese military occupation, a bitter revolutionary struggle for independence, or mass murder. While he and his immediate clique dominated the state, the military as such did not form a ruling caste, not least because they had available to them a centralized, reasonably professional civilian bureaucratic apparatus inherited from absolutism, whose authority had never been fatally undermined, as Indonesia's had been, by collaboration, inflation, and revolution. The survival of the monarchy meant that there was no possibility, even under his dictatorship, of a Sukarno- or Suharto-style monopolistic leadership-for-life. The high rate of assimilation of immigrant Chinese into Thai society and the absence of a characteristic colonial racialized economic hierarchy also meant that when the Thai bourgeoisie began to feel its oats it was not structurally divided along racial/religious lines as in Indonesia.

Suharto dominates a highly centralized state apparatus, which is largely his own creation over the past quarter of a century. But it is far more deeply penetrated by the military than Sarit's bureaucracy ever was. It has little self-confidence and no tradition of autonomy. It is not fundamentally based in law, as is the Thai civil service. (It is useful to compare the prestige that the judiciary enjoys in Siam with the general contempt felt for its opposite number in Indonesia.) In this sense, the future of the Indonesian state apparatus in the post-Suharto era is highly uncertain. It seems much less likely than the Thai civil service to evolve into the sort of structure that made the promises of electoralism in Western Europe attractive.

CONCLUSION

It is at least superficially ironic that uncolonized Siam, which began to have elections well after they had been instituted in the American Philippines and the Dutch Indies, has today the nearest approximation to Western-style bourgeois democracy. But only superficially. The sunny face of Janus offers the expectation that elections will have real policy outcomes satisfactory to substantial sections of the voting population. This means the necessity of a coherent civil bureaucracy capable of enforcing electorally generated policies: that is, a strong state. There are good historical reasons for thinking that it is hard to build such a state *after* the spread of mass electoralism. Siam was probably fortunate therefore to have electoralism begin half a century after the initiation of a modern-style bureaucracy by a Thai monarch. Colonial states were, for all their absolutist pretensions, typically weak because of external domination from distant metropolises and because of their rigidly racial internal hierarchies. For reasons already described, the Philippines has had an exceptionally weak state in modern times, while electoralism was instituted very early in this century. In Indonesia the huge native component of the late colonial apparatus was always vulnerable to the accusation of treason, and it came close to disappearing in the early revolution. In that sense, too, electoralism preceded the creation of a genuinely powerful and national civil apparatus, and part of the price has been the effective nullification of any serious form of popular representation for the past quarter of a century. Under conditions where elections have no visible positive policy outcomes for substantial social groups, one should not be surprised to find that they are meaningful only when, under rare favorable historical circumstances, their tallies can be read as a fundamental repudiation of the rulers. The most striking examples in modern Southeast Asia come not from the three countries here under analysis, but from Burma: the rejectionist returns of the elections of 1960 and 1990.

The shadow face of Janus is pacification, and the tendency toward the delegitimation of a vast range of popular participatory practices. This is one reason why in our times dictatorial regimes like those of the People's Action Party in Singapore, and of the New Order in Indonesia, think it useful to stage elections regularly. One can thus easily understand the ambivalence of the radical left toward electoralism in general and to the subnational electoral successes of the mainstream Italian and Indian Marxist parties in particular. For these successes come at the price of the leaderships' assimilation into the political class, and the marginalization of that popular participation that has always been central to the radical project.

2

A useful fiction:
Democratic legitimation in
New Order Indonesia

R. WILLIAM LIDDLE

But when electorates are aware of manipulated campaign procedures, when law and practice do not provide a level playing field but, rather, distort the process strongly in favor of the incumbents, what kind of legitimacy is created?[1]

INTRODUCTION

Measuring accurately the legitimacy of an authoritarian government is a formidable task, if by legitimacy we mean the positive belief of members of society in that government's right to rule.[2] Virtually all modern governments claim legitimacy. Representative democracies by their openness to challenge in free elections and to inspection by disinterested observers make it easy for political scientists to learn at least the expressed views of the citizenry. Autocracies by their constraints on their own people and on social-scientific analysts construct Herculean barriers against both the articulation of opinion and its observation.

In the case of President Suharto's "New Order," the authoritarian government that has ruled Indonesia since 1966, it is nonetheless possible to conceive an argument about legitimacy and to collect evidence for it. In essence, the argument is that adherence to democratic norms, including but not limited to the holding of general elections, is only the New Order's second-line claim to legitimacy. Its primary or first-line

---

[1] R. H. Taylor in the Introduction to this volume.
[2] Max Weber, *The Theory of Social and Economic Organization* (New York: Oxford University Press, 1947), 124.

34

claim is that it is a developmental regime, dedicated to the achievement of a modern industrial economy, including a high standard of living for all Indonesians.

Few politically active or aware Indonesians genuinely believe that their government is democratic. A small group denies it legitimacy on that ground. Many people, however, believe that the regime is developmental and accord it legitimacy for that reason. Many others are committed instead to the pursuit of personal or group agendas and give democracy and development either lower or zero priority on their preference scales.

For both the believers in developmentalism and the pursuers of other goals, acceptance of the government's claim to democratic legitimation is a useful fiction. The developmentalists can present themselves to their own people and to foreigners in the beautiful robe of democracy rather than the ugly cloak of dictatorship. Those with other agendas are able to exploit for their own purposes the institutions created by the New Order to make credible its claim to democratic legitimacy. The result is a fragile but nonetheless so far perdurable "ruling formula," in Mosca's sense of the set of basic principles through which a government claims legitimacy.[3]

My evidence for these propositions comes largely from the public discourse, as recorded in newspapers and magazines published in Indonesia, supplemented by interviews and informed by my sense as a long-time observer of what lies behind government statements and actions and public responses to them. These sources are of course imperfect. The Indonesian media have been systematically enjoined for most of the New Order from amplifying the voices of a wide range of political intellectuals and activists. Supporters of representative democracy, an Islamic state, regional separatism, and Marxism have been regarded as "outside the national consensus" by the government. The media have frequently been prevented from reporting on antigovernment movements, public disturbances, the corrupt behavior of high officials—especially the president's family and close associates—and so on. The government also expects the media to serve as cheerleaders, spreading the good news of government policies and programs.

At a less conscious level, the media have often reflected inadequately the concerns of people least familiar to the urbanized bureaucratic, military, intellectual, and journalistic elites that monopolize the national

[3]Gaetano Mosca, *The Ruling Class* (New York: McGraw-Hill Book Company, 1939), 70.

communications network. These include the urban lower class and rural people in general, but especially the rural poor. The attitudes and opinions of the millions of Indonesians whose consciousness is still basically circumscribed by regional language and culture are also hardly audible in the national discourse. These limitations are substantial, but I hope not disabling for the argument I shall make.

LEGITIMACY THROUGH DEVELOPMENT

The New Order government's primary claim to legitimacy is its commitment to the principle of development. In official statements, such as the president's annual independence eve address or the Broad Outlines of State Policy adopted by the People's Consultative Assembly every five years, development is typically defined as a trilogy of goals: growth (*pertumbuhan*), equalization (*pemerataan*), and stability (*stabilitas*).[4] The first two of these goals are entirely economic in content, while the third is largely political.

This standardized development trilogy (*trilogi pembangunan*) formulation goes back to the mid-1970s, when the government first came under sustained attack for economic policies believed by many Indonesians to emphasize growth at the expense of equal distribution of the benefits of growth. Following the student demonstrations of late 1973 that led to rioting in Jakarta in early 1974, the government began to adopt and self-consciously promote a series of policies designed to channel some of the benefits of growth to the poorer sections of the population.

From the very beginning of the New Order in the mid-1960s, however, the goals of development (*pembangunan*), understood to include both growth and equality dimensions plus stability, had been central to the image of itself presented by the government to both domestic and foreign audiences. The New Order was born in the wake of the killing in the early morning of October 1, 1965, of six senior army generals by a group of junior officers in alliance with leaders of the Communist Party (PKI). Major General Suharto, at the time in command of strategic troops in Jakarta, immediately rallied anticommunist forces in the army and society. He then began an offensive against the Left that ended with

---

[4]See, for example, "Pidato Kenegaraan Presiden Republik Indonesia Soeharto di depan Sidang Dewan Perwakilan Rakyat 16 Agustus, 1993" [The State Address of Republic of Indonesia President Suharto Before the Session of the People's Representative Council, August 16, 1993], published as a supplement in *Kompas* 29, no. 51 (August 18, 1993).

the banning of the PKI, the killing of perhaps five hundred thousand party members and supporters, and his own accession in 1967 to the presidency.[5]

The larger political context in which these events took place was a two-decades-long struggle for power between the army, in a broad sense representative of the postcolonial social status quo as it existed in the 1950s and early 1960s, and the Communist Party, which was expanding in size and influence and threatening to overturn the established order and the army's place in that order. The larger economic context was a rate of growth that had been steadily falling and a rate of inflation that had been rapidly climbing since the mid-1950s. In the chaotic political situation of late 1965 and 1966, the growth rate turned negative and the inflation rate soared out of control.

General Suharto began to take command of the civil government in March 1966, when he forced President Sukarno to sign an order effectively ceding executive authority to him. Suharto's first political moves were to destroy his archenemy, the Communist Party, and to consolidate control over the army and the armed forces. (The navy and air force leadership had been much more left-leaning than that of the army.) These were followed in the late 1960s and early 1970s by the gradual extension of his power over noncommunist civilian groups, such as the university and high school students, Muslim intellectuals, and political activists who had provided much of the popular base for his challenge to Sukarno.

The justification for these actions was first couched as anticommunism, but this was soon broadened to become antiextremism, in which the extremism of the communist left was balanced by that of the Muslim opposition, accused of wanting to establish a state based on *syari'ah* (Islamic law). The Suharto government thus began early to present itself as the middle ground between extremes (as indeed the Sukarno government before it had done), and to legitimate its repressive actions in the name of maintaining the stability of a centrist regime.

Suharto's conception of centrism included a democratic component, glossed as Pancasila[6] Democracy, which I will describe in the next sec-

---

[5]For the history of this period, see Harold Crouch, *The Army and Politics in Indonesia* (Ithaca: Cornell University Press, 1978).
[6]Five Principles of "Belief in the One and Only God, Just and Civilized Humanity, the Unity of Indonesia, Democracy Guided by Inner Wisdom in Unanimity Arising out of Deliberation among Representatives, and Social Justice for All the People of Indonesia." *Indonesia 1990: An Official Handbook* (Jakarta: Department of Information, Republic of Indonesia, 1990), 13.

tion. It also incorporated a Javanist concern with order, as reflected in the frequent reference to concepts such as *tata tentrem* (peaceful order) and similar phrases familiar to most Javanese through popular historical texts and the shadow play (*wayang*) tradition.[7] These concepts were in turn linked to economic development, defined both in Javanese terms— as, for example, in the slogan *gemah ripah loh jinawi* (peaceful, prosperous, agriculturally fertile)—and in modern, Western-derived ones— the image of a schooled population living in an urban society based on an industrial economy.

The idea of development projected by the Suharto government from its earliest years was thus multidimensional. Economic goals, growth and distribution, quickly became paramount, the raison d'être of the regime. The disastrous condition of the economy in the mid-1960s was both a challenge that the new leadership could hardly avoid and an opportunity to stake a claim for its long-term legitimation. In order to appeal to a broad cross section of the population, these goals were described in both traditional and modern terms.

Political stability was a legitimating principle in its own right, reflecting popular anxiety over the recent instability and threat of a communist takeover plus the belief on the part of regime leaders that militant Islam was the main threat, after communism, to the social status quo and to their own continued rule. Political stability was also claimed to be an instrument for achieving the more basic economic goals. After the regime's initial consolidation in the late 1960s and early 1970s, stability came more and more to be defined in this instrumental way.

Finally, economic stability also became by the early 1970s a part of the government's overall conception of stability. This reflected both continuing concern over the recent hyperinflation and negative growth and the belief of domestic and foreign businesspeople that economic development requires not only the right kind of market-stimulating and -regulating policies but also long-term consistency in their implementation.

What has the government done to make good on its claim to developmental legitimacy? The policy history of the New Order, now more

---

[7]A collection of Javanese sayings compiled by Suharto himself as moral instruction for his children and published by his daughter is Hardiyanti Rukmana, ed., *Butir-Butir Budaya Jawa* [Grains of Javanese Culture] (Jakarta: Yayasan Purna Bhakti Pertiwi, 1987). For a scholarly treatment of these ideas, see Soemarsaid Moertono, *State and Statecraft in Old Java* (Ithaca: Cornell University Modern Indonesia Project, 1968).

than a quarter-century old, is well known.[8] By 1967 Acting President Suharto had adopted the advice of a group of mostly American-trained professional economists, led by Widjojo Nitisastro of the University of Indonesia. The Widjojo group's views were backed by the World Bank, the International Monetary Fund, and the governments of the industrialized world, to which the Sukarno government in its last years had been unable to repay its debts. Payment was rescheduled as part of a package that included massive new assistance, given with the assurance that the Suharto government would follow neoclassical development policies designed to induce growth through encouraging private investment, both foreign and domestic.

The mutually beneficial connection among Suharto, the Widjojo group, and the industrialized, capitalist world has continued, with relatively little friction, ever since.[9] New assistance has been given on an annual basis by a consortium of Western governments and Japan, until 1992 chaired by the Netherlands and called the Inter-Governmental Group on Indonesia, and now chaired by the World Bank and called the Consultative Group on Indonesia.

Within Indonesia, however, the technocrats' path has not always been smooth. Opposition has come primarily from two quarters: those who favor more rapid, state-led growth versus the market- and comparative advantage-oriented technocrats; and those who advocate more egalitarian growth. Until the mid-1970s the statists were represented most effectively by Ibnu Sutowo, then head of the national oil company. Today their flag is carried by Minister of Research and Technology B. J. Habibie, a German-trained aeronautical engineer intent on committing the state to invest heavily in capital-intensive, high-technology import-substitution projects. This group gets much of its support from within the bureaucracy and from businesspeople who hope for state contracts or other government favoritism. There is also a powerful predisposition in Indonesian political culture, dating to the pre–World War II nationalist movement, to favor state intervention and oppose private capitalism, either foreign or domestic. Then and now, the domestic business community has been heavily Sino-Indonesian.

[8]The best recent account is John Bresnan, *Managing Indonesia* (New York: Columbia University Press, 1993).
[9]R. William Liddle, "The Relative Autonomy of the Third World Politician: Suharto and Indonesian Economic Development in Comparative Perspective," *International Studies Quarterly* 35, no. 4 (December 1991): 403–27.

Opponents of neoclassical growth who desire more egalitarian policies are a complex group. Some are middle-class, indigenous (*pribumi*) Indonesians, who see their path to success as businesspeople blocked by Sino-Indonesian dominance of the private sector. Their policy preferences are generally protectionist, within a mixed-economy framework. Others are regionalists, officials and businesspeople in the provinces who oppose what they see as excessive centralization of policy formulation and implementation. This group has so far tried largely to achieve its goals by working within the bureaucracy.

Still others think in class terms, arguing in traditional Marxist fashion that capitalist development necessarily benefits only a small business elite. In today's political climate, it is impossible to mobilize openly for a revolution to overthrow capitalism, though undoubtedly there are would-be political activists ready to do so. Other class-oriented egalitarians believe in correcting the biases of capitalism from within the system, for example through credit or intermediate-technology programs directed at the urban and rural poor. This group includes many of the leaders of the nongovernmental organizations that have proliferated in the 1980s and 1990s.

Despite these differences and the resulting tensions and conflicts over government policy, the response to the New Order claim to legitimacy through development seems to be basically positive. That is, the regime is in fact legitimate in the minds of probably a majority of members of the politically aware public because of its developmental record. Evidence for this assertion, given the authoritarian nature of the regime, is largely circumstantial. It includes the absence of any substantial underground mobilization against the government, and also of many signs of prerevolutionary hostility within the political public, or for that matter in the populace as a whole.[10] More positively, the public record of eco-

---

[10]This is not to argue that there are no signs or no hostility. For example, urban middle- and lower-class resentment of Sino-Indonesians has undoubtedly grown since the late 1980s, when the government began to adopt what is now a long series of deregulation-policy packages. One effect of deregulation has been, as Indonesian Marxists would predict, to enable the already rich to become richer. Signs of mostly Sino-Indonesian corporate wealth are visible in the explosion of expensive housing and shopping malls in Jakarta and other major cities. In April 1994 massive worker protests in Medan, North Sumatra, against low wages, poor working conditions, and political repression turned into anti-Chinese riots. See Human Rights Watch/Asia, *The Limits of Openness* (New York: Human Rights Watch, 1994), Chap. 5. The blatant favoritism shown in the awarding of government contracts to the president's children is also a cause of middle-class resentment. This anger is directed more toward the president himself, however, than toward the regime.

nomic policy debate in the mass media, again making allowances for the authoritarian climate, suggests that differences are mainly over details— more versus less protectionism, more versus less attention to the regions, indigenous entrepreneurs, or the poor, and so on—rather than over the government's basic development policy orientation.

What accounts for the government's success in obtaining developmental legitimation? First, there is real personal experience corroborated by statistical evidence.[11] The incomes of most Indonesians have risen substantially in the last two decades, and so has the general quality of life— in tangible facilities, such as schools, health care, housing, public and private transportation, roads, and in such intangibles as personal security, religious freedom, trust in price stability, the availability of goods, and the sense that the economic situation is likely to continue to improve.

Second, there is a widely accepted logic, or story, that connects this success to government policy. This is the logic of the market mechanism. The most recent illustration of its effectiveness is the connection between the government's series of deregulation policy packages, adopted since the mid-1980s, and the subsequent dramatic rise in Indonesia's nonoil exports.[12] The market logic has tended also to attribute failures in development to factors outside the government's control. Examples are the negative impact of a strengthening yen on Indonesia's balance of payments, or more generally and severely the effect on the growth rate of the world recession and falling oil prices in the early 1980s.

Third, the government's economic policies come complete with a powerful foreign imprimatur. Suharto chose to adopt the market-centered, export-oriented approach favored by the World Bank, the International Monetary Fund, and the governments of the industrialized world at just the time this approach was beginning to show results in places such as Korea and Taiwan. Other development theories, such as the total state control of communist economies, the isolationism of *dependencia*, the internationalist politics of the New International Economic Order, the localism of Basic Human Needs, and the import substitution popular in Latin America, were either failing in practice or stillborn. Put differently,

[11]Anne Booth, ed., *The Oil Boom and After: Indonesian Economic Policy and Performance in the Suharto Era* (Singapore: Oxford University Press, 1992).
[12]See for example Ross Chapman, "Indonesian Trade Reform in Close-Up: The Steel and Footwear Experiences," *Bulletin of Indonesian Economic Studies* 28, no. 1 (April 1992): 67–84.

the New Order has been riding an international neoclassical development wave that after more than a quarter century still has not crested.

Finally, a word must be said about the relation of coercion to developmental legitimacy. Suharto and his agents have not shrunk from using force unsanctioned by law or the constitution against political opponents or in other circumstances. Examples include the killing and jailing of communists in the mid-1960s, the brutal suppression of political demonstrations on many occasions, the repression of regional and religious groups that have challenged state authority, ostracism and other measures constituting "civil death" for elite dissidents, the vigilante-style execution of recidivists in the early 1980s, continuing state terrorism against the people of East Timor, recently tightened constraints on the press,[13] and so on.

These actions both contribute to regime legitimacy—that is, they constitute a fourth reason for successful legitimation—and fill the gap between legitimacy and stability. To regime supporters, they provide proof that the government is strong, willing to back up its commitments by coercing those who oppose it. To regime opponents and troublemakers of various kinds, on the other hand, they erect a physical barrier against instability. The measure of order that the government cannot obtain willingly, in the form of voluntary acceptance offered by those who agree with its development policies, it acquires by the threat or the use of force majeure.

ELECTIONS AND DEVELOPMENTAL LEGITIMATION

How do electoral and, more broadly, democratic legitimation relate to the developmental legitimation described above? In my view, popular elections and the political and governmental institutions whose personnel are chosen through election-related processes have been subordinated to the larger claim of developmentalism. Pancasila Democracy, the general term used by the government to describe these institutions, is only one dimension of stability, which is in turn only one-third of the devel-

[13]Press controls, tight for most of the 1980s, were relaxed in the early 1990s, leading many observers to suggest that the New Order government might be beginning to democratize itself, either out of confidence in its own popularity or in response to growing demands from an increasingly educated and sophisticated middle class. In June 1994, the period of openness abruptly ended when the government closed Indonesia's leading newsweekly, *Tempo*, and two other weekly magazines. See Human Rights Watch/Asia, *The Limits of Openness*, Chap. 2.

opment trilogy of legitimating principles. Nonetheless, it is also true that a great deal of independent effort has been put into its promotion.

Suharto's concept of Pancasila Democracy, like his idea of development, has both modern or Western-derived and ostensibly traditional components. General parliamentary elections are the quintessentially modern democratic institution. The fact that they have been held five times in the New Order—compared with once during the representative democracy period of the 1950s and not at all during the Guided Democracy of President Sukarno in the early 1960s—is a source of great pride to government spokespersons.

Elections are linked to the parliament or DPR (Dewan Perwakilan Rakyat, People's Representative Council), 400 of whose 500 members are elected; the remainder are military appointees. The DPR meets annually and must approve all proposed legislation, including the government's budget. There is also a superparliament, the MPR (Majelis Permusyawaratan Rakyat, People's Consultative Assembly), which consists of all members of the DPR plus an additional 500 appointees. It meets quinquennially to elect the president and vice president and to set the Basic Outline of State Policy (Garis Besar Haluan Negara) for the coming presidential term.

The duties of both the DPR and the MPR (but not, curiously, the procedure by which their members are selected) are specified in the Constitution of 1945. This constitution was unilaterally and unconstitutionally decreed back in force by President Sukarno in 1959, after nearly a decade of representative democracy under the Constitution of 1950.[14] New Order spokespersons have claimed for it the kind of sacredness attributed by most Americans to their constitution.

In Pancasila Democracy, Pancasila is intended to be an indigenizing modifier. President Suharto has himself claimed that Pancasila, despite the obvious derivation of most of the five principles from the vocabulary of nineteenth and twentieth century European politics, is the product of thousands of years of Javanese history.[15] He also links it to other con-

[14]On the representative democracy period see Herbert Feith, *The Decline of Constitutional Democracy in Indonesia* (Ithaca: Cornell University Press, 1962).
[15]"Laporan Stenografi Amanat Presiden Soeharto pada Malam Ramah Tamah Dengan Pengurus K.N.P.I. [Komite Nasional Pemuda Indonesia] Tanggal 19 Juli 1982 di Jalan Cendana No. 8 Jakarta" [Stenographic Report of the Address of President Soeharto at an Informal Evening with the Officers of the National Committee of Indonesian Youth July 19, 1982, at 8 Cendana Street, Jakarta], typescript. This is an unofficial transcription of an extemporaneous speech, in which the president spoke at great length to mostly non-Javanese youth leaders about the glories of ancient Javanese values.

cepts, such as *musyawarah* (discussion) and *mufakat* (consensus), for which deep cultural roots are claimed. The point of this indigenization is to buttress the assertion that the New Order version of elections and election-related institutions is both genuinely Indonesian and authentically democratic, though admittedly different from the history and current practice of the Western democracies. It is used to justify every departure from Western democratic practice, of which there are a great many.

How do members of the Indonesian political public respond to the government's claim to be practicing Pancasila Democracy, particularly in light of their positive reaction to the claim to developmental legitimation? I will organize my answer in two parts: a discussion of four general considerations, which will make up the remainder of this section; and, in two additional sections, a description and analysis of the divergent responses of four specific groups in the public.

My first general point is that the empirical credibility of the claim to successful democratic practice is vastly weaker than the claim to developmental success. It is widely understood that the party system, the electoral process, and the DPR and MPR are so rigged, structured and managed from above, that they allow little genuine representation from below. The effect is to make it very difficult for most politically aware Indonesians to accept the government's claim that the New Order is a democracy, even a Pancasila Democracy.

Only three political parties are granted the right to compete in elections: the government's own Golkar (Golongan Karya, Functional Groups), the PDI (Partai Demokrasi Indonesia, Indonesian Democracy Party), and the PPP (Partai Persatuan Pembangunan, Development Unity Party). In every New Order election, Golkar has achieved well over 60 percent of the vote, reaching its peak of 73 percent in 1987. PPP, intended to represent the Islamic community, won nearly 30 percent in early elections but has recently dropped to half that because of the withdrawal of its one truly mass-based component organization, the Nahdlatul Ulama (Awakening of the Traditional Religious Teachers). In the last two elections PDI has risen from a single- to a double-digit vote percentage, but it remains the smallest of the three.

Golkar is not a political party at all, in the sense of an organization in society that competes electorally with similiar organizations for control of the government. It is rather the electoral face of the civilian bureaucracy and the armed forces, mobilized every five years to get out the vote for the ruling group led by Suharto. PDI and PPP are artificial fusions of, respectively, five nationalist and Christian parties and four Islamic parties. They were forced to combine by the government in 1973. Their leaders are approved, and sometimes hand-picked, from above. Leadership struggles in the parties usually reflect high-level conflicts among government officials more than genuine differences among party factions. Virtually all of PDI's income and a substantial proportion of PPP's are direct grants from the government.[16]

In the context of the developing world and even the Southeast Asian experience, the New Order conducts elections in which the ballots are cast and counted honestly, with few exceptions.[17] The elections' primary undemocratic feature is the party system, which gives voters few and unattractive choices. Another is the government regulations on political organizations and campaigns, which give the advantage to Golkar and prevent PDI and PPP from mobilizing effectively either prior to or during the campaign period.[18]

For example, PDI and PPP are not allowed to maintain organizations below the district level, whereas Golkar-supporting subdistrict and village heads and territorially based military officers are in constant contact with the voters. Most district- and provincial-level leaders of Golkar are also retired military officers, and even apolitical villagers know that the armed forces provide the backbone, and the muscle, of the government's party.[19] During the 1971 elections, the military's presence was overt and palpable. In subsequent elections, the military has been able to play a more back-seat role because the voters know what is expected of them.

Military influence extends to the DPR and MPR, where there are formally organized armed forces "fractions," one of four in the DPR (together with Golkar, PPP, and PDI) and one of five in the MPR (Regional Delegates constitute the additional fraction). A separate doctrine, the

[16]During campaigns, PPP is able to solicit funds and services from devout Muslims, even those with relatively little wealth, while both Golkar and PDI are in practice limited to what the state provides. In the case of Golkar, this is a lot, for virtually the whole state apparatus is mobilized on its behalf.
[17]After each election, the parties have charged ballot stuffing and other irregularities in some parts of the country, particularly outside Java, where press and other observation is not so close. They have never been able to provide much evidence, however. My own observation of elections in 1971 (a village in Yogyakarta) and 1987 (an urban polling place in Banda Aceh) suggests that the government scrupulously observes its own electoral regulations.
[18]On these restrictions, see Afan Gaffar, "The Javanese Voter" (Ph.D. dissertation, Ohio State University, 1988), Chap. 4.
[19]Author's field notes: Brosot, Kulon Progo, Yogyakarta, 1971; Banda Aceh, Aceh, 1987.

"twin functions" (*dwi-fungsi*) of the armed forces to not only defend the country against external enemies, but also play a domestic sociopolitical function, is used to justify this legislative role, as well as intervention in many other areas of national and local political life.[20]

From a democratic perspective, however, the biggest shortcoming of the MPR and DPR is that they are not representative bodies autonomous of the state but instead are totally dominated by President Suharto and his bureaucratic and military agents. Most members of the political public are fully aware that 50 percent of the MPR membership is selected in a process ultimately controlled by the president, and that all candidates for the DPR—from Golkar, PPP, PDI, and the armed forces—are screened by the president's office.[21] Neither body has ever passed a law or resolution not sent to it by the president.

Second, there is no history of democratic practice and resulting commitment in prewar colonial Indonesia.[22] This tends to mitigate what might otherwise be the very negative impact of the lack of government credibility. Two close neighbors, India and the Philippines, had considerable experience under the British and the Americans with elections, political parties, and legislatures from early in the twentieth century. The effect was to create both a political climate favorable to representative democracy and a perceived positive match between the specific interests of social groups and the democratic process.

The Dutch in Indonesia, on the other hand, allowed democratic institutions to begin to develop only at the very end of the colonial period, and then with a minuscule suffrage. No significant social or political group ever developed a commitment to these institutions. In 1950, at the end of the revolution for independence, a democratic constitution was adopted for reasons of international fashion, the desire for support from Western nations, and the absence of any alternative on which the major political forces could agree. When it was challenged mid-decade, its few true believers could not mobilize enough resources to defend it against its enemies.

[20]See Hasnan Habib, "The Role of the Armed Forces in Indonesia's Future Political Development," in Harold Crouch and Hal Hill, eds., *Indonesia Assessment 1992* (Canberra: Department of Political and Social Change, Research School of Pacific Studies, Australian National University, 1992), 83–94.

[21]Prior to the 1992 election, President Suharto as chair of the Guidance Council of Golkar quite openly scratched a number of names from the final candidate list. See "Golkar," *Tempo* 21, no. 29: 21–33.

[22]J. S. Furnivall, *Netherlands India: A Study of Plural Economy* (Cambridge: Cambridge University Press, 1944), Chap. 9.

Third is a widespread fear of the abyss, which tends to harden what might otherwise be at least a neutral attitude toward representative democracy. During the several years of democratic practice in Indonesia, roughly 1950–7, the nationalist elite faced three challenges to its values and indeed to its very existence. These came from regionalists, some of whom wanted separation from Indonesia; from politically self-conscious Muslims, some of whom wanted an Islamic state; and from the Indonesian Communist Party, which wanted a people's democracy.

Separatists and more moderate regionalists were put down by a combination of force and negotiation in the late 1950s and early 1960s. The Islamic state idea was defeated at the ballot box in 1955, when all Muslim parties combined received a little over 40 percent of the vote, and again in 1959, when President Sukarno reestablished executive supremacy over parliament and subsequently banned Masyumi, the largest Islamic political party. The Communist Party was destroyed in the mid-1960s through the combined efforts of the army and anticommunist, especially Muslim, forces in society.

The conduct and results of the 1955 parliamentary elections, the only free elections ever held in Indonesia, probably did not convince many people of the merits of democracy. The preelection parliament, in part a product of concessions made to the departing Dutch, had been unrepresentative, fragmented, and incapable of producing stable coalitions or coherent and consistent policies. The exaggeratedly high hopes of many members of the political public that an election would solve these problems began to give way to despair during a campaign that tended to polarize voters, particularly along religious lines. Hostility to elections and to democracy deepened when the four parties that dominated the new parliament appeared still to be incapable of creating a stable coalition or of developing effective policies to address pressing national issues.[23]

This history is very much alive in the minds of Indonesians today. One reason, to be sure, is that officials in the ministries of information and education keep it alive, for example, with three different history-plus-ideology courses taught at every level from primary through sec-

[23]For recent reinterpretations of this period, see David Bourchier and John Legge, eds., *Indonesian Democracy 1950s and 1990s* (Clayton: Monash University Centre of Southeast Asian Studies, 1994). The four major parties were the Indonesian Nationalist Party with 22.3 percent, the modernist Islamic Masyumi with 20.9 percent, the traditionalist Islamic Nahdlatul Ulama with 18.4 percent, and the communist PKI with 16.4 percent.

ondary school, obligatory workshops for officials, endless showing of films and speechifying on national holidays, and so on. More important, however, is that the issues themselves are to some extent unresolved. To what extent is of course difficult to ascertain in the absence of open politics. Separatist movements still exist in Aceh and Irian Jaya, and the apparent unwillingness of the East Timorese to accept Indonesian sovereignty is regarded by most Indonesians, certainly by most government officials, as a separatist problem. If a more democratic center were to relax the current iron grip on the regions, separatists and regionalists would certainly be emboldened to act. The breakup of the Soviet Union is frequently offered by officials as evidence of the need to maintain tight control.

Practicing Muslims are probably a much larger proportion of the Indonesian Islamic community today than they were thirty years ago. This raises fears on the part of nonpracticing Muslims and non-Muslim minorities, such as Christians and Hindu Balinese, that in a democratic Indonesia Muslim parties might win a majority of legislative seats and reopen the Islamic state issue. Some Muslim groups would certainly do so.

Finally, many Indonesians believe that a new radical movement from below might use democracy to advance its members' interests much as the communists did in the 1950s. Economic growth has created a large industrial workforce, concentrated in the area around Jakarta but present in other cities as well.[24] Dissatisfaction with low wages and poor working conditions, combined with anger at the government's attempt to silence workers with state-controlled unions and readiness to call out the troops, has led to an explosion of wildcat strikes in the 1990s. Many small farmers and laborers in the rural areas also have gained little from New Order–style development. In a democratic setting, skillful politicians with an ear to the ground could certainly mobilize large numbers of disadvantaged urban and rural workers.

The lack of any historic commitment to representative institutions plus fear of the abyss make many Indonesians unresponsive to complaints that the New Order is insufficiently democratic. But there is at least one

[24]Hal Hill, "Indonesia's Industrial Transformation, Parts I and II," *Bulletin of Indonesian Economic Studies* 26, nos. 2 and 3 (August and December 1990): 79–120 and 75–110; Chris Manning, "Structural Change and Industrial Relations during the Soeharto Period: An Approaching Crisis?" *Bulletin of Indonesian Economic Studies* 29, no. 2 (August 1993): 59–95.

factor, my final general consideration, working in the other direction: the poor fit and the resulting tension between the outside world's conception of democracy and that of the Suharto government. One way to put this point is to contrast the relationship between the World Bank and the New Order on the issue of developmentalism with that between, say, Amnesty International or Human Rights Watch and the New Order on the issue of democracy. For more than a quarter century, the Indonesian government and the World Bank have traveled the same developmental road, including a shared commitment to political stability, not to democracy. The substantial benefits have included the annual aid package, now over U.S.$5 billion, and also the world's approbation in the form of prizes, awards, and editorials in the newspapers of leading industrial nations.

Amnesty International and Human Rights Watch, in the short period they have existed, have never been particularly friendly to the Indonesian government. But they have also not been nearly as central to the formation of world opinion about democracy as the World Bank has been concerning development. Only in the last decade, and particularly since the end of the cold war and the election of President Bill Clinton in the United States, has that situation been changing. Prodemocracy organizations and voices have gained substantially in resources mobilizable against authoritarian governments.

The filming by foreign media of the Santa Cruz massacre, where 75 to 200 unarmed East Timorese demonstrators (the figures are Asia Watch's, which suggests the power of its information-gathering capacity) were gunned down by Indonesian troops in November 1991, also turned a harsh and unflattering light on Indonesian domestic politics.[25] The juncture of these and other developments—such as the turn to democracy in Southern Europe, Latin America, and parts of East Asia, and the communications revolution that has brought CNN and BBC television broadcasts to living rooms everywhere—appears to be creating a powerful new worldwide prodemocracy tide against which it will be increasingly hard for New Order officials to fight.

Another way to think about the impact of the changing international situation on Indonesia is in terms of the anthropologist's concepts of myth and ritual. The idea of development is a modern Western myth,

[25]Asia Watch, "East Timor: The November 12 Massacre and its Aftermath," *Indonesia Issues* 17–18 (December 1991).

rooted in the Enlightenment notion of progress, and its rituals are the macroeconomic policies and programs of ministers of finance and central bankers. The idea of representative democracy is also a modern Western myth, rooted in ancient Athens but reaching us via eighteenth-century liberalism and nineteenth-century nationalism, both European ideologies. Its rituals are the activities of parties, elections, and legislatures in open societies. Both of these myths have great attractive power in their societies of origin and in much of the developing world as well.

The Suharto government has little influence over the international meaning and persuasive power of either the myths or their attendant rituals. If it is to use them for its own purposes, it must take them more or less as it finds them. In the case of developmentalism, this has worked well enough, for the international and domestic meanings do not vary significantly in practice. Indonesia has thus not come in for much criticism from abroad on its development policies. When it does, small-scale and specific reform measures can be taken, such as deregulation or tax reform. In the case of democracy, on the other hand, the New Order has borrowed the language, but not the content, of the outside world's conception of democracy and has thus made itself vulnerable to foreign criticism.

This comparison helps us to understand why the New Order leaders emphasize the indigenousness of Pancasila Democracy. To the degree to which it is indigenous, the product of thousands of years of Javanese history, its current implementation cannot be judged by foreigners who have no independent measure of (or indeed any real interest in) what is or is not Pancasilaist. Anti-Suharto Indonesians often complain that Pancasila is a moving target, redefined at will by the president to suit whatever purpose he has in mind. But they have not had the political resources to make their own definition compete effectively for national attention. In the much less hegemonic international arena, in contrast, Human Rights Watch and Amnesty International have been able to build their impressive data banks on widely accepted definitions of human rights and democracy.

ATTITUDES TOWARD DEMOCRATIC LEGITIMACY

Members of Indonesia's political public have responded to the government's claim to be democratic in one of four ways: acceptance, rejection, feigned acceptance by people who actually consider the government to be legitimate on developmental grounds, and feigned acceptance by people who actually support or are at least willing to work with the government on other, typically more narrow, interest-based grounds.

Given the number of ways in which the government's implementation of Pancasila Democracy deviates from the foreign practice of representative democracy, it is hard to believe that there are any Indonesians who believe their government to be genuinely democratic. I have met several representatives of two subtypes, however: government officials whose responsibilities virtually require them to believe it, at the cost of severe cognitive dissonance; and politically inexperienced but school-educated and more-or-less middle-class Indonesians who swallow the government's propaganda whole.

In the case of government officials, it is of course ultimately impossible for an observer to know, even after repeated interviews, to what extent they are serious in their defense of the genuineness of Pancasila Democracy. President Suharto's autobiography[26] and other writings suggest that he has convinced himself, and I have interviewed many officials, on national, district, and village levels, who also appear to be true believers. Perhaps one powerful psychological force at work here is the need for a distinctive social identity, which in the Indonesian setting has found expression in the vocabulary of Pancasila and Javanism.

More apolitical Indonesians also find this vocabulary appealing as a way of convincing themselves that they live in a morally upright world. I once lectured in Jakarta on the prospects for post–New Order democratization and was surprised to be asked by a young man in the audience to explain what it was exactly that was undemocratic about Pancasila Democracy.[27] The tone of the question suggested not hostility to the know-it-all American expert but a kind of pained wonderment that the New Order might not be democratic after all. I suspect that many school-educated Indonesians, who have been exposed to twelve or more years of indoctrination but have not themselves been politically engaged, share this attitude. It is of course held without any deep conviction and can probably be reversed easily.

Rejecters are much more politically sophisticated and active. They evaluate the New Order's democratic claim from an informed knowledge of democratic ideals and practices elsewhere. The most vocal ones,

[26]Soeharto, *Pikiran, Ucapan dan Tindakan Saya: Otobiografi* [My Thoughts, Statements and Deeds: Autobiography] (Jakarta: PT Citra Lamtoro Gung Persada, 1988).
[27]The talk was at the Centre for Strategic and International Studies, March 1993.

like the human rights lawyers Buyung Nasution and Mulya Lubis or the medical-doctor-turned-political-activist Marsillam Simandjuntak, are all necessarily outside the government.[28] They tend to be highly educated, usually in American or European universities, and are often the children of equally highly educated parents. Government spokespersons find it easy to dismiss this group as excessively Westernized. The charge has perhaps greater force in Indonesia than in other Southeast Asian countries, like the Philippines or even Malaysia and Singapore, because of the historically small size and relative social isolation of the foreign-educated elite.

There may nonetheless be many rejecters, so far inactive because of the danger of speaking out, who do not fit a Westernized social profile. The most prominent example of an active one is the current national chair of the traditional, rural-Java-based Islamic social and educational organization Nahdlatul Ulama, Abdurrahman Wahid. The son and grandson of prominent NU leaders, Abdurrahman Wahid received his formal education in Indonesia, Egypt, and Iraq. He is an autodidact who reads, socializes, and travels widely.

Abdurrahman Wahid's commitment to representative democracy is deep and of long standing. For much of the New Order period he has preferred for tactical reasons to cooperate with the government. He has recently become public, however, and now heads the Forum Demokrasi (Democracy Forum), a discussion group and protoparty that supports representative democracy and opposes political organizations based on religious affiliation. In a democratic Indonesia, it is virtually certain that a party led by Abdurrahman Wahid would attract a mass following, especially from the villages of east and central Java.

It is worth pointing out that in terms of the connection between Indonesia and the outside world, the rejecters are to Amnesty International as the technocrats are to the World Bank. To any Indonesian reader, the impact of this comparison must be to demonstrate the weakness of the rejecters. For the technocrats are influential domestically in their own right, as possessors of knowledge and skills valued by the government, and they enjoy in addition the borrowed resources of the world's most respected development agency. The rejecters, on the other hand, are iso-

[28]Nasution's recently completed doctoral dissertation is a powerful attack on the legitimating myth of Pancasila Democracy. Adnan Buyung Nasution, "The Aspiration for Constitutional Government in Indonesia: A Socio-legal Study of the Indonesian Konstituante 1956–1959" (Riijksuniversiteit Utrecht, 1992).

lated by their own government and have been able to get little help from financially, organizationally, and politically weak international human rights organizations. This situation has begun to change in the last decade, but the technocrats are still by far the more powerful of the two.

Developmentalists are a large group, at least within the state bureaucracy. They believe wholeheartedly in the New Order, but as a developmental, not a democratic regime. They often privately take a two-stage position, arguing that authoritarian stability is necessary in the short run until successful development has created the social foundations, particularly a politically moderate middle class, for democracy. South Korea and Taiwan are cited as examples of this process. In public, however, they rarely deviate from the government's Pancasila Democracy line. They, too, want the legitimacy boost that recognition as a democracy brings or at minimum seek to avoid the criticisms that the New Order represses popular participation and violates basic human rights.

The developmentalists can perhaps be divided into two subgroups: the technocrats themselves and other officials with policy-formulating and -implementing responsibilities in the development area; and other members of what we might call the development-policy community, including academics, private consultants, and so on. It overdraws the picture only a little to argue that virtually all of these individuals, though well educated and fully knowledgeable about the differences between foreign democratic practice and Pancasila Democracy, maintain a kind of conspiracy of public silence on the subject.

For example, a well-known younger private economist once confided that he had been warned by a leading senior economist not to have political thoughts of his own. "We have succeeded so far," the younger man was told, "because we have left politics to the generals."[29] A prominent social scientist and policy adviser illustrated his conviction that authoritarianism and development are connected by comparing Indonesia with India, "where the government is immobilized by too many conflicting demands from below."[30] In Jakarta today the consensus remedy among developmentalists for the declining influence of the technocrats is not democracy. Rather it is more insulation—the word most heard is institutionalization—for key macroeconomic policy officials

[29]Interview, Jakarta, October 1989.
[30]Interview, Yogyakarta, November 1990.

from the predations of rent-seekers, import-substituters, and other advocates of more state intervention in the economy.

My final category is a gallimaufry of many different groups that publicly accept the government's claim to be democratic in return for benefits bestowed upon them. A few of these groups are political elephants, major players who use democratic rhetoric to advance their own individual or group interests. The most prominent example is the military, which now heads the great majority of Golkar district and provincial branches. In terms of democratic legitimation, it is particularly important that it does so in a period when an aging president might need to be replaced. The logic is that whoever controls Golkar, the political organization that has repeatedly won a large majority of the popular vote in parliamentary elections, will be able to stake the strongest constitutional claim to the succession. The military also fields the best organized and disciplined fraction in the DPR. Since 1988 its leaders have been arguing on democratic grounds for an expanded role for the legislature.

Most supporters of other causes who feign acceptance of the government's democratic claims, however, are political mice, small-time players who offer a few rupiahs worth of legitimation in return for a few rupiahs worth of reward. Only in total do they constitute a major force for New Order legitimacy. They include those old politicians who once headed nine independent political parties but now must live under very tight constraint in two fused parties and the younger generation of party leaders to whom this is the normal way of doing political business.

The government's own Golkar is an umbrella party that subsumes many function-specific organizations for civil servants, youth, women, workers, farmers, and so on. Each of these has a monopoly, communist- or Latin American–corporatist-style, in its particular area of activity. There is only one state-controlled organization for civil servants, one civil servants' wives' affiliate, one labor union, one farmers' organization, one peak association for youth organizations. There are also several once-independent organizations, such as cooperative associations led by old revolutionary fighters, that have been part of Golkar since its founding in the early 1960s. The activists and members of all these groups offer political support to the government in return for material and status benefits.

Most ostensibly autonomous, nonstate, professional groups have lost the right to criticize the government, even in their area of expertise, and to freely choose their own leaders in return for organizational monopoly and financial subsidization. These include the associations of doctors, lawyers, journalists, engineers, teachers, and so on.[31] Catholic and Protestant churches, the national association of Protestant churches, Islamic associations, such as Nahdlatul Ulama and Muhammadiyah, the leading modernist Islamic social and educational organization, and other religious groups such as Hindu Balinese and Buddhists have greater autonomy but must tread carefully to avoid government intervention.[32] For the Islamic majority, there is a government-created Majelis Ulama Indonesia (Indonesian Council of Islamic Religious Teachers), which serves mostly to explain and justify government actions to the Islamic community.

Two potentially more influential forces are the nongovernmental organizations or LSM (Lembaga Swadaya Masyarakat) and LPSM (Lembaga Pengembangan Swadaya Masyarakat) organized independently of the state, and ICMI (Ikatan Cendekiawan Muslim se-Indonesia, All-Indonesian Association of Muslim Intellectuals). The LSM and LPSM work in a variety of fields, from the defense of human and consumer rights to protection of the environment and village-level community development. There are now thousands of these private organizations and tens of thousands of cadres who work in them and have been trained by them. Their importance is both as an alternative source of values, certainly more democratic than New Order values, and as a network of political activists. At present, however, most LSM and LPSM leaders appear willing to get along by going along, since the government monopolizes so many of the resources that they need to operate effectively.[33]

ICMI is a patron-client network of Muslim bureaucrats, plus some university intellectuals and private businesspeople, who have tied their

[31]Some of these arrangements are contested by rejecters, however. For many years there have been two competing organizations of private advocates, only one of which is recognized by the government. In mid-1994, after the government's closing of *Tempo* and two other newsmagazines, a dissident Alliance of Independent Journalists was formed.

[32]A current case is the intervention of the North Sumatran military commander in a leadership dispute in Indonesia's largest protestant church, the Huria Kristen Batak Protestan. See Human Rights Watch/Asia, *The Limits of Openness*, Chap. 7.

[33]Eldridge's most recent work on the LSM and LPSM argues that their leaders cannot be counted on to promote democracy. Philip J. Eldridge, *Non-government Organizations and Democratic Participation in Indonesia* (Singapore: Oxford University Press, 1995). New restrictions on foreign financing, imposed in the wake of the 1991 Santa Cruz massacre, make most of these groups even more dependent than before on the government. In mid-1994 they were also being threatened by a proposed presidential regulation that will tighten government supervision over them.

fate since 1990 to the rising star of Minister of Research and Technology Habibie.[34] Habibie's primary substantive interest is in the promotion of state industries that promise to make Indonesia a center for the development of new, high-value-added technologies. He heads the state aircraft, shipbuilding, and munitions industries and the government agency in charge of technology development, and holds more than twenty other high government positions.

Habibie's interest in Islam as a political or social philosophy appears to be minimal, but he has been willing to associate himself, probably at Suharto's request, with Muslim activists who have heretofore been considered outside and in many cases opposed to the New Order. These individuals are the sometimes biological but more often spiritual descendants of the politicians and intellectuals affiliated in the 1950s with Masyumi, a political party that brought together a wide spectrum of Islamic organizations and individuals but whose core support was in the urban, Western-educated, modernist Muslim community. Of the four major political parties of the parliamentary period, Masyumi was the second largest with more than 20 percent of the vote in the 1955 elections. It also drew most heavily among voters outside the Javanese cultural area.

In 1960 Masyumi was banned by President Sukarno because some of its leaders participated in the regional rebellions of the late 1950s. The new Suharto government, led by generals who had fought the rebels, refused to rehabilitate the party or its old leaders. This section of the Muslim community has thus been politically alienated for the last thirty years. It has also been growing in numbers with the general trend toward a more urbanized and educated Muslim population, both in Java and in the other islands.

In allowing or encouraging the formation of ICMI, President Suharto seems to have intended to coopt this large and growing group of potential dissidents. This is also the interpretation of Abdurrahman Wahid, whose nonreligious Democratic Forum is a direct response to ICMI. According to Abdurrahman Wahid, much of the human talent in the Islamic community that should be available for the demanding intellectual and political task of making post-Suharto Indonesia more democratic has unfortunately been absorbed by the regime-supporting ICMI.[35]

[34]For the history of ICMI, see M. Syafi'i Anwar, "Islam, Negara, dan Formasi Sosial Dalam Orde Baru" [Islam, the State, and Social Formation in the New Order], *Ulumul Qur'an* 3, no. 3 (1992): Supplement, 1–28; Robert W. Hefner, "Islam, State, and Civil Society: ICMI and the Struggle for the Indonesian Middle Class," *Indonesia* no. 56 (October 1993): 37–66.
[35]Interview, March 1993.

ICMI members themselves make one of two claims. Some express pleasure at having finally been invited to play inside the state, which they believe is the only game in town and likely to remain so for a long time to come. Others see themselves as the opening wedge of a democratizing and/or Islamizing force that will soon, perhaps with the departure of President Suharto, transform Indonesian politics.[36]

DEVELOPMENTALIST ACCEPTANCE OF PANCASILA DEMOCRACY

It seems probable that the developmentalists and the other groups who for reasons of self-interest pretend to accept Pancasila Democracy are much larger in numbers and, until now, have proved to possess more durable political resources than the authentic accepters and rejecters. If I am correct, what explains this distribution of attitudes? Six factors, in rough descending order of importance, perhaps account for most of the imbalance.

First, the long record of development success has been crucial. For the developmentalists, it constitutes continuing proof that they are on the right track, that the policies they promote and the theory behind those policies do in fact produce development. They are thus morally justified in continuing to pretend in public—which includes such actions as accepting Golkar nomination as election vote-getters and appearing before DPR committees to defend their policies—that Pancasila Democracy is a genuine form of democracy. For many of the other groups, the balance of exchange—what they get in return for their acceptance of Pancasila Democracy—is heavily material and is thus also dependent on a continually growing economy.

Second, the concentration of resources used to dispense rewards and sanctions in the central government, and finally in the hands of President Suharto himself, makes cooperation with the government extremely attractive and dissent from it extremely costly. Many individuals and groups have felt the sting of presidential displeasure, some for more than twenty years. It is widely appreciated that the government is fully cognizant of the extent of its resources and knows how to use them to maximum advantage to itself. This factor, of course, is also dependent, particularly on the reward side, with a high economic-growth rate.

Third, Pancasila Democracy provides a set of stable institutions and

---

[36]Columns in the ICMI daily newspaper *Republika*, founded in January 1993, frequently hint at this possibility.

divides resources fairly widely among individual players within the system below Suharto himself. Conflict over the distribution of spoils is thus resolved in a way that leaves both winners and losers capable of fighting another day. Recent examples are the post-1992 election battles among active military, retired military, civilian bureaucrats, and others over regional governorships, legislative chairs, and Golkar leadership positions. Defeated candidates tend not to withdraw from the system but to look for another opportunity to advance within it.[37]

Fourth, the ideological construction of Pancasila Democracy is loose and incorporative enough, a mentality rather than an ideology in the language of Juan Linz, that few groups feel unable to associate themselves with it in principle.[38] By comparison, to accept communist ideology meant to reject both religious belief and a major role for private enterprise in the economy. The biggest battles against Pancasila in the New Order have been fought by Muslim groups who accuse the government of trying to turn Pancasila into a religion. In the 1980s, many Muslims bitterly opposed the implementation of regulations requiring all political and social organizations to make Pancasila their *asas tunggal* (sole principle). Almost all were forced to capitulate and have since discovered that the regulations make no difference in their ability to practice their faith. Indeed, they have learned that acceptance of Pancasila has made it easier for them to advance their interests within the regime.

Fifth, the institutions of Pancasila Democracy provide many stages—bureaucratic, legislative, mass media, even the arena of the street—at many levels—national, provincial, district, village—where social groups usually outside the system can seek redress for grievances against officials or other groups. Examples in the 1990s have included: complaints by the people of Eastern Indonesia that the rate of growth in their region is too slow, which have been brought to Jakarta both by provincial officials and by private businesspeople and traditional leaders; protests by villagers in West Java against the low compensation they receive when they are forced to sell their land for housing developments, golf courses, and shopping malls; and protests by middle-class urbanites against a new law imposing prohibitively high fines for traffic offenses. My point is not that the protesters in each of these cases succeeded in

---

[37]A case in point is Major General (ret.) Basofi Sudirman, who became governor of East Java after losing out in the competition for the governorship of Jakarta.

[38]Juan Linz, "An Authoritarian Regime: Spain," in E. Allardt and I. Littunen, eds., *Mass Politics* (New York: Free Press, 1970), 251–83.

reversing government policy but rather that some action was usually taken and the majority of the protesters then felt that there is a measure of flexibility in the system.

Finally, even some of the most diehard anti–New Order dissidents question only the implementation, not the principle, of Pancasila Democracy. I am thinking in particular of the Petition of 50, a group of prominent retired military officers and civilian intellectuals and activists who have been hammering away at the government for decades on issues of democracy, human rights, and the political role of the military. Their complaint is not against Pancasila, the Constitution of 1945, or even the twin functions doctrine of the armed forces, but rather that Suharto operates a personal dictatorship under cover of these high principles. Even as they criticize the government, therefore, their words and actions help to legitimate the basic institutions of the regime.

INAUTHENTIC AND AUTHENTIC LEGITIMACY

What kind of legitimacy has the New Order created with its quinquennial elections and legislative institutions that are so obviously not democratic? My answer has been: a kind of second-order or inauthentic legitimacy, in which most members of the political public accord authentic legitimacy to the regime on other grounds and seek to please officials and domestic and foreign audiences by feigning belief in the government's democraticness.

Because it is so dependent on developmental success, democratic legitimation must be inherently fragile. Moreover, the government's reliance on the substratum of development must be, in the language of game theory, a lose-lose proposition. If economic growth slows or stops, a significant portion of the developmentalists and the other progovernment groups will cease being supportive and demand a new government, perhaps even a genuinely democratic one. If economic growth continues, the probability is that new middle-class groups—as in South Korea, Thailand, and Taiwan—will begin to demand autonomy and a decision-making process more responsive to their interests.

Though fragile, this combination of authentic developmental and inauthentic democratic legitimation has nonetheless lasted for more than a quarter century. Reasons for perdurability include the six factors limned above, the personal political skills of Suharto, who has governed for the whole of the New Order, and at the bottom line what we might call an effective legitimacy-coercion balance in the political system.

When developmental plus democratic legitimacy have not been enough to win the day, there has been no hesitation to use force. At the same time, the government has always tried to shift away from coercion and back to developmental and democratic legitimation as quickly as possible. The need for an effective balance is evident from the experiences of Suharto's neighbors: Ne Win in Burma and Ferdinand Marcos in the Philippines, who once had it but lost it; and Mahathir Mohamad in Malaysia and Lee Kuan Yew in Singapore, who, like Suharto, have always been able to restore it.

Is democratic legitimation likely to become more or less fragile in the future? Most signs point toward increasing fragility. Pancasila Democracy as conceived and promoted in New Order Indonesia is an oxymoron, two contradictory halves in irreconcilable tension with each other. The meaning of the Pancasila half is for the present under the government's control, but a number of circumstances—the end of the Suharto presidency, an increase in armed-forces concern about future political stability, the rise of new social and political groups—could change that.

The meaning of the democracy half, which derives originally from outside Indonesia, is definitely not under the government's control, and the foreign and domestic forces promoting genuinely representative democracy are growing. The firestorm of international protest fanned by the 1991 Santa Cruz massacre required all of Suharto's diplomatic skill to contain.[39] The government faces more international condemnation not only on the East Timor issue but also for its repressive labor policy and continuing violation of the human rights of its citizens. Within Indonesia, the banning of the three newsmagazines in mid-1994 prompted a modest increase in dissident activity. Perhaps more importantly, it provided compelling new evidence to the magazines' millions of readers, who constitute a large majority of the political public, that it has little tolerance for a free press and even less interest in genuine democratization. For how many of these readers and for how much longer can the New Order's version of Pancasila Democracy remain a useful fiction?

[39]R. William Liddle, "Indonesia's Threefold Crisis," *Journal of Democracy* 3, no. 4 (October 1992): 60–74.

3

Ｏ＝■Ｉ

Elections without representation:
The Singapore experience under the PAP

GARRY RODAN

INTRODUCTION

In Singapore, regular and open elections have existed alongside authoritarianism for decades.[1] In this situation, elections have not given effect to broader democratic representations or processes. Rather, extraparliamentary constraints on challenges to the policies and ideologies of the ruling People's Action Party (PAP) have generally rendered elections a stunted political expression—not the periodic culmination of many contests over social and political power, but the only contest. Nevertheless, in the PAP's historical struggle for, and subsequent consolidation of, political supremacy, elections have been a significant institution. They have afforded the PAP government a political legitimacy not enjoyed by other authoritarian regimes, especially important in limiting the impact of external criticism. Ironically, elections have thus enabled the PAP to claim a mandate in operating outside democratic processes between ballots.

There has never been any pretense on the part of the PAP leadership that the formal appearances of liberal democracy in Singapore reflect the actual substance of the political system. In the early years of self-government Prime Minister Lee Kuan Yew declared that "Western type parliamentary democracy has to be adapted and adjusted to suit the practical realities of our position."[2] Lee expressed deep reservations

---

[1] Under the Constitution, elections are required at least every five years. In practice, the People's Action Party (PAP) has not gone the full five years since 1968, tending to call elections a year earlier than required.
[2] Quoted in Alex Josey, *Lew Kuan Yew: The Struggle for Singapore* (Sydney: Angus and Robertson, 1974), 229.

about the capacity of political oppositions in the Asian context to play
a constructive role. Added to this was the view that Singapore, like other
developing countries, ran a certain risk with universal suffrage because
the requisite strong leadership and policies promoting economic growth
could not be guaranteed popular support.[3] Following the failed merger
with Malaysia and Singapore's political independence, the imperatives
of nation building also entered into the list of caveats about the democratic process.[4] These arguments formed the basis of the PAP's justification not just for a host of constraints on the activities of opposition
political parties and dissident individuals in a dominant-party system[5]
but also for a virtual merging of the institutions of party and state, which
to a large extent afforded the mechanisms to effect such constraints.

The considerable power enjoyed by the ruling elite in this authoritarian system is further rationalized by an elaborate ideology of elitism,
which is now deeply embedded in the social structure of Singapore and
dominant within the political culture. According to this ideology, Singapore must be, and indeed as a result of reforms by successive PAP
administrations actually is, an uncompromising meritocracy. In this
view, government as a technical process is emphasized over government
as a political process, leading Chan to describe Singapore as an "administrative state."[6] Such an ideology is antithetical to any concept of
political representation that emphasizes the obligations of government
to reflect and/or respond to the aspirations and concerns of the electorate. Rather, it reinforces a strict Hobbesian notion of representation
as the authority to act, an authority in which elections provide formal
and periodic acknowledgment of the intrinsic merit of the leadership.
This elitism manifests itself not just in a rejection of interest-group representation in the political process, but it also shapes the selection of
candidates for the ruling party through an almost exclusive preoccupation with formal educational and technical qualifications. The ide-

[3]Ibid., 229–31.
[4]Chan Heng Chee, *Singapore: The Politics of Survival* (Singapore: Oxford University Press,
1971).
[5]Thomas Bellows, *The People's Action Party of Singapore: The Emergence of a Dominant
Party System* (New Haven: Southeast Asian Studies Monograph 13, Yale University Press,
1973), and Chan Heng Chee, *The Dynamics of One-Party Dominance: The PAP at the
Grassroots* (Singapore: Singapore University Press, 1976).
[6]Chan Heng Chee, *Politics in an Administrative State: Where Has the Politics Gone?*
(Singapore: Occasional Paper Series No. 11, Department of Political Science, University
of Singapore, 1975).

ology of meritocracy is thus a rationale for a very exclusive political process.

With the PAP enjoying a parliamentary monopoly from 1966 to 1981, elections were unproblematic for authoritarian rule. However, a sustained electoral decline since the early 1980s, though not suggestive of a change of government in the foreseeable future, has aroused serious concern within the PAP. Yet precisely because elections have been the only sanctioned avenue for political contestation, and because the PAP has itself drawn so readily on their existence for its legitimacy, elections are now entrenched in the political system; they could be emasculated only at serious political cost to the PAP. Instead, the government has responded with a number of institutional reforms to the political system, including the electoral process, and modifications to the ideological justification for a virtual one-party state in Singapore.

Although these responses have their limitations and even contradictions, we should be careful not to overstate the immediate democratic possibilities in Singapore and the role elections might play in this. In particular, opposition political parties remain constrained in their ability to form meaningful power bases. The PAP's continued hostility to any notion of political representation mitigates against the involvement of non-state-sponsored organizations in the political process, however indirectly. But a less recognized constraint is the ideological success the PAP has had with opposition parties themselves. Their implicit acceptance of elitist PAP assumptions about the purpose and process of government also stifles the development of an alternative politics that could find expression through the ballot and offer voters a significant choice. At both the structural and the ideological levels, politics as a process of representation has yet to achieve legitimacy within Singapore.

POSTWAR ELECTIONS AND PAP ELECTORAL DOMINANCE

The attainment of Singapore's self-government and independence was channeled through the electoral process and political parties. After administrative separation from Malaya and Singapore's declaration as a Crown Colony in 1946, a legislative council was inaugurated in 1948, which comprised six elected seats and a further sixteen ex officio and nominated members. New elections in 1951 raised the proportion of elected seats to nine out of twenty-five. However, it was only with the advent of the Rendel Constitution of 1955 that elections began to assume meaning for the general population. The Rendel Constitution, while retaining defense, finance, and internal security matters in the hands of the governor, introduced automatic voter registration and a new thirty-two-member legislative assembly, twenty-five seats of which were directly elected by the people in April of that year.

Prior to this, the party of the domestic bourgeoisie, the Singapore Progressive Party and the Singapore Labour Party, led by middle-class, English-speaking Indians, had enjoyed electoral success because the process was largely exclusive of the non-English-educated working class and petite bourgeoisie. The early parties failed to reflect anything but the narrow interests and aspirations of the elite.[7] However, the prospect of self-government set in train a flowering of political parties, including the PAP and the Singapore Labour Front—both formed in 1954 and both quickly commanding genuine popular support.[8] The PAP, a convenient alliance between radical representatives of the Chinese working class and a group of English-educated, middle-class nationalists, engaged selectively in the electoral process leading up to 1959, keeping the pressure on for complete, rather than partial, self-government. By the time this materialized, compulsory voting had been introduced. This, combined with a first-past-the-post system, gave the PAP reason to embrace the 1959 elections wholeheartedly. In the event, it won forty-three of the fifty-one legislative seats with 53.4 percent of the total vote.

It should be understood that the establishment of the electoral process and multiparty politics before self-government was not indicative of any common set of political values about the broader political process itself. Rather, elections represented a means by which a party might assert political dominance. Hence, when in office, the PAP felt no constraint in engaging in various violations of democratic principles and had no commitment to the building of democratic political institutions that might support the electoral process.

Despite its resounding win, the early 1960s were years of considerable internal turmoil for the PAP. The intensity of the power struggle between its two economically diverse factions was exacerbated by the issue of merger with the Federation of Malaysia, resulting in the formation in

---

[7]Yeo Kim Wah, "A Study of Three Early Political Parties in Singapore," *Journal of Southeast Asian History* 10, no. 1 (1969): 115–41.
[8]Five parties contested the 1955 elections and by 1959 there were ten contesting elections for self-government.

1963 of a new party, the Barisan Sosialis (BS). The consequent exodus of the Left from the PAP depleted the party of its grassroots base and threw its electoral viability into question. However, rather than abandon the electoral process, the PAP government exploited its executive powers to impair the capacity of its new formal opponents. Most conspicuous in this was the use of the state-owned Singapore Broadcasting Commission for propaganda and the exercise of the Internal Security Act to intimidate activists in the trade union movement, journalists, and others.[9] Understandably, the BS's base in the trade union movement was a priority target. But at the same time, the government introduced further social reforms in housing and education to cultivate greater support within the working class.

The split also precipitated the integration of the PAP and the state. This involved more than just an alliance between the PAP and senior civil service bureaucrats who accrued greater power as the public sector's importance to social and economic development increased. Freed of the necessity to respond to grassroots policy initiatives, and indeed wary of newcomers within party organizational ranks, the PAP leadership transferred and assigned various political functions to the bureaucracy. Over time, the politicization of the civil service resulted in such a close relationship between its upper echelons and the government that the two became almost indistinguishable. Increasingly, recruitment into government occurred via the civil service.[10] But more than just asserting the leadership's control over the party organization, the intermeshing of the government and the public bureaucracy established new forms of social and political control for the PAP. In this project, community centers and Citizens' Consultative Committees became important institutions through which the policies and values of the technocratic elite were transmitted.[11]

As the electoral record shows, the above formula managed to hold the PAP in office in 1963 and consolidate its power thereafter. Instead

---

[9]T. J. S. George, *Lew Kuan Yew's Singapore* (London: Andre Deutsch, 1973); and Dennis Bloodworth, *The Tiger and the Trojan Horse* (Singapore: Times Books International, 1986).

[10]Khong Cho Oon, "Managing Conformity: The Political Authority and Legitimacy of a Bureaucratic Elite," revised paper presented at the workshop on Political Legitimacy in Southeast Asia, Chiangmai, February 23–6, 1993, 12–4.

[11]Seah Chee Meow, *Community Centres in Singapore* (Singapore: Singapore University Press, 1973); and Seah Chee Meow, "Parapolitical Institutions" in Jon S. T. Quah, Chan Heng Chee, and Seah Chee Meow, eds., *Government and Politics in Singapore* (Singapore: Oxford University Press, 1987), 173–94.

of weakening the government, the political and economic uncertainty created by the failed merger with Malaysia was used to rationalize new levels of state control in the name of safeguarding the national interest. Lee Kuan Yew stressed the centrality of a "very tightly organized society" in surviving the precarious situation Singapore now faced.[12] Furthermore, the new export-oriented industrialization program had shown significant results by the time of the 1968 elections, with manufacturing employment rising from 45,535 in 1965 to 73,059 three years later.[13] Meanwhile, by October 1966, the PAP's major opponents, the BS, had withdrawn from the parliamentary process altogether. It called on the PAP to act on eight demands relating to the conditions for serious political opposition, including the release of political prisoners, freedom of speech, and the abolition of detention laws. But if the BS felt it was impaired in the parliamentary process, party leader Lee Siew Choh's call to advance the "struggle outside Parliament,"[14] which would have tested the full force of the PAP state, never got off the ground. In the 1968 election, the PAP won fifty-one of the fifty-eight seats unopposed and picked up the remaining seven with comfortable majorities. The remarkable subsequent economic transformation of Singapore ensured that the PAP's electoral stocks remained exceptionally high, with the party averaging 72 percent of the total vote for the next three general elections and a total monopoly of parliamentary seats.

This period of absolute political dominance by the PAP went hand in hand with the institutionalization of rigid hierarchical structures throughout both the political and social spheres, aided greatly by the supportive ideology of meritocracy. This ideology is neatly encapsulated in Lee Kuan Yew's 1967 observation that in every society there is some five percent of the population "who are more than ordinarily endowed physically and mentally and in whom we must expend our limited and slender resources in order that they will provide that yeast, that ferment, that catalyst in our society that alone will ensure that Singapore shall maintain its pre-eminent place in the societies that exist in South and Southeast Asia."[15] Very quickly, and without any serious debate over the criteria of merit, formal educational and professional qualifications

---

[12]Chan, *Singapore: Politics of Survival*, 51.
[13]Garry Rodan, *The Political Economy of Singapore's Industrialization: National State and International Capital* (London: Macmillan, 1989), 99.
[14]Quoted in Chan, *Singapore: Politics of Survival*, 22.
[15]Quoted in George, *Lee Kuan Yew's Singapore*, 186.

Table 3.1. *Parliamentary elections since 1955*

Date	Number of seats	Number of parties contesting	Party returned	Number of seats won	Percentage of votes won[a]
Legislative Assembly					
1955 April 2	25[b]	5 and 11 independents	Labour Front	10	26.74
1959 May 30	51	10 and 39 independents	PAP	43	53.40
1963 September 21	51	8 and 16 independents	PAP	37	46.46
Parliament					
1968 April 13	7 + (51)[c]	2 and 5 independents	PAP	58	84.43
1972 September 2	57 + (8)	6 and 2 independents	PAP	65	69.02
1976 December 23	53 + (16)	7 and 2 independents	PAP	69	72.40
1980 December 23	38 + (37)	8	PAP	75	75.55
1984 December 22	49 + (30)	9 and 3 independents	PAP	77	62.94
1988 September 3	70 + (11)	8 and 4 independents	PAP	80	61.76
1991 August 31	40 + (41)	7 and 7 independents	PAP	77	59.31

[a]Refers to total votes cast, not total valid votes cast.
[b]The 1955 Legislative Assembly consisted of one Speaker, three ex officio members, 25 elected members, and four nominated members.
[c]Uncontested seats in parentheses.
Source: *Singapore 1992* (Singapore: Ministry of Information and the Arts, 1992), 234.

were adopted as the almost absolute and universal measure of elite entitlement. Accordingly, the primary and secondary education systems embarked on streaming programs to identify and nurture the gifted. This necessarily produced a very competitive and stressful education system but one that was expected to generate excellence and achievement. Despite the pretense of meritocracy, access to elite positions in general was not removed from systems of patronage. Within the PAP itself, access to the upper echelons was heavily controlled and anything but competitive, so that the party's leadership was self-appointed and unaccountable to any broader party forum. The criteria for entry into this political elite were of course internally determined.[16]

PAP ELECTORAL DECLINE

The PAP's parliamentary monopoly was not broken until October 1981, when Joshua Jeyaretnam of the Workers' Party (WP) prevailed in the predominantly low-income seat of Anson. In the subsequent 1984 gen-

[16]Bellows, *People's Action Party*, 24; James Cotton, "The Limits to Liberalization in Industrializing Asia: Three Views of the State," *Pacific Affairs* 64, no. 3 (1991): 316.

eral election, not only was Jeyaretnam returned, but Chiam See Tong of
the Singapore Democratic Party (SDP) won the seat of Potong Pasir—
by comparison with Anson, a seat with a greater share of lower-middle-
class voters.[17] More important, the PAP suffered a 12.6 percent fall in
its share of the total vote. Further but less substantial drops in support
for the PAP of 1.12 percent and 2.0 percent occurred respectively at the
1988 and 1991 elections. Given the first-past-the-post system, this translated into just one successful opposition candidate in 1988 and four in
1991. However, the point remains that the PAP begrudgingly recognized
the unlikelihood of restoring its share of the vote to the levels of the
1970s. By 1991, the collective vote of opposition parties was approaching 40 percent. The realistic objective became that of arresting the decline and ensuring the PAP's ability to condition the form political
opposition would take.

Although it is not the aim of this essay to analyze in any detail the
factors accounting for the erosion in the PAP's vote, the leadership has
until very recently operated from the assumption that the rapidly expanding middle class has been pivotal. Certainly in the wake of the
1984 general election there was a perception that Singapore's younger,
better-educated voters were more sympathetic to the PAP's opponents
than the previous generation of voters.[18] The party's analysis of the
1988 general election also led to a suspicion that Malay voters were
disproportionately receptive to the appeals of opposition parties. However, the 1991 election results revealed a different political dynamic.
Aside from the SDP's retention again of Potong Pasir, PAP losses occurred in the seats of Bukit Gombak, Nee Soon Central, and Hougang,
with slender government margins in the additional seats of Bukit Batok,
Nee Soon South, Braddell Heights, Changi, and Eunos. On top of this,
heavy swings against the government were recorded in Ulu Pandan, Ju-
rong, Bukit Merah, and Yu-Hua. Of all these electorates, only Ulu Pandan and Braddell Heights could be described as middle class. Support
for the opposition was largely coming from satellite towns on the outer

---

[17]The indicator being used here is the level of private housing and educational qualifications of the electorate. See John W. Humphrey, *Geographic Analysis of Singapore's Population* (Singapore: Department of Statistics, Census Monograph No. 5, 1985).
[18]By 1990, the middle class constituted around a quarter of Singapore's population, a
trebling of its 1957 proportion. See Garry Rodan, "The Growth of Singapore's Middle
Class and Its Political Significance," in Rodan, ed., *Singapore Changes Guard: Social,
Political and Economic Directions in the 1990s* (Melbourne: Longman Cheshire, 1993),
55.

edge of the city center, constituencies with high percentages of people with average and below-average incomes from a range of semiskilled and unskilled white- and blue-collar occupations. To the PAP's consternation, its so-called heartland of Chinese-educated, working-class voters had apparently defected in significant numbers. Rising living costs, growing inequalities, and, to a lesser extent, lingering animosities toward the government for its ethnic policies underlay much of this discontent. Although there has been an element of middle-class alienation with the PAP's repressive and paternalistic practices, this has been tempered by the knowledge that their social and economic positions are well served by PAP policies and the ideology of meritocracy. Class factors were certainly becoming more important to voting patterns, but not in the way hitherto perceived by the leadership of the ruling party. Rather, a growing consciousness of inequalities was developing among both the working and lower-middle classes. This was fueled by both a rise in conspicuous consumption among the privileged classes and a slowdown in the opportunities for social mobility as stratification became more rigid.

Although there is room for debate over the political roles of different social classes in contemporary Singapore, there can be no denying that rapid capitalist development in the city-state has generated a host of social and economic changes that have combined with demographic, ethnic, and cultural dynamics to produce a more differentiated electorate. The electoral trend necessarily called into question the effectiveness of the established political formula of the PAP. If Singapore was becoming more socially diverse, was the PAP capable of doing justice to its claim to national-movement status without dismantling its elitist structures and ideologies? Could it be taken seriously any longer in its pretense as the only institution capable of expressing the national interest?

THE INSTITUTIONAL RESPONSE

The PAP response to the shock loss in the Anson by-election was less than gracious. Not only was Jeyaretnam subjected to harsh treatment both inside and outside parliament, but government leaders also embarked on a new verbal offensive against political systems characterized by strong parliamentary oppositions. Concerned that younger Singaporeans in particular might be attracted to the notion of a stronger opposition presence in parliament,[19] Lee Kuan Yew asserted that at best an opposition makes no difference to good government. He went on to warn that "if we are unlucky, like most developing countries, an opposition can make for confusion by raising false expectations of unattainable benefits from greater welfare spending, as in Britain and so many Third World countries."[20] Lee's conflation of the principle of oppositions in general with welfare policies reflected another preoccupation of equal importance to the then prime minister. Second Deputy Prime Minister Sinnathamby Rajaratnam subsequently went even further to claim that "the role of an opposition is to ensure bad government."[21] The initial response to the breaking of its parliamentary monopoly, then, was a resolve that Jeyaretnam's feat should not, and would not, be repeated. This approach simply generated greater public sympathy and admiration for Jeyaretnam and set in train unprecedented criticism of the PAP through letters to the daily, English-language newspaper, the *Straits Times*. Soon the PAP revised its strategy, turning its attention to institutional reforms.

The first such reform involved amending the constitution in July 1984 to provide for a new category of parliamentary member—the nonconstituent member of parliament (NCMP)—under which the three highest vote-getters among the unsuccessful opposition could be invited to enter parliament. NCMPs were unable to vote on money bills, bills altering the constitution, or no-confidence motions in the government, but they could speak on these issues and vote on all other bills. The intention was to alter public perceptions of the PAP as intolerant of political opposition and to appease what it suspected was rising sentiment among the English-educated middle class for some form of opposition for its own sake. However, this did not prevent a dramatic swing against the government in the December election of that year. The offer of an NCMP seat after the election was also turned down by opposition parties, who, at this stage, were united in the view that neither their problems nor the problems of the political system could be alleviated by the scheme.[22]

---

[19]About 200,000 people cast votes for the first time in the 1984 election and more than one-third of the electorate was below thirty years of age.

[20]*Straits Times* (ST), December 15, 1981, p. 1.

[21]Quoted in *Far Eastern Economic Review* (FEER), May 7, 1982, p. 21.

[22]This unified position only lasted until the next general election in 1988. On this occasion, the Workers' Party accepted an offer of two NCMP seats for Francis Seow and Lee Siew Choh. However, Seow was disqualified before parliament convened owing to a tax-eva-

The immediate response to the 1984 election gave expression to the peculiarity of the PAP's conception of elections and their relationship to government accountability. Lee raised the possibility of modifications to the one-person-one-vote system: "It is necessary to try and put some safeguards into the way in which people use their votes to bargain, coerce, to push, to jostle and get what they want without running the risk of losing the services of the government, because one day, by mistake, they will lose the services of the government." Rajaratnam virtually chastised the electorate and warned that "if it is an attempt by voters to blackmail the government (to compromise on important issues or principles), then we must show that we cannot be blackmailed."[23] Soon, however, the PAP's soul-searching resulted in a strategy, largely under the aegis of the so-called New Guard leaders groomed to take over the reins from Lee Kuan Yew and his generation of colleagues, to accommodate apparent aspirations for a less authoritarian political system. They, and Goh Chok Tong in particular, projected themselves as a force for a more consultative style of government that would take heed of constructive criticism. The substance to the claim was provided by such initiatives as the establishment within the Ministry of Community Development in 1985 of a Feedback Unit, an extraparliamentary institution both taking suggestions from the public and explaining government policies at the grassroots level; the adoption of Government Parliamentary Committees in 1987; the introduction of Town Councils progressively between 1986 and 1991 to decentralize administration of public housing estates and related activities; and the establishment of the Institute of Policy Studies to involve professionals in public policy discussion. With the exception of the Town Councils, the theme of these initiatives was the PAP's preference for direct dissent from its policies, particularly by the English-educated professionals, either through institutions that it could control or through means by which public policy debate might be depoliticized.

Town Councils, while opening up opportunities for greater participation in public affairs, had another angle to them. Because responsibility for Town Councils rested with the local MP, their establishment gave concrete expression to Lee Kuan Yew's view that constituencies rejecting PAP candidates should not be insulated from their "bad choices." So far,

---

sion conviction. No NCMP seats were offered after the 1991 election, so Lee is to date the only person to enter parliament as an NCMP.
[23]Both quotations from ST, December 24, 1984, p. 1.

however, there is no evidence of inferior administrative performance by opposition-run Town Councils and no public perception of such. That is not to say the opposition-run Town Councils have not had their special problems in dealing with government bureaucracies.[24] Prime Minister Goh Chok Tong has also indicated that priority in the projected upgrading of public housing estates will be given to constituencies with PAP members.[25]

These reforms were complemented by the introduction in 1990 of yet another category of MP—the nominated MP (NMP). Up to six NMPs could be appointed to parliament by the president, on the advice of a special select committee of parliament. The voting rights of NMPs were restricted in the same way as those of NCMPs, but their terms would be limited to two years rather than the life of a government.[26] As explained by then Deputy Prime Minister Goh Chok Tong, parliament could appoint publicly-nominated people who had excelled or had special expertise in the professions, commerce, industry, cultural activities, social services, or people from underrepresented constituencies, such as women. But unlike elected MPs, these people were expected to be nonpartisan. Importantly, the emphasis was on the contribution eminent individuals could make to parliament. It was not the government's intention to foster the idea of interest group representation. Once again, the PAP was trying to steer disaffection with it away from the formal opposition in favor of co-optation.

The concept of meritocracy permeates and shapes the government's initiatives even in oppositional politics. The PAP had always objected to the existing opposition on various grounds, but a recurring theme was its poor-quality personnel. Through the NMP scheme, the government projected itself as providing a responsible and, most importantly, capable opposition. However, the major attraction of NMPs for the PAP over the NCMP scheme is that they are an alternative to party representation. The NCMP did not work to dissuade voters from increasingly supporting opposition candidates, but the NMP scheme, government

---

[24]Among other problems, opposition-run councils experience inordinate delays in project approvals from authorities. One consequence of this has been the build-up of unspent funds. A recent change to the Town Councils Act has, however, increased the compulsory contribution each council is required to make to a Sinking Fund, thereby limiting the scope for surpluses.

[25]FEER, May 14, 1992, p. 15.

[26]This does not rule out the possibility of a candidate's being renominated and reappointed for a further two-year term.

leaders hope, may yet do that. For all intents and purposes, then, the NMP scheme has supplanted that of the NCMP.

Initially, two people were appointed to parliament under this new arrangement—a heart specialist and associate professor at the National University of Singapore, Maurice Choo, and the president and chief executive officer of the United Industrial Corporation Limited, who was also chair of the Singapore Tourist Promotion Board and former chief executive officer of the Trade and Development Board, Leong Chee Whye.[27] Neither made much impact on parliamentary debate nor attempted to speak on behalf of particular interests or groups. However, rather than abandon or downplay the scheme after the 1991 elections, when opposition membership in parliament rose from one to four, the government significantly boosted the number of NMP seats to six in 1992, as if to partially counter formal opposition gains and to test the scheme's potential seriously.

In the process, the government appears to have modified its original position on the impartiality of NMPs. Of the next six NMPs, three indicated a desire to speak on behalf of specific interests before entering parliament and have acted accordingly, even if an official charade is maintained that publicly emphasizes individual qualities and statuses of NMPs. In this group was Kanwaljit Soin, an orthopedic surgeon who is also a past president of the Association of Women for Action and Research (AWARE), the primary organizational advocate of women's interests in Singapore; Robert Chua, executive chairman of the air conditioning company A.C.E. Daikin and president of the Singapore Manufacturers' Association; and Tong Kok Yeo, secretary general of the Union of Telecoms Employees.[28] Another NMP, Chia Shi Teck, is managing director of the Hesche garment chain and has pursued matters of concern to local business.[29] To differing extents, party and state structures already incorporate organizations involving business, labor, and

[27]Leong Chee Whye died in 1993.
[28]The other MPs include an academic lawyer, Walter Woon, who had already enjoyed a high public profile notably through his challenging the prevailing official denunciations of Western values in a series of articles in the local press; and Toh Keng Kiat, a medical practitioner. While Toh has contributed little to parliamentary debate so far, Woon has made an impact. Among other things, he has called in parliament for legislation to enforce filial piety—a position that came as a surprise after his contributions to the earlier debates about liberalism.
[29]Chia created a stir when, after asserting that senior civil servants were inflexible in their dealings with the private sector, he claimed to have been advised by government backbenchers against taking too critical a stance.

women's groups. The most conspicuous of these is the National Trades Union Congress (NTUC), which, on behalf of organized labor, is supposedly involved with the PAP in a symbiotic relationship.[30] The PAP has also long had a Women's Wing, and although it has never been particularly active, attempts were made to revive it in 1988. While local business has never enjoyed an especially sympathetic ear from the PAP, since the mid-1980s there have been attempts to increase the channels of communication between it and the government.[31] The 1992 NMP appointments implicitly acknowledge, however, that such structures have not given adequate expression to the concerns of the groups to which they are linked. That inadequacy should come as little surprise, since these structures—particularly those linking the NTUC and the PAP—were designed to enhance the effectiveness of the government's message and not to solicit ideas about policy.

On the surface, the 1992 NMP appointments appear to concede some measure of legitimacy to the concept of interest group representation. However, this is not the intention of the exercise. There may be a calculation that it is politically expedient to make some concession to certain interests, but this should not be read as indicative of shifting political values within the PAP leadership. Rather, these appointments are a preemptive move to ensure that any disaffection with the government from de facto interest groups does not translate into greater support for opposition parties. In any case, the form of interest representation here remains a very indirect and qualified one. None of this rules out critical individuals' being appointed as NMPs. Indeed, the scheme will have no credibility if NMPs do not demonstrate a sufficient independence of mind from the government. Importantly, though, the government will be able to set the limits of this criticism through its control over appointment.

Alongside the above changes intended to provide alternatives to formal opposition parties, the PAP has also adjusted the rules under which elections are contested and introduced potential constraints on the policy options open to parties that win office. The former involved the establishment in 1988 of group representation constituencies (GRCs), whereby various constituencies are lumped together and contested as a

[30]Frederic C. Deyo, *Dependent Development and Industrial Order: An Asian Case Study* (New York: Praeger, 1981).
[31]Ian Chalmers, "Loosening State Control in Singapore: The Emergence of Local Capital as a Political Force," *Southeast Asian Journal of Social Science* 20, no. 2 (1992): 57–84.

group. Constituents thus vote for a team rather than an individual candidate. At least one in the team of GRC candidates fielded by a party, or alliance of parties, must be a member of an ethnic minority.[32] Initially each team involved three candidates, but this has since been raised to four. The pretext for this move was the need to guard against underrepresentation of minority groups. However, opposition parties complained it would stretch their limited resources and open up the scope for weak PAP candidates to be shielded through team membership. Coincidentally or otherwise, the troublesome seat of Anson disappeared in the redrawn boundaries, making way for the GRCs.

Ironically, given the declared intent of GRCs, Goh Chok Tong complained after the 1988 general election that a disproportionate number of Malays had supported opposition candidates. Opposition parties did relatively well in constituencies like Eunos and Bedok, where Malays constituted significant minorities. In a 1989 measure that seemed motivated by the desire to dilute the political impact of the Malay vote, the government implemented strict quotas for the ethnic mix of communities in public housing estates.[33] Because 85 percent of Singapore's residents live in these estates, the government has considerable control over the ethnic composition of electorates.

Another change to the political system is the elected presidency, something first publicly alluded to by Lee Kuan Yew in 1984. It was not until 1991, however, that the constitution was amended to provide for this. The new office involves such powers as the right to veto all senior civil service appointments and government expenditures, which draws on the considerable (currently US$47 billion) national financial reserves. The explanation for this significant constitutional modification was the need to guard against what Lee calls irresponsible (read "welfare-oriented") governments that would go down the path of deficit budgeting. Incidentally, the powers could conceivably be used to curtail any new-look PAP government that chose this course as much as they could restrain a non-PAP government. The new interest in institutional con-

---

[32]According to the Singapore Census of Population 1990, Singapore's population of just over 3 million is accounted for by the three major ethnic groups: Chinese 74.68 percent; Malays 13.53 percent; and Indians 7.61 percent.

[33]This did not require people to move, but meant that people selling flats might have to find a buyer from a nominated ethnic community. The actual quota, controlled at both the neighborhood and individual-apartment levels, puts a general ceiling of 80 percent for Chinese, while 22 percent at neighborhood level and 25 percent at the apartment level for Malays. For further details see FEER, March 9, 1989, p. 24.

straints on, and procedures for, government is thus to some extent a commentary on Lee Kuan Yew's concern with the possibility of some future internal deviation from established PAP policy fundamentals.

Eligibility for presidential candidacy effectively rules out any individual not part of the PAP establishment. Prospective presidential candidates must have a minimum of three years' experience in one of the following positions: cabinet minister, chief justice, speaker of parliament, attorney general, auditor-general, chairman of the public service commission, permanent secretary in the civil service, or chairman or chief executive officer of a company with a paid-up capital of at least S$100 million (US$62.5 million). A clause in the constitution also permits the presidential commission to grant eligibility for others to stand who do not qualify under the above, but this power can be exercised as much to limit as to open up candidacy. Former opposition MP Jeyaretnam applied unsuccessfully for a certificate of eligibility under this provision.

In the first presidential elections in 1993, the government persuaded a reluctant former auditor-general and executive chairman of POSBank, Chua Kim Yeow, to compete against the otherwise sole candidate—government minister and secretary-general of the NTUC, Ong Teng Cheong. Chua described his candidature as "an act of duty" and stated at the outset that he considered Ong "a far superior candidate."[34] As it turned out, Chua managed an amazing 41.3 percent of the vote.

The possibility of further significant institutional modification over the longer term was recently fueled by Lee Kuan Yew's proposal that, in fifteen to twenty years, it might be appropriate to give married men aged between thirty-five and sixty years two votes each—to reflect what he sees as their greater responsibilities and contributions to society. In particular, he is concerned that demographic trends might otherwise result in a disproportionate-aged voter population susceptible to welfare overtures.[35]

In reflecting on the various institutional changes to the political process since the early 1980s, two points warrant underlining. First, it is clear that the New Guard PAP leadership is no more relaxed about parliamentary opposition than its predecessors and uses new forms of institutionalized co-optation to stymie support for opposition parties. Second, these various forms of co-optation do not signal any intention

[34]*Straits Times Weekly Edition* (STWE), August 7, 1993, p. 1.
[35]See STWE, May 14, 1994, p. 6.

on the leadership's part to compromise on the elitist ideology of meritocracy. The case of the NMPs suggests, however, that the PAP's strategy runs a certain risk of inadvertently legitimizing notions of political representation at odds with "meritocracy." The ideological campaigns that have accompanied these institutional initiatives indicate the PAP's awareness of this sort of tension and a firm commitment that there be no challenge to the dominant political culture.

IDEOLOGICAL ADJUSTMENTS

In tandem with the establishment of new mechanisms of co-optation, the PAP set about updating its arguments for a distinctive form of democracy and consolidating its case against liberal democracy. Given the flurry of institutional modifications, the actual principles or values underlying the PAP's alternative to liberal democracy were in need of clarification and elaboration. Here the concepts of "consensus" and "communitarianism" loom large, and the idea of a distinctive "Asian democracy" has been important.

In the 1960s and 1970s, PAP leaders focused on what they saw as the historical and geopolitical obstacles to liberal democracy in Singapore. Reference to such obstacles has not disappeared, although there is necessarily some shift in emphasis. After all, Singapore is no longer the developing country with a problematic political existence it was in the 1960s. Recent statements by the Minister for Information and the Arts, George Yeo, who has taken over Rajaratnam's mantle as chief authority on matters ideological and philosophical, evidence this. According to him, the city-state of Singapore is simply too small to have two or more parties competing all out for government.[36] Yeo has written, "Democracy in Singapore must take into account our need to plan long-term, our small size, our social divisions and the importance of human resource development in maximizing the potential of every citizen."[37] Now it appears that continuing economic development, rather than the problems of initiating it, militates against liberal democracy.[38]

[36] *Straits Times Overseas Edition* (STWOE), October 31, 1992, p. 8.
[37] George Yeo, "Young PAP—Recasting the Net," *Petir* (May/June 1993): 19.
[38] It is not the suggestion here that competitive elections among parties are the definitive feature of democracy, only that the PAP's rationale for rejecting liberal democracy has shifted somewhat. For an attempt to define democracy in such a way that liberal democracy is but one variant, see Philippe C. Schmitter and Terry Lynn Karl, "What Democracy Is . . . And Is Not," *Journal of Democracy* 2, no. 3 (1991): 75–88.

In 1988, Goh Chok Tong observed that over the last decade there had
been a clear shift in societal values in Singapore, from "communitarianism" to "individualism."[39] As Goh saw it, the importance attached to
collective interests—including national interests—was being down-
graded, as self-seeking individuals increasingly adopted values more consistent with so-called Western liberalism. Undoubtedly Goh suspected
that the PAP's electoral decline had something to do with this perceived
change in values. Subsequently, not only was there a new verbal assault
by the PAP leadership on liberal-democratic models, but the party produced a formal document outlining a set of values that should under-
write Singapore's political system. A 1991 parliamentary White Paper,
entitled *Shared Values*, identified five values: nation before community
and society above self; family as the basic unit of society; regard and
community support for the individual; consensus instead of contention;
and racial and religious harmony. According to the government, it was
simply giving official recognition to established and dominant values,
but the debate leading up to the document witnessed widespread reservations and suspicion from the public. The non-Chinese communities
were particularly concerned that the Confucian flavor of the so-called
shared values represented a new assertion of Chinese cultural dominance.

Clearly, the two most important shared values are nation and community ahead of self, and consensus over contention. They are perceived
by the authors to be most directly pitted against liberal values. The former emphasized individual obligations to the state, not rights to be respected by the state. Explicit references to Confucian philosophy were
readily used by the leadership to distinguish Singapore's Asian brand of
government. Goh Chok Tong asserted, for example, that obligations to
the state along with

many Confucian values are still relevant to us. An example is the concept of
government by honourable men *(junzi)*, who have a duty to do the right for the
people, and who have the trust and respect of the population. This fits us better
than the Western concept that a government should be given as limited powers
as possible, and always treated with suspicion, unless proved otherwise.[40]

[39]Goh Chok Tong, "Our National Ethic," *Speeches* 12, no. 5 (1988): 13.
[40]"The National Identity—A Direction and Identity for Singapore," ibid. 13, no. 1 (1989):
34.

Many observers have questioned the new interest within the PAP leadership in Confucian philosophy. Chua describes the trend as "a conceptual foil to reinterpret the hitherto practices of the state."[41] Among other things, this promotion of Confucianism involved the Singapore government's enlisting the help in the early 1980s of eight overseas scholars to incorporate Confucianism into the secondary-school syllabus. Cotton refers to the exercise as an attempt to "reinvent Confucianism for a population never especially familiar with it."[42]

The other core PAP value, nation and community ahead of self, was central to the rationale behind the various institutions of co-optation, prescribing a particular form of oppositional politics devoid of interest group involvement. The document, however, did not address the question of how consensus is to be determined or what structures or processes might be involved.[43] Clammer notes that the political culture the PAP is attempting to institutionalize through *Shared Values* is antithetical to political pluralism and leaves little room for significant political participation other than that sanctioned by the PAP.[44] Consensus, therefore, is not so much a working out of compromises between different interests and perspectives as an ideology that represses differences per se. What matters in political terms, though, is not that consensus exists, but that governments can portray their policies in this light. George Yeo's reference to democracy as "a process which forces governments to engage the enthusiasm of increasing numbers in order to govern effectively" is perfectly consistent with this.[45]

The substantial recent ideological investment of the PAP in the concept of consensus not only reflects concern about the possibility of further

[41]Chua Beng Huat, "Confucianization in Modernising Singapore," paper presented at the Beyond Culture? The Social Sciences and the Problem of Cross Cultural Comparison Conference, Evangelical Academy at Loccum, Germany, October 1990, p. 19.

[42]Cotton, "The Limits to Liberalization," 320. Also see Kernial Singh Sandhu and Paul Wheatley, eds., *Management of Success: The Moulding of Singapore* (Singapore: Institute of Southeast Asian Studies, 1989), 1096, which challenges the notion that Confucianism has been central to Singapore's economic success.

[43]Chua Beng Huat, in "Towards a Non-Liberal Communitarian Democracy," unpublished paper presented at Murdoch University, June 9, 1993, also makes the point that the mechanisms for consultation that might evidence the commitment to arriving at consensus don't exist. However, he sees democratic potential in this to the extent that the government's rhetoric may yet come back to haunt it.

[44]John Clammer, "Deconstructing Values: The Establishment of a National Ideology and Its Implications for Singapore's Political Future," in Rodan, ed., *Singapore Changes Guard*, 39–40.

[45]STWOE, September 3, 1991, p. 8.

opposition party gains; it also has important implications for the interpretation of election results. While on the surface the number of votes for opposition parties may appear unthreatening, especially if many of these votes are actually protest votes against the PAP rather than wholehearted endorsements of opposition parties, they nevertheless testify to the absence of consensus. As Chua puts it, "Electoral support is thus not about how well the opposition parties do but rather how united is the nation behind the PAP leadership and the party's self-conception as a 'people's movement'."[46] It is thus difficult to see how the PAP's brand of consensus can be reconciled with strong opposition political parties.

The simultaneous and heightened attacks on "Western liberalism" are tied to the PAP's attempt to reinforce the ideology of meritocracy. Its fear is that Singapore's meritocratic structures would be a casualty of any notion of representation legitimizing interest groups as political actors. The leadership and the government-owned media take every opportunity to depict the economic decline or stagnation of countries with liberal-democratic systems as a fundamental consequence of the responsiveness of governments to the misguided and self-proclaimed rights of individuals and groups. Possibly the second most pejorative term (after liberalism) in the PAP lexicon is "welfarism," seen as the quintessential manifestation of this process. Hence, Prime Minister Goh refers to "the democratic distemper which afflicts peoples whose economies have become sluggish because of subsidies."[47] Liberal societies are also seen to be in a broader moral or social decay and here much store is made of neoconservative critiques from within that invariably lament the decline of values supportive of more hierarchical social and political orders.[48]

The PAP's fear of welfarism is more a political than an economic one. Although the categories of social security and welfare in the Singapore budget represent a minuscule component of total expenditure,[49] the proportion of government spending on education and housing is well above

---

[46]Huat, "Toward a Non-Liberal Communitarian Democracy."

[47]Goh, "My Urgent Mission," *Petir*, November/December 1992, p. 9. Also see Goh's contribution to the debate on the President's Address in *Parliamentary Debates Singapore* 59, no. 5 (January 16, 1992): columns 354–55, in which he elaborates on his government's case against welfarism and expounds on the policies of "levelling up," which he distinguishes from welfare.

[48]See, for example, Barbara Dafoe Whitehead, "The Case of the Vanishing Parent," *Sunday Times* (London), May 2, 1993, Focus section, p. 7.

[49]In 1988, for example, they represented just 2.01 percent of total budget expenditure, compared with an international average of around 30 percent. See STWOE, February 29, 1992, p. 13.

world averages. In fact, Prime Minister Goh estimated in 1993 that an average Singaporean owning a three-bedroom flat would receive about S$70,000 in direct government subsidy over a lifetime.[50] What the government has resisted is the principle of redistribution as a means of redressing social and economic inequalities. Such a course, it has repeatedly warned, would kill the goose that lays the golden egg—the talented elite upon whom all Singaporeans are dependent. According to Goh, "If you level down society, you want everybody to be equal, you are not sharing prosperity. You are sharing poverty."[51] Hence, a new PAP slogan has been popularized in an attempt to dampen debate about social and economic inequalities: "the politics of envy."[52] There is a certain resonance here with Plato's derisive reference in *Republic* to democracy as the government not of the people but of the poor against the rich.

Yet at the same time, and in the wake of the 1991 election, which evidenced significant alienation from the PAP by low-income voters, the PAP has actually embarked on programs and policies that, however indirectly, amount to increased welfare spending targeting those on lower incomes. For example, through its dollar-for-dollar sponsoring of ethnic community organizations established to assist lower-income Singaporeans—namely Mendaki (Malay), Sinda (Indian), and the Chinese Development Assistance Council—the government is allocating several hundred million dollars per year now in welfare spending. Voluntary welfare organizations can receive up to 80 percent of construction and 50 percent of operating costs from the government, as well as state help in securing land and premises at nominal cost and in granting tax exemptions. The government has also extended direct assistance to low-income families through the Small Family Scheme. In cases where parents each earn below S$750 per month, the government is now committed to providing a grant of S$800 per year into the mother's Central Provident Fund for twenty years or until she reaches forty-five years of

[50]STWOE, March 20, 1993, p. 5.
[51]STWOE, August 17, 1991, p. 4.
[52]This slogan was popularized following a letter to the "Forum" column of *The Straits Times* on February 17, 1993 by the assistant secretary-general of the SDP, Chee Soon Juan, in which a number of points were made about the unequal benefits of Singapore's prosperity. This aroused stern criticism in parliament from various PAP members, including Prime Minister Goh, who claimed that if the SDP "succeeded in pushing the politics of envy, Singapore would go down the drain. The middle class will envy the upper classes. The poor will envy everyone else" (as quoted in STWOE, March 13, 1993, p. 5). Thereafter, PAP MPs and journalists have used the phrase with great frequency.

age, whichever is earlier. The grant is conditional, however, on the family's size being limited to two children, and thus it has a significant social engineering element to it. In another gesture of positive discrimination in favor of the underprivileged, the government has paid the December monthly service and conservancy charges for lower-income people living in public flats for both 1992 and 1993.

But although it is prepared to spend more money alleviating the conditions of the poor—and, of course, keen to capitalize politically on this—it simultaneously condemns welfarism. There are several interrelated reasons for the government's extreme sensitivity over debate about social and economic inequalities and its eagerness to distinguish its role in welfare from that of Western counterparts. Certainly Singapore's leaders are convinced that there is an economic imperative underlying the case for meritocracy. As Prime Minister Goh reiterated, "It is this practice of meritocracy in the civil service, in politics, in business and in schools, which has allowed Singaporeans to achieve excellence and to compete against others."[53] But more fundamental political considerations underscore the hostility to welfarism. None is more serious than Goh's concern that "the disadvantaged do not expect and cannot demand that they be looked after by the State as a matter of right."[54] The notion of rights infers a very different set of political relationships. Most important, it calls into question the political preeminence of experts in the policy process because it is grounded in a notion of political representation as a legitimate aspiration in public policy that is unrelated to any technical credentials.

POLITICAL OPPOSITION

Aside from the general pervasiveness of the PAP state, there are numerous problems for opposition parties in competing with the PAP in elections. First, they cannot match the PAP's strategic propaganda advantage of sympathetic government-owned and -controlled domestic media.[55] Second, there is a strong fear of persecution for involvement with opposition parties. The long list of candidates and activists taken to

---

[53]Goh, "My Urgent Mission," p. 15.
[54]STWE, September 18, 1993, p. 1.
[55]The editor of *The Straits Times*, Leslie Fong, publicly acknowledges his pro-government stance and makes no apology for it. For comments by Fong and a general discussion of the press in Singapore see *Asiaweek*, September 25, 1992, pp. 45–55.

court by government members serves as a strong negative example to would-be participants in the political process.[56] The sacking of a National University of Singapore academic, Chee Soon Juan, for alleged misuse of research funds not long after he contested the December 1992 by-election in Marine Parade is likely to have reinforced the belief that opposition politics remains a personally risky affair. In a city-state where the government is not only a substantial employer, but also the major dispenser of commercial contracts, there is a perception that careers and business interests can easily be jeopardized by association, however indirect, with opposition parties. Third, and this is not completely unrelated, as a legacy of decades of authoritarian rule, alienation from politics in general is high in Singapore.[57] But despite these and other odds,[58] opposition parties have made some progress over the last decade. But can more substantive gains be made in the near future? And what are the prospects of elections becoming a more meaningful exercise in democratic choice in Singapore?

Although there are twenty-two registered opposition political parties in Singapore,[59] many fewer are consistently active in contesting elections and promoting their causes. Those that are include the SDP, WP, National Solidarity Party, Singapore National Malay Organization, and Singapore Justice Party. Only the WP and the SDP have actually won seats from the government since the BS abandoned the parliamentary process in 1966. All of these parties, however, are very limited in structure and resources and are comparatively dormant between elections. Given that the PAP usually provides little more than the minimum required nine-days' notice of election, campaigning itself is often a brief

---

[56]Lee Kuan Yew himself has sued as many as thirteen people for libel (Stan Sesser, "A Reporter at Large (Singapore)," *The New Yorker*, January 13, 1992, p. 64). The most noteworthy case is that of J. B. Jeyaretnam, whose latest spat with Lee Kuan Yew cost him a total of more than S$800,000 in damages and costs after he was found guilty of defamation for comments at an election rally in 1988.

[57]The PAP itself is worried about the implications of this for its own organizational future. It has recently set up Young PAP in an attempt to stimulate more interest in the party. See Yeo, "Young PAP," 10–29.

[58]For a discussion of other odds, see Chan, *Dynamics of One-Party Dominance*, 185–220; and R. S. Milne and Diane K. Mauzy, *Singapore: The Legacy of Lee Kuan Yew* (Boulder: Westview Press, 1990), 91–5.

[59]At the time of writing (August 1994), a breakaway group within the SDP has made application to form a separate party—the Singapore People's Party. The official recognition of this party would bring the total to twenty-three. For a discussion on the moves to form the Singapore People's Party, see STWE, July 9, 1994, p. 4. Some consideration has also been given to a merger between the WP and the National Solidarity Party, but as yet this has not transpired. See STWOE, January 9, 1993, p. 13.

affair. Cooperation between opposition parties in determining who will contest which electorate has been one way of maximizing limited resources. Significantly, the most successful opposition strategy was that of the 1991 general election in which the government was unopposed in just over half (forty-one) of the total (eighty-one) seats. On this basis, the PAP could not play up the idea of a freak result (that is, the unforeseen removal of the government through protest votes), and the desirability or otherwise of opposition per se came into central focus.

The current official memberships of the SDP and the WP are 491 and 2,557 respectively,[60] but active membership must be distinguished from mere registration. Only about 100 of these within the WP, and even fewer within the SDP, could be described as active. Party cadres number around sixty-five for the WP and fifty-two for the SDP. But if the limited personnel involved are striking features of the two parties, even more so are the organizational structures: Both are elitist along PAP lines. Like the PAP model, the executives of the SDP and the WP appoint cadres (referred to as organizing members in the case of the WP),[61] who in turn elect the executive, referred to as the central executive committee in the case of the SDP and the council in the WP case. There is a significant centralization of power within each party's structure. In organizational practice, then, neither party gives expression to a democratic alternative to the PAP.

Another parallel between the PAP and the major opposition parties is the premium placed on the recruitment of professionals as election candidates. This is part of the reason behind the special importance attached by the SDP to the recent attraction of neuropsychologist and Ph.D. Chee Soon Juan into its ranks. Certainly much of the general population has internalized the PAP's ideology of meritocracy and measures the suitability of candidates almost exclusively in terms of formal educational qualifications. Opposition parties cannot ignore this reality. Yet, the elitist assumption underlying such an expectation is not a matter of serious political contest. They try to match the PAP's credentials. In the 1991 general election, much was made by the SDP that its nine candidates all boasted tertiary education qualifications.

Of the two major parties, the WP comes closer to an explicit ideolog-

---

[60]Registry of Societies, Singapore, 1993. These figures predate the formation of the Singapore People's Party.
[61]The proposed Singapore People's Party also intends to adopt a cadre system.

Table 3.2. *WP and SDP in general elections, 1976–91*

	1976	1980	1984	1988[a]	1991
WP					
Seats contested	22	8	15	32	13
% of votes in constituencies contested	28.0	29.2	41.9	38.5	41.1
SDP					
Seats contested	—	3	4	18	9
% of votes in constituencies contested	—	30.7	46.1	39.5	48.6

[a]Workers' Party merged with Barisan Sosialis and Singapore United Front
Source: STWOE (September 1, 1991): 24

ical posture. Since its formation in 1957, the WP has, as its name suggests, projected itself as the custodian of the working class. However, while it is philosophically guided by a social-democratic conception of social justice, it is by no means a radical party. It produced a reasonably detailed party manifesto for the 1988 election that outlines a series of proposed programs to improve the conditions for lower-income earners and to enhance civil liberties generally. The rigid streaming within the education system is also challenged. At the same time, it emphasizes the need for "responsible trade unionism" and asserts that "trade unions must never be so powerful as to promote sectional interests at the expense of the rest of society." The importance of the private sector is also underlined, with a commitment to "ensure that the public sector does not crowd out local entrepreneurs through unfair competition."[62]

The SDP though not established until 1980 under the leadership of Chiam See Tong, who has held the seat of Potong Pasir since 1984, has now surpassed the WP in terms of the percentage of the vote it attracts and the number of parliamentary seats it holds. However, whereas the WP may appear a little confused about its ideology, the SDP does not seem to have consciously addressed the question at all. It has campaigned heavily for the desirability of a check against government arrogance, thus actively cultivating the so-called protest vote, and played on the theme of excessive government charges in areas like health, ed-

---

[62]For further discussion of the Workers' Party see Chan Heng Chee, "Political Parties," in Quah, Chan, and Seah, eds., *Government and Politics of Singapore*, 164–7; and Carolyn Choo, *The PAP and the Problem of Political Succession* (Kuala Lumpur: Pendaluk, nd), 50–75.

ucation, and transportation. But the SDP has not yet articulated any clear alternative vision for Singapore—either in concrete policy terms or in terms of political philosophy. Until very recently, it did not actually have a document even approximating a party manifesto.[63] Significantly, in recent SDP calls for more government spending in health, education, and housing, it has voluntarily distinguished these reforms from welfarism.[64] Chiam has also gone out of his way inside and outside parliament to praise the PAP for its achievements. Accordingly, Chiam has been spared the hostile treatment meted out to Jeyaretnam by the PAP.

Neither major opposition party represents a coherent ideological alternative to the PAP, and certainly neither directly challenges or scrutinizes the PAP's central ideological concept of meritocracy. While this need not mean that there is a conscious acceptance of the PAP's ideology, it does at least reflect a limited ability to formulate alternatives. This is a potent aspect of the ruling party's hegemony. Ironically, the recent success at the polls by the SDP has brought with it problems and challenges that render the immediate future a more difficult one. First, the PAP has gone all out to expose the deficiencies of the SDP as an alternative government, particularly in view of the absence of any coherent economic policy statement. Apart from a broad, declared aim to achieve economic union with Malaysia, little has been proposed. Second, tensions among the opposition parties surfaced after the 1991 election, with the SDP promoting itself as the symbol of an emerging two-party, rather than multiparty, system.[65] Third, an internal SDP dispute threw the party itself into disarray. The immediate electoral prospects of the SDP, if not

---

[63]The first attempt at something like this was a 156-page book written by an acting SDP secretary-general, Chee Soon Juan (1994), and entitled *Dare to Change*.

[64]See the speech by SDP MP for Nee Soon Central, Cheo Chai Chen, in *Parliamentary Debates Singapore*, 59, no. 9, March 10, 1992, columns 683–4.

[65]See, for example, STWOE, December 12, 1992, p. 4; ST, December 12, 1992, p. 26; and ST, December 17, 1992, p. 22. In a sensational move, Chiam resigned as secretary-general of the SDP in May 1993 and subsequently made a public attack on a number of Central Executive Committee members. This culminated in Chiam's expulsion from the party in August 1993, a decision that, under the Singapore Constitution, required him to vacate his parliamentary seat. However, Chiam took out an injunction that held his seat until a court challenge against the expulsion was decided in Chiam's favor in late 1993 (ST, December 11, 1993, p. 1). The effect of this was that Chiam retained his parliamentary seat but was only an ordinary member of the SDP, as opposed to being either on the CEC or a cadre. Other legal writs were exchanged between factions, including an unsuccessful attempt by pro-Chiam forces to have the collective leadership headed by Ling How Doong declared null and void (STWE, May 7, 1994, p. 12). Not surprisingly, Chiam's supporters moved in mid-1994 to form a separate party, the Singapore People's Party (STWE, July 9, 1994, p. 4).

the opposition more generally, are not likely to have been aided by this splintering.

If the recent relative electoral success by opposition parties has thrown up immediate problems, their continued separation from social bases remains a major obstacle and one that will complicate their ability to respond effectively to some of the challenges just identified. One of the constants in Singapore politics throughout the leadership transition has been the insistence that political and nonpolitical activities should remain clearly demarcated—at least so far as this involves opposition parties and groups or organizations outside the PAP's extensive umbrella. This has crucial implications because civil society is a site for various economic, social, ideological, and religious conflicts. But challenges to PAP policies or philosophies not transmitted through formal opposition parties are rarely tolerated by the ruling party. The activities of nongovernment organizations of all types are subjected to strict controls through the Societies Act, first introduced as law in 1967, which enforces a rigid distinction between political and nonpolitical activities. In the wake of public positions taken by the Law Society in the late 1980s, legislation covering professional organizations was also amended to enforce further the government's insistence that, in the words of then Minister for Communications and Information Wong Kan Seng, "public policy is the domain of the government. It isn't the playground of those who have no responsibility to the people, and who aren't answerable for the livelihood or survival of Singaporeans."[66]

This atmosphere of sensitivity to the activities of nonstate organizations makes it very difficult for opposition parties to cultivate the sort of support bases common to parties in liberal democratic societies. In such societies, political parties play a fundamental role in giving selective political expression to the interests and views emanating in civil society. The control over organized labor exercised by the PAP has obviously, and quite intentionally, undercut the social base of any other political party hoping to lay claim to the representation of the working class.[67] But peak employer bodies, professional organizations, and interest groups in areas like consumer affairs, environmentalism, and women's issues are also out of bounds for political parties. Generally speaking, non-state-sponsored civil organizations are poorly developed in Singa-

[66]*Asiaweek*, June 15, 1985, p. 20.
[67]Only nine of the eighty-one registered employee trade unions are not affiliated with the NTUC. Singapore Ministry of Labour Annual Report, 1993, p. 19.

pore because of the pervasiveness of the paternalistic state, which has stifled community initiatives. Lately, however, some independent organizations have emerged and achieved reasonable public profiles in advancing concerns. The Association of Women for Action and Research (AWARE) and the Nature Society of Singapore (NSS) have, for instance, not only developed significant memberships by Singapore standards, but made strong representations to government on policy issues. The continued development of these organizations and the preparedness of the government to tolerate them are, however, contingent upon observance of the restrictions laid down in the Societies Act. The NMP scheme may increasingly become a mechanism through which the government attempts to co-opt such organizations, preempting the need for proscription under the Societies Act. Co-optation, it should be noted, is not without its attractions to nongovernment organizations where no effective alternatives are immediately available. Where co-optation takes forms like the NMP scheme, however, there is the risk of inadvertently legitimizing a politics that acknowledges representation for distinct interests—precisely what the PAP is determined to avoid.

Whatever the tensions in the PAP's management of these organizations, for the time being at least, it will remain very difficult for the establishment of even loose functional links between the activities of nongovernment organizations of any ilk and opposition political parties. For opposition parties, however, such connections are prerequisites for the development of more mass-based, rather than elitist, organizational structures and access to resources useful in the formation of detailed alternative policies.

CONCLUSION

It has been argued in this chapter that elections in Singapore have never been indicative of any shared political culture supportive of democracy. They have, nevertheless, served a very important function in the legitimization of the PAP and are now a seemingly permanent feature of the political system. This is not to suggest that the ruling party does not have reservations about elections. Indeed, it retains a deep mistrust in the judgment of the bulk of electors, whom it believes could be so easily seduced by a less honorable and less rational political opposition. In guarding against this possibility, the PAP has embarked on a range of measures at both the institutional and ideological levels, which further condition the form that opposition takes. These measures are intended to simultaneously defend and consolidate rational decisionmaking and the ruling party's political supremacy. Increased social heterogeneity and a population that is more educated, in both the general academic and electoral senses, have apparently only reinforced the PAP's reservations about electoral politics.

Underlying the various initiatives in the last decade is a resolve by the PAP that the political process must not move toward the incorporation of any notion of representation that compromises the structures or ideology of "meritocracy." It is this ideology that rationalizes the hierarchical social and political order built up over the last three and a half decades in Singapore. Yet without a challenge to the elitism embodied in meritocracy it is difficult to see how the political process can be altered in such a way as to render elections a more meaningful exercise in democracy. So long as government is regarded the preserve of experts, the permissible extent and form of political opposition, both formally and informally, will necessarily result in restricted choices available to the electorate. But, at the same time, opposition parties themselves have found it difficult to break out of the PAP's ideological framework, in no small part because of the institutionalization in Singapore of a comprehensive set of mutually supportive ideological concepts in which meritocracy is pivotal.

Despite the obstacles to an effective challenge to elitist politics under the PAP, the increasing diversity and plurality of Singapore society is nevertheless likely to place greater pressure on the PAP leadership to demonstrate its capacity as the only valid expression and competent adjudicator of the national interest. Current tendencies suggest this will be accommodated through more extensive mechanisms for co-optation rather than the tolerance of a genuine civil society. If the apparent contradictions in this process prove manageable, electoral politics may become even more a political epiphenomenon.

4

Elections' Janus face:
Limitations and potential in Malaysia

JOMO K. S.

In the course of the following discussion of the significance of Malaysian elections, it is argued that the circumstances and conduct of Malaysian elections have changed significantly since the 1950s.[1] Malaysian elections have increasingly served to maintain and legitimize those already in power, with national political leadership determined by the contest for the United Malays National Organization (UMNO) leadership, rather than the national electoral process.

These developments have been accompanied by the uneven and probably unsystematic erosion of democratic institutions, human rights, civil liberties, and the rule of law in Malaysia, largely because of a growing concentration of power in the hands of the executive, more specifically the prime minister, especially since the 1980s. This has adversely affected the roles, status, powers, and independence of the bureaucracy, the legislature, the judiciary, and even the nine constitutional monarchies.

The period since the 1980s has also seen the growth of rent appropriation and other abuses of power by politicians with business interests and by politically well-connected businessmen. This phenomenon of politics in business is popularly referred to as "money politics." It includes the award of lucrative contracts to companies controlled by the ruling party, especially its dominant faction(s), the use of political influence and

[1]A much earlier version of parts of this paper was presented at the Asian Peace Research Association conference, "Deepening and Globalizing Democracy," Yokohama, Japan, March 17–22, 1990, and will be published by the Malaysian Social Science Association in a festschrift for S. Husin Ali. I am grateful to Yoshikazu Sakamoto, Harold Crouch, and Paul Lubeck for critical comments on the earlier paper, but responsibility is mine alone.

connections to further business interests, the use of government resources to advance particular political interests of the ruling party, and the use of executive and legislative powers to facilitate and advance political and business interests.

The final section of this chapter outlines desirable electoral reforms that would enable elections to contribute to, rather than undermine, democracy and active citizenship. While it is difficult to imagine such reforms being voluntarily undertaken by those in power, it is very likely that they would enhance the credibility and hence the legitimacy of Malaysia's electoral system.

It has been suggested that the convenient, but simplistic, identification of democracy with elections and ostensible majority rule is because of the absence of a historical tradition of democracy in the dominant ethnic Malay culture, as well as the other non-Western cultures that have influenced Malaysia's political development. According to this line of argument, British colonialism is to be credited with bringing democracy to Malaysia.

This superficial view is particularly appealing because it appears to be supported by historical evidence. But it ignores significant popular traditions in Malay and other indigenous Asian cultures. While it is true that the great or elite traditions of the ruling classes have dominated historically, the "little traditions"—especially of the peasant masses—survived and undoubtedly contributed to the democratic impulse that moved the peoples of Malaysia to resist colonialism and to demand civil rights, albeit sometimes expressed in non-Western idioms. British colonialism appropriated for itself legislative and executive powers, with nominal deference to collaborating Malay rulers through the creation of a fiction of continued Malay authority, at the expense of the precolonial systems of Malay political authority. Popular resistance to colonial expansion, particularly in the late nineteenth and early twentieth centuries, was not insignificant, though admittedly often led by disenfranchised members of the previously privileged equivalents of an aristocracy or nobility. The anticolonial struggles also contributed a great deal to strengthening and spreading this democratic tendency.

Although largely illegal until 1940, labor organizing, particularly after the decline of indenture beginning in the 1920s, contributed significantly to the emergence of an increasingly self-conscious working class with more than economic aspirations. Inspired by developments in the neighboring Netherlands East Indies, the emergence of pan-Malay radical nationalism in the 1930s, especially among educated youth, must also have contributed to an increasingly active civil society, albeit an ethnically fragmented one.

However, British colonialism managed to fend off and suppress the nascent Malayan radical nationalist movement that emerged in the immediate postwar years through a variety of measures, including ethnic divide-and-rule tactics and, most important, outright repression, culminating in the counterinsurgency war, fictionalized as the "Emergency" primarily for the purposes of insurance claims. Instead, it created conditions that enabled the elitist, multiethnic conservative or "moderate" nationalists—embodied by the Alliance—to take over the reins of power as decolonization became inevitable.

The Alliance had been established in the mid-1950s—as negotiations for independence became imminent—as a coalition of the three main ethnic political parties. Though initially supportive of UMNO founder and president Onn Jaffar's efforts to form a single conservative multiethnic party after leaving UMNO in 1951, the British later backed the Alliance leaders from the UMNO, MCA (Malayan Chinese Association) and MIC (Malayan Indian Congress) over more radical nationalist forces, some of whom had been driven underground in the late 1940s.

Elections in the British Empire were first held several decades earlier on the Indian subcontinent. Throughout the colonial period, there was never any initiative from the British authorities to seriously enhance popular political participation until the failure of the first three years of the counterinsurgency campaign from 1948 necessitated concessions to "win hearts and minds." Hence, it was only in the 1950s that social reforms, including greater political participation and elections, were reluctantly incorporated into the colonial political heritage. An important factor apparently contributing to the first Malayan elections was the desire to secure greater legitimacy for nonviolent political processes, organizations, and personalities in the face of the continuing communist-led armed insurgency for national liberation from imperial rule.

Thus, since the late colonial period, Malaysia has had regular elections for the lower house of the federal parliament, known as the Dewan Rakyat, as well as for state legislative assemblies. Before independence (Merdeka) in 1957, the British colonial government held colonial Malaya's first federal legislative elections in 1955. Since then, federal elections have been held in 1959, 1964, 1969, 1974, 1978, 1982, 1986, 1990, and 1995. State elections have generally been held together with federal elections for the eleven states of Peninsular Malaysia, whereas state elections in Sabah and Sarawak—usually held over more than one day—have been held at different times since 1969, when they were suspended after the results in the peninsula came in.

The states of Sabah and Sarawak on the island of Borneo were not integrated with Malaya and Singapore to form Malaysia until September 1963 as an attempt to bring together Britain's disparate colonial possessions in the region under a stable and friendly regime. Local political developments and considerations there have been quite different from those prevailing in the peninsula. Perhaps more important, voting considerations and patterns in these states tend to diverge much more between federal and state elections than on the peninsula.

DEMOCRACY AND ACCOUNTABILITY

Democracy in Malaysia has largely been defined and popularly understood in electoral terms, that is, the regular conduct of multiparty elections, in which the continued incumbency of the UMNO-dominated ruling coalition since the first national elections in 1955 has rarely been in doubt. Democracy is thus identified mainly with the right to vote and the notion of majority rule, sometimes interpreted ethnically in terms of rule by the Muslim Malay majority over the rest of the population.

Hence, although it suggests some accountability of elected rulers to the ruled, democracy also implies the apparently voluntary surrender of control over public life by the ruled to the rulers. By reducing the meaning of democracy to voting in highly circumscribed circumstances offering limited choice (where the possibility of changing the regime, let alone the terms and nature of governance itself, is very rarely a serious option), elections have been largely reduced to what may well be a ritualistic and orchestrated exercise legitimating the surrender of many other democratic rights.

The popular suspicion remains that if an election should really offer the serious possibility of replacing the regime—currently determined by other processes, especially the UMNO party-leadership elections—it would not be held (as happened with municipal elections, largely won by the opposition, and which have not been held since the mid-1960s). In the event of outcomes unacceptable to those in power, various legal devices have been employed to suspend constitutional processes until more acceptable alternative arrangements have been made, as happened after the May 1969 general election. Similarly, after the 1990 elections, when opposition parties captured the state governments of Sabah and Kelantan, the federal government resorted to fiscal and other means to undermine their ability to govern.

Recognizing the importance of the first elections as precedent setting, it might be noted that the form of parliamentary democracy introduced mimicked the Westminster model, ostensibly adapting it to colonial Malayan conditions, particularly to favor the Alliance leadership, who offered the prospect of a conservative multiethnic consociationalist leadership understandably preferred by a colonial power anticipating imminent decolonization in its most lucrative colony. Typically, considering the political, cultural, and jurisprudential heritage involved, the constitution of the postcolonial state promised balance among the legislature, the executive, and the judiciary.

Over the years, various amendments have been made to the constitution and the laws of the country to consolidate further the position of the ruling coalition, especially the UMNO leadership that dominates it. By the late 1960s, current Prime Minister Mahathir Mohamad—then an UMNO back-bencher—bitterly complained of the concentration and consolidation of power in the hands of the executive, especially the prime minister.[2]

Over the years, too, the electoral system itself has changed greatly, again primarily to consolidate the dominance of the ruling Barisan Nasional (BN), or National Front coalition, especially its dominant partner, UMNO. After every other election, the number of parliamentary constituencies has been increased and their boundaries redelineated, generally to the advantage of the ruling coalition, especially UMNO (sometimes with inadvertent advantages to the ethnic, Chinese-based opposition Democratic Action Party or DAP), with the number of registered voters in the largest constituency much greater than in the smallest parliamentary constituency. Election rallies have been banned since 1978, ostensibly owing to the communist threat, while the campaign period has been progressively shortened through legislative reform.

The print media are almost all owned by companies controlled by political parties and politicians of the ruling coalition. The broadcast

---

[2]Mahathir Mohamad, *The Malay Dilemma* (Singapore: Donald Moore, 1970).

media were a state monopoly until 1984, when a private television broadcasting license was awarded to an UMNO-controlled company. In fact, by early 1993, this process of media control had gone so far that those aligned with the then UMNO deputy president (Ghafar Baba) and two of the three UMNO vice-presidents (Abdullah Badawi and Sanusi Junid) were publicly complaining that the other vice-president at the time (now Deputy President Anwar Ibrahim) had a virtual media monopoly of private television broadcasting and the major Malay and English daily newspapers.

Some government agencies have also been effectively transformed into political machinery for the ruling BN coalition, especially UMNO politicians. These include the Information Department, Kemas (Community Development), the Tatanegara (Civics) Bureau, and the Islamic Center of the Prime Minister's Department, certain agencies of other ministries, as well as other agencies of the state governments and regional authorities. All this is legitimized by invoking the national interest, developmental needs, subversive threats, or requirements for maintaining Malay political hegemony.

These trends have grown since the 1960s, with new implications arising from greater UMNO hegemony and the related growth of the public sector and state intervention from the 1970s. One consequence of this has been the emergence and consolidation of money politics and its various consequences, including corruption.[3] It has frequently been observed that the concentration of power in the hands of the executive has been taken to new heights under Mahathir's leadership since 1981,[4] with the bureaucracy and then the judiciary taking a particularly serious battering in the 1980s,[5] followed by Malaysia's constitutional monarchies in early 1993.

MONEY POLITICS

In the early years before and after independence, the MCA financed the Alliance's electoral and other expenses. Since then, especially from the

---

[3]E. T. Gomez, *Money Politics in the Barisan Nasional* (Kuala Lumpur: Forum, 1991).
[4]Chandra Muzaffar, *Freedom in Fetters* (Penang: Aliran, 1987); Committee against Repression in the Pacific and Asia (CARPA), *Tangled Web: Dissent, Deterrence, and the 27th October 1987 Crackdown in Malaysia* (Sydney: Committee against Repression in the Pacific and Asia, 1988).
[5]Self published by the Lawyers Committee for Human Rights, *Malaysia: Assault on the Judiciary* (New York, 1989).

early 1970s, UMNO has consolidated its own political finances, which were used to secure control of the *New Straits Times Press* and to build the Fleet Holdings conglomerate around it. In the mid-1980s, however, the UMNO political fund changed from being a relatively passive port-folio investor by becoming an increasingly active corporate player with apparently declining accountability to the UMNO leadership except for the UMNO treasurer, and perhaps president. The flurry of corporate activity since the mid-1980s, ostensibly in favor of UMNO, has also personally benefited the UMNO trustees involved.[6]

The growth of money politics has not only involved UMNO, but its BN coalition partners as well. Already, two presidents of BN coalition parties have been convicted for criminal breach of trust involving cor-porate assets built up through political means. One of these prosecutions and the collapse of the MCA-initiated deposit-taking cooperatives (DTCs) in late 1986 were conveniently delayed—with the connivance of the Singapore government—until after the August 1986 general elections in order to protect the MCA, which might otherwise have fared much worse electorally.[7]

Political involvement and intervention in business are now so exten-sive that it is generally believed that most new fortunes built since the mid-1970s have been due to "know-who" (political influence and connections), rather than "know-how" (technical ability or entrepre-neurship). This widespread pervasiveness of money politics is a general phenomenon, involving national, state, divisional, and even branch party leadership, as well as the women's and youth wings of the parties con-cerned. Inevitably, it has touched upon many businesses and other ec-onomic activities, causing fairly serious distortions and undermining the likelihood of enhancing efficiency to ensure international competi-tiveness. Such developments could not proceed inexorably without coming up against problems of their own creation, albeit unintentional-ly.[8] The public sector and opportunities for privatization have since

[6]E. T. Gomez, *Politics in Business: UMNO's Corporate Investments* (Kuala Lumpur: Fo-rum, 1990); E. T. Gomez, *Political Business: Corporate Involvement of Political Parties in Malaysia* (Townsville, Australia: Centre for Southeast Asian Studies, James Cook Uni-versity, 1994).
[7]Gomez, *Money Politics.*
[8]Jomo K. S., *Growth and Structural Change in the Malaysian Economy* (London: Mac-millan, 1990).

become the main focus of attention by the new breed of enterprising rent seekers.

The regularity of elections in Malaysia has also ensured some sort of accountability among those elected, if only in order to secure reelection, retain office, and thus hope to gain access to power. This has obliged politicians, especially from the ruling coalition, to deliver at least some goods in trying to maintain and increase electoral support. This has resulted in constantly evolving, complex, and varied systems of political-economic patronage, involving much of the electorate, particularly the rural indigenous population.[9]

Greater popular awareness and sensitivity in recent years to money politics and other abuses of power have heightened consciousness about the need for greater political transparency and accountability among some fractions of the middle class and for Malaysian democracy to embody a more effective system of checks and balances, particularly in the face of increasing executive powers. In the 1980s, money politics in Malaysia came to be associated with blatant abuses of power for self-aggrandizement, such as the Bumiputera Malaysia Finance scandal in Hong Kong (involving the loss of RM2.5 billion), the DTCs scandal involving RM1.5 billion taken from almost 600,000 depositors, mainly by MCA-connected politicians, and the North-South Highway scandal (involving the privatization of very lucrative highway toll collection rights for thirty years to an UMNO-associated company).[10]

THE MAHATHIR ERA

In the early 1980s, the public-sector budget deficit grew rapidly as the government first tried to spend its way out of the recession—due to the collapse of commodity prices—during 1980–82, and then heavily financed new nonfinancial public enterprises that were set up to develop heavy industries—at the prime minister's behest—until the mid-1980s. This spending spree was largely financed by foreign borrowings from commercial sources after interest rates had risen because of American

[9]Shamsul A. B., *From British to Bumiputera Rule* (Singapore: Institute of Southeast Asian Studies, 1986); Marvin Rogers, *Local Politics in Rural Malaysia: Patterns of Change in Sungai Raya* (Boulder: Westview Press, 1992).

[10]Jomo K. S., et al., *Mahathir's Economic Policies* (Kuala Lumpur: IMSAN, 1989); Gomez, *Politics in Business*; Gomez, *Money Politics*; Gomez, *Political Business*.

intervention to tighten international financial liquidity. During this period, Malaysia's public debt, especially the foreign debt component, grew rapidly.[11] When the major industrial powers decided to depreciate the U.S. dollar against Japanese, German, and other strong currencies in late 1985, Malaysian authorities chose to depreciate the ringgit even against the U.S. dollar. The result was the ballooning of the cumulative foreign debt, especially the relatively recent component denominated in Japanese yen taken to finance new heavy industries. Hence, the Malaysian foreign debt continued to grow until the late 1980s, although net borrowings had virtually ceased in mid-decade.

Economic policies introduced by Daim Zainuddin, finance minister from mid-1984 until early 1991, have often been attributed to Mahathir, rightly or wrongly. Hence, the regressive fiscal reforms since the mid-1980s, apparently inspired by supply-side economic philosophy, plus related policies such as privatization, have been identified with Mahathir. Likewise, the reduction of subsidies ostensibly for the poor and the increased incentives for private investments, especially from abroad, are identified with the prime minister.[12]

Although Mahathir did not explicitly renounce the New Economic Policy (NEP), he announced its suspension in early 1986, during the midst of the mid-1980s recession, in an interview with the Australian Broadcasting Corporation, reported in Malaysia only by the Chinese vernacular press. Quite understandably to those who recognize implications of the ethnically segmented nature of Malaysian society, such an announcement was to be made only for foreign and domestic Chinese consumption for political reasons. In other words, while Mahathir politically could not afford to abandon the NEP explicitly, by the mid-1980s he was prepared to go about prioritizing his own economic policy agenda, necessarily at the expense of the NEP.

The fiscal crisis was further exacerbated by the regressive tax reforms instituted in the mid-1980s by the new finance minister. On the one hand, the tax base diminished considerably as direct taxes (income tax and estate duties) were reduced, while indirect taxes on consumption were increased. The reduction in public expenditures from 1982 cut military, social services, and welfare funding (subsidies ostensibly for the

[11]Jomo, *Mahathir's Economic Policies.*
[12]Jomo K. S., *Beyond 1990: Considerations for a New National Development Strategy* (Kuala Lumpur: Institute for Advanced Studies, University of Malaya, 1989).

poor). Hence, the impact of the fiscal system became increasingly regressive from the mid-1980s.

This adversely affected the previously rapid progress in poverty reduction, as well as government efforts since the early 1970s to create a Malay business community and middle class through public expenditure and state intervention. This situation was aggravated by the severe recession of 1985–6, precipitated by the collapse of primary commodity prices and worsened by the effectively deflationary new fiscal policies. For that reason, most of the progress toward the NEP objectives took place in the 1970s and early 1980s, while the 1985–6 recession apparently reduced overall income inequality by squeezing higher and more variable Chinese incomes more than others.

Not surprisingly, then, while official poverty incidence fell from 49 percent in 1970 to 18 percent in 1984, it declined only to 15 percent in 1990. Similarly, the Bumiputera (Malay and other indigenous peoples) share of corporate wealth rose from 2.4 percent in 1970 to 18.7 percent in 1983, but increased only to 19.4 percent in 1988, though the proportion of Bumiputera wealth in private hands rose from 41 percent in 1983 to 67 percent in 1988,[13] reflecting Mahathir's enthusiasm for individual, rather than collective, wealth accumulation.

These economic developments were reflected in parallel political developments, including new political cleavages in UMNO, the dominant party in the ruling coalition. In early 1986, Musa Hitam shocked the nation by resigning as deputy prime minister after enjoying Mahathir's political support against Tengku Razaleigh Hamzah in both the 1981 and 1984 party contests for the deputy presidency.

For the April 1987 UMNO General Assembly, Musa ran with Razaleigh, who challenged Mahathir for the presidency of the party. The Razaleigh-Musa team lost by less than 2 percent of the total votes to Mahathir and his new deputy, Ghafar Baba, amid charges of electoral fraud. Those who supported the Razaleigh-Musa partnership, then popularly known as Team B, were subsequently marginalized by Mahathir's victorious Team A, despite the latter's unconvincingly slim victory in an election heavily favoring the incumbent.

In October 1987, the authorities arrested more than a hundred activists from a wide range of dissident groups, including the opposition Is-

[13]Jomo, *Beyond 1990*.

lamic Party (PAS), DAP and Malaysian Peoples Socialist Party, the Chinese education movement, and Christian evangelists, as well as a variety of more progressive social activists.[14] Over a third were subsequently held without trial for many months, with the parliamentary opposition leader, Lim Kit Siang, and his son released last in April 1989.

In February 1988, the lawyers representing the UMNO leadership under Mahathir caused the deregistration of UMNO when it was challenged in the courts by party dissidents who alleged electoral fraud. Mahathir's camp acted swiftly to establish a new party with a similar name (UMNO Baru or New UMNO), but with a different constitution consolidating the position of the incumbent leadership. In response, the Razaleigh camp began to organize separately politically, ostensibly to reestablish the old UMNO by legal means; these efforts have failed so far and are unlikely to succeed.

Soon after the UMNO deregistration, as a number of important cases were about to come before the supreme court, the prime minister and the attorney-general moved swiftly to replace the lord president, the highest judge in the land, after he expressed dissent over the prime minister's attitude toward the judiciary. Some of the other judges who came to his defense were later also removed. This so-called assault on the judiciary is widely believed to have resulted in a bench far more intimidated by and amenable to the executive.[15]

Shahrir Samad, a former minister then aligned with the dissident UMNO faction, precipitated a by-election in August 1988 by resigning his own seat, ostensibly in protest against and to test support for Mahathir's leadership. His resounding victory probably forced Mahathir to reconsider his tactics and to compromise with the Musa camp in an attempt to isolate and weaken the Razaleigh-led movement. With this reconciliation and other efforts to project a more liberal and tolerant image, popular antagonism toward Mahathir began to subside.

A NEW OPPOSITION BLOC?

Meanwhile, the strong and sustained economic recovery from 1987 had improved economic conditions more generally, further softening anti-

[14]CARPA, *Tangled Web.*
[15]Lawyers Committee for Human Rights, *Malaysia.*

Mahathir sentiment. By 1989, the new political alignments began to consolidate. The Razaleigh-led faction was finally allowed to register a political party known as Semangat 46 (Spirit of 1946, referring to the year of the establishment of the original UMNO). From late 1988, the Razaleigh group had begun to enter into discussion with PAS and other smaller Muslim, and hence Malay-based, parties with a view to closer political cooperation.

In 1989, these groups came together to formally announce the establishment of the Angkatan Perpaduan Ummah (APU) or Movement of (Muslim) Community Unity. After APU was formed, Semangat 46 initiated parallel discussions for cooperation with other opposition political parties in Peninsular Malaysia not confined to Muslims. Despite the inability of PAS and the DAP to cooperate directly, a de facto multiethnic and multireligious opposition coalition in Peninsular Malaysia—led by Semangat 46—emerged, albeit not without serious organizational and image problems, exacerbated by government propaganda, harassment, and efforts to undermine it.

This effectively meant the emergence of two rival, multiethnic and multireligious political coalitions in Peninsular Malaysia, both under Muslim-Malay leadership. With the official end of the communist-led, armed insurgency in December 1989, new checks on communal politics and some increasing sophistication in Malaysian political culture, political differences along policy, rather than ethnic, lines began to reverse the previously unchecked growth of communal politics after the virtual elimination of the multiethnic parliamentary left in the mid-sixties. Although such a situation would still not prevent all efforts at irresponsible racial or religious politicking, it is already clear that protagonists on both sides have been effectively deterred from the extremist ethnic/religious posturing in which they were previously more inclined to indulge.

Such extremism used to be justified by BN politicians, who could refer to the existence of the predominantly Chinese DAP on the one hand and the exclusively Muslim PAS on the other hand. With these two erstwhile antagonists effectively allied, albeit only indirectly, politicians on both sides of the new divide became less wont to play the old racial and religious games. Undoubtedly, many still do, whether because of force of habit, continuing differences, or political desperation. But the trend is clear and unlikely to be reversed in the near future if the two-coalition situation holds. If for nothing else, this alone would be an important reason to welcome the development of opposition cooperation and the consequent emergence of the two ethnically similar rival political blocs offering policy alternatives.

One might cynically argue that since both Semangat 46 and Mahathir's New UMNO share their origins in the old UMNO, there is really no significant difference between the two rivals. At one level, this is true, insofar as both claim to be representing and advancing the Malay interest, and neither would explicitly criticize, let alone oppose the NEP, which has dominated economic policymaking and political debate more generally over the last two decades.

There are important differences beyond this point, however, at least judging by past policy and practice associated with the two main protagonists, Mahathir and Razaleigh. Since 1982, Mahathir has been identified with and has been responsible for drastic cuts in public spending and efforts to eliminate what he terms the "subsidy mentality" by reducing public welfare expenditures except insofar as they are considered necessary to finance the system of political patronage over which his UMNO prevails. Razaleigh, on the other hand, was associated with the growth of public expenditures in the late 1970s as well as the counter-cyclical, deficit-budget spending of the early 1980s, causing him to be described as more Keynesian in economic-policy temperament. Of course, to be fair, Mahathir, too, was a big spender so far as heavy industrialization was concerned, a policy to which Razaleigh was lukewarm at most. Mahathir also appears to be far more enthusiastic about foreign investments, probably because he sees foreigners as preferable partners for the ascendance of Malay capital, compared to Chinese business interests.

The difference between the two has since emerged more clearly as Razaleigh continued to call for the continuation of the NEP, while Mahathir has formulated new economic policies for the period after 1990, when the NEP's Outline Perspective Plan for the period 1971–90 ran out.[16] Although Mahathir has been anxious to get on with his own new economic policy priorities—though, of course without forsaking his political support, especially from the Malay community, by abandoning the NEP—Razaleigh is keen to reaffirm the NEP's original philosophy and objectives while criticizing defects in its implementation, especially since Mahathir became chief steward. This stance may well prove pop-

[16]Jomo, *Growth and Structural Change.*

ular with a generation of Malays brought up on and dependent on the NEP. Yet, by reaffirming the NEP's philosophy and objectives, which are broadly acceptable even to non-Malays, while distancing himself from much of what has been done in the name of the NEP, Razaleigh's commitment to the NEP may not alienate the non-Malays, though this kind of fine-tuning is difficult to practice with virtually no media access, let alone control.

The challenge for Razaleigh and his supporters in the near future will be to try to gain support from Malay voters disillusioned with the economic and cultural liberalization associated with the Mahathir regime since the mid-1980s and especially since 1991 without alienating traditional urban non-Malay support for the opposition. Mahathir's limited liberalization has won significant non-Malay support away from the opposition, especially with the sustained economic boom since 1987. But after decades of state patronage and related privilege, it has also inadvertently weakened Malay confidence in the UMNO-dominated state, though favorable economic conditions and continued ethnic privilege have checked this erosion.

The differences do not end here. Although some of those who joined Semangat 46 did so because of failure within the old UMNO or rejection by Mahathir or other incumbent leaders, key leaders recognize that they cannot get very far simply by wanting to replace Mahathir's personal leadership without offering any substantive or significant policy change. In other words, they understand that they must offer a combination of both leadership and policy change and hence are more amenable to alternative policy proposals. Most of those in the old UMNO with damaging skeletons in their closets generally did not dare risk the sanctions that they had good reason to fear might be imposed against them if they broke with Mahathir's New UMNO and joined the opposition. Those who dared to make the break were probably reasonably confident that they could survive the political, business, and other pressures after breaking ranks with those in power. In this sense, there is some difference between those who joined and remain with Semangat 46 and those who opted to join Mahathir's UMNO regardless of their personal sentiments about his leadership.

Perhaps more important, Semangat 46 does not dominate the opposition to the same extent that UMNO dominates the BN. While UMNO is able to impose its political, economic, and other agendas on the rest of the ruling coalition, Semangat 46 is not in such a commanding position. The cooperation among opposition parties is therefore among partners who mutually need one another, and hence is far more equitable than what prevails in the BN.

Historically, PAS has been identified with providing a supposedly Islamic alternative to contemporary Malaysian problems. For many years, under Asri's leadership, especially in the 1960s up to the mid-1970s, its rhetoric was as much Malay as Muslim. With the Islamic resurgence sweeping the country beginning in the 1970s, however, more authentically Islamic ideas became influential. Asri was ousted in 1982 by a new, more *ulama'* leadership somewhat influenced by the then recent Iranian Revolution. Among other things, the new PAS leadership increasingly made calls for socioeconomic justice and even talked of mobilizing the *mustadh'afin* (the meek) against the *mustakbirin* (the arrogant). In the mid-1980s, PAS also began to criticize narrow Malay chauvinism, misleadingly termed *assabiyah* (communal solidarity). In mid-1986, PAS forged a limited electoral pact with the smaller opposition parties in Peninsular Malaysia besides the DAP (which explicitly rejected cooperation, ostensibly because of PAS's call for an Islamic state), consistent with this line of reasoning. In short, by the mid-1980s, PAS had begun to espouse a more populist socioeconomic position once again, and at least rhetorically rejected Malay chauvinism in favor of more universal and progressive Islamic values.

In the 1986 election, PAS secured 17 percent, or one-sixth, of the votes. The government's Islamization policy has enabled UMNO to outflank PAS on a range of Muslim issues, driving PAS into an ideological corner. Fortunately for PAS, its leadership has thus far avoided adopting overly dogmatic and doctrinaire positions, which have ensured minimal mass support for foreign counterparts such as the Jama'at Islami in predominantly Muslim Pakistan, which secured only 3 percent of the votes cast in the 1993 national election. It is increasingly clear that PAS has enjoyed electoral support mainly because it has been the main Malay-based opposition party and has taken the moral high ground, rather than because of its Islamic ideological platform. In the less likely event that it develops a better-informed and more comprehensive critique of the status quo, premised on progressive and universal Islamic values, and compromises on its rhetorical and theologically unnecessary demand for a theocratic state, PAS will not only be strengthened, but existing ideological obstacles to closer cooperation with non-Muslim opposition parties may be less difficult to overcome.

Besides Semangat 46 and PAS, the other two component parties of APU are Berjasa (To Serve) and Hamim (Muslim Party). Both are splinters from PAS. Berjasa broke away during the 1977–8 Kelantan crisis and joined the BN to defeat PAS, then under Asri's leadership. Hamim, on the other hand, was established by Asri when he sensed impending marginalization by the younger *ulama'* leadership in 1982. Berjasa supported and joined APU from the outset. After Asri unsuccessfully tried to dissolve Hamim to facilitate joining UMNO directly, the new Hamim leadership opted out of the Barisan Nasional to join APU. APU then has all the Islamic parties in the country in its camp, plus Semangat 46, which is composed entirely of Muslim Malays.

During the 1980s, the DAP also underwent some transformation. Originally, the DAP was the Peninsular Malaysian component of Singapore's ruling People's Action Party (PAP), left in the peninsula after Singapore seceded in August 1965. During Singapore's brief stint as part of Malaysia, the PAP espoused a "Malaysian Malaysia," while hoping to replace the MCA as UMNO's Chinese partner and also offering itself as an anticommunist alternative to the strongest opposition party outside the East Coast then, the Socialist Front. This seemingly just demand for a "Malaysian Malaysia," with which it has secured considerable non-Malay support, seems to threaten the vast majority of Malays. The DAP continued to be identified with this slogan and corresponding demands through the 1970s. However, after its poor performance in the April 1982 elections, it also began to emphasize a new role and image as the main parliamentary opposition party, as a safeguard against the abuses and corruption rapidly growing with the spread of money politics.

Furthermore, the DAP is, at least nominally, multiethnic, and has occasionally made serious efforts to recruit Malays into its leadership, which is far more than the non-Malay-based BN parties (including the nominally multiracial ones, such as the Gerakan), can say for themselves. Also, the DAP has a social-democratic political program inherited indirectly from the PAP's early days as an anticolonial movement in the 1950s. By taking its official social democratic platform more seriously and by continuing to expose and reject corruption and other abuses of power (usually associated with money politics), the DAP can become more broadly acceptable, as has already begun to happen in recent years, and it can develop more meaningful cooperation with the other opposition parties, including PAS. The DAP secured one-fifth of the total votes cast in the 1986 general elections.

Since PAS has already conceded that it does not envisage the immediate establishment of an Islamic state, while APU is committed to upholding Islam only as a way of life (*ad-deen*), the DAP can cooperate with PAS without either side compromising its principles. A sizable splinter faction from the MIC under the leadership of M. G. Pandithan—the former MIC vice-president sacked by MIC president, Samy Vellu—formed the All-Malaysian Indian Progressive Front, or IPF, in mid-1990. The IPF succeeded in mobilizing many Indians in a relatively short time, mainly from among relatively poor, working-class communities. While the Indians do not constitute a demographic majority in any electoral constituency, they have a significant presence in some urban and rural plantation areas.

The Partai Rakyat Malaysia (PRM), or People's Party, has long advocated the idea of opposition cooperation, having actively participated in the limited electoral pact of 1986. Though some of its leaders have been closely identified with opposition unity efforts since late 1986, it could mount good candidates in only a few areas. Moreover, it is unclear to what extent people voted for the credible opposition candidates it fielded rather than for the party's radical nationalist platform.

Given the repression against the Left over several decades, PRM's lack of access to the mass media, the declining credibility of socialism, both nationally and internationally (especially since the 1970s in Malaysia), and the overwhelming significance of ethnic and religious politics in recent decades, it correctly recognized that there is not a tremendous socialist groundswell waiting to be tapped. In trying to be more relevant to the contemporary political situation, after appraising that situation, the PRM moderated its socialist goals and dropped the word "socialist" from its name in early 1990, thus resuming its original, populist name. It has pledged to work for feasible progressive social change, in cooperation with other existing opposition political parties as well as other sympathetic and open-minded political forces.

The complex and different political considerations in Sabah and Sarawak have inhibited active and direct participation in the peninsula-based opposition coalitions, but have, at the same time, left open the possibility of potential political allies if the electoral contest in the peninsula is deadlocked.

Thus, it is clear that the new political formation involves a split through Malaysian society involving all ethnic groups. The emergence of two Malay-led, multiethnic, multireligious blocs is a development without precedent in the Malaysian context. The effort that came closest historically was probably the Socialist Front (SF), which thrived from the late 1950s until the mid-1960s, before it broke up under pressure from official repression (when most of its national leaders were arrested and detained indefinitely without trial), as well as interethnic suspicions and differences on ethnic, language, and other related issues. However, the SF enjoyed more support from the Chinese, compared with the other ethnic groups, diminishing its credibility as an alternative in the eyes of the other communities, particularly the Malays.

The 1987 split within UMNO, resulting in the emergence of Semangat 46, was undoubtedly a development of great significance. It seems that the split is irreconcilable, at least while Mahathir continues to lead the New UMNO. Consequently, the entire Malaysian political scenario may well have changed, with the possible consolidation of a variant of bipartisan politics, with two rival Malay-led, multiethnic coalitions. Even if the two UMNO factions are essentially similar politically (which does not seem to be the case from a policy point of view), the very fact of open competition between the two factions is likely to continue to widen political space, as well as to introduce some political constraints into a system that previously seemed to undermine inherited elements of institutional accountability.

Although this development could still be temporarily reversed by competing Malay claims to legitimacy, involving more extremist posturing, it already seems to have resulted in a longer-run decline in ethnic politicking, as policy issues and governance practices increasingly become subject to debate between ethnically similar rival camps. Mahathir's recent willingness to publicly declare an official commitment to forging a Malaysian nation—transcending ethnic, including Malay, loyalties—and much of the rest of his political agenda would probably have been more mutely expressed, if at all, if not for the changed political circumstances brought about by the coalescence in 1990 of the previously ethnically polarized political opposition.

But by doing so, Mahathir has once again successfully claimed the center ground for the political forces he represents, casting the opposition once again as extremist, negative, and even antinational for a population with an apparently short political memory, especially with limited opposition access to the mass media. As noted earlier, the apparent success of his economic and cultural liberalization efforts has had divisive and problematic consequences for the still nascent and poorly consolidated opposition party cooperation.

In the October 1990 general election, there was a significant decline in Malay political support for the ruling Barisan Nasional, as well as a further decline in Chinese electoral support for it. But the gain in Malay support for the opposition in a heavily gerrymandered first-past-the-post electoral system was insufficient to deprive the BN of success in the elections. In Malaysia's electoral system, the opposition was able to secure open support only in Sabah—arguably at the expense of Muslim Malay support in the peninsula—but was unable to do so in Sarawak because of the different political context there. Furthermore, cultural prejudices and suspicions as well as the virtual monopoly of print and broadcast media enjoyed by the BN have continued to undermine a more comprehensive coalescence of the opposition involving both the DAP and PAS.

The apparently irrepressible rise of Anwar Ibrahim, especially during 1993, poses new challenges for all concerned. His overwhelming defeat of the incumbent deputy leader of UMNO and the government, Ghafar Baba, suggests that he may well enjoy greater support from within the party than even Mahathir, whose previous claims that he remained in office only to unite the disparate factions in the party will probably increase pressures for an early succession, notwithstanding Mahathir's probable private reluctance. Mahathir is believed by many, besides himself, to possess a much broader and deeper view of national developmental priorities than his cabinet colleagues (including Anwar), especially after the exit of Razaleigh and Musa.

Anwar's ascendance also poses new challenges for the still nascent opposition cooperation. His close association with PAS leaders during his years as an ostensibly independent and critical Muslim social activist in the 1970s, especially after PAS's virtual expulsion from the ruling BN coalition in 1977, reputedly at the instigation of Razaleigh, will inevitably raise the prospects of the revival of his old alliances, especially in view of his remarkable success in preserving his Islamic reputation despite making various compromises since joining UMNO in 1982. Mahathir's departure from center stage in such circumstances would eliminate Razaleigh and his supporters' bête noire and, some would argue, their raison d'être as well. Unlike Mahathir, Anwar seems more likely to try to broaden the political and social base of the regime, conceivably with initiatives even bolder than Razak's in the early 1970s leading to the formation of the Barisan Nasional. It is premature, however, to speculate meaningfully on what shape such initiatives might take and what implications they portend.

ELECTORAL REFORM

While resistance to electoral reform from the incumbent ruling coalition, especially the dominant UMNO, is to be expected, one should not exaggerate the opposition to change, especially from the rapidly growing middle class. This middle class is ethnically divided, especially between the Malays, who have been encouraged to believe that they owe their own material and other achievements entirely to Malay political hegemony as embodied by UMNO, and their non-Malay counterparts, who have inevitably come to believe that they would be better off if not for intervention by the Malay-dominated state.

Nevertheless, there is a growing moral repugnance to the increasing abuses associated with the money politics that pervades Malaysian society. This ethical dismay has probably also been encouraged by the various religious revivals in the country over the last two decades. Hence, measures to develop a fairer electoral system—with reduced attendant abuses—are likely to be broadly welcomed, even among Malays, if Malay political preeminence per se is not threatened.

But such concerns in themselves are unlikely to bring about electoral reform and ensure greater political accountability. Instead, considerations of credibility and legitimacy are more likely to be decisive in bringing about such change. If the very legitimacy of the government is at stake because of widespread and profound doubts about the fairness of elections, and such doubts encourage destabilizing and delegitimizing behavior and action, it is more likely that reform-minded elements may have an opportunity to bring about change that might otherwise appear threatening to the incumbent regime.

There is, of course, a very broad range of possible electoral reforms. Some, such as proportional representation, seem most unlikely in the medium term in view of the advantages inherent in the present Westminster-type first-past-the-post system gerrymandered to ensure overwhelming UMNO hegemony and the arguments invoking Malay political hegemony likely to be invoked in defense of these arrangements. Instead, the following proposals draw on existing electoral concerns and related suggestions for reform that appear to enjoy some popular support and articulation:

1. The urgent need for strict restrictions on electoral campaign financing. Limited campaign financing by the government alone or mandatory public declaration of all political contributions will be well received by a population increasingly disgusted by money politics.

2. The overhaul of inaccurate electoral rolls, alleged double registration, continued registration of long-deceased persons, and the reform of the elections commission, currently unable to function effectively to ensure that all citizens desiring to vote can actually do so. In these circumstances, it may be desirable to eliminate the separate exercise of voter registration and simply to rely on existing national registration to determine voter eligibility.

3. The revision of various unfair restrictions on campaigning, especially those imposed on or to the disadvantage of the opposition parties. For example, the election campaign period has been significantly reduced over time to less than two weeks. Also, public rallies, which were disallowed from 1978, ostensibly because of the communist insurgency, should now be allowed with the government's peace treaty with the Communist Party of Malaya in December 1989.

4. The prohibition of abuse of government personnel, machinery, and other resources, especially by political parties and candidates of the ruling Barisan Nasional coalition. On the other hand, existing restrictions on political participation by trade unionists, academics, and students should be withdrawn in the interest of fuller democratic participation.

5. Changes in ownership and regulation of the print and, especially, the broadcast media, now dominated mainly by political and business interests associated with the ruling coalition, as well as by the government itself. This is related to allegations and clear evidence of biased and tendentious reporting, on the one hand, and lack of coverage of political statements and developments, on the other—both in favor of the ruling coalition. This problem can be overcome only by ensuring greater freedom to publish and broadcast, regulated by journalist ethics, rather than by political preferences or ownership.

6. The elimination of abuse of voting and vote-counting procedures. Postal votes—of uniformed service personnel—do not seem to be freely made and have been overwhelmingly in favor of the ruling coalition. The new procedures for vote counting at the polling stations themselves will favor parties and candidates with large machines and the ruling

coalition because voters may fear penalties to their communities for voting for the opposition.

7. The election of members on the basis of proportional representation to the Dewan Negara (Senate, or upper house of parliament), currently all appointed. Some members of the upper house can be elected by certain restricted constituencies or special interest groups for more effective representation of their particular interests, for example, women, trade unions, small minority-ethnic groups (such as the aboriginal Orang Asli and the smaller tribal communities in Sabah and Sarawak), the disabled, religious communities, and so on.

8. The election of municipal, village, and other councils, with their proceedings open to the public and well covered by the media. This can help ensure greater participation, transparency, and accountability of elected representatives in much smaller and more intimate communities, compared to elected representatives in the state assemblies and federal parliament.

Besides such measures to strengthen checks and balances, many other reforms affecting other spheres of Malaysian political life are urgently required to create conditions for more truly participatory democracy. The existing heritage of repressive legislation, which has been arbitrarily abused by those in power to consolidate their own positions, must be systematically dismantled. Legislation such as the Internal Security Act, the Printing Presses and Publications Act, the Police Act, the Universities and University Colleges Act, the Official Secrets Act, the Broadcasting Act, the Societies Act, various labor laws, and so on must be repealed or amended drastically to ensure basic freedoms, civil liberties, and human rights.

CONCLUSION

There is a great deal of work that has to be done to create the political and cultural conditions for the citizenry to participate actively in democratic life. The most obvious areas of urgent reform in this regard are clearly the educational system and the media, but a great number of other institutions and practices will also have to be subject to profound progressive transformation to create an institutional framework conducive to popular democratic initiatives. The problem, of course, is that all these changes are unlikely to be initiated without effective pressure. So long as Malaysians continue to be manipulated by politicians playing ethnic bogeys, it is difficult to envisage such pressures for democratization.

Yet, quite unexpectedly, the political crises of the second half of the 1980s have undermined the old ethnic political-institutional framework, heightened some democratic sensibilities, and may have inadvertently strengthened checks and balances in the long run (by increasing and changing the character of political competition) because of the desperate or self-aggrandizing abuses of power that have come to public attention. All the political forces responsible for these developments are not particularly democratic or progressive-minded.

There is little doubt that these developments have brought about a profound sea change in Malaysian, especially Malay, politics. Whether the democratic agenda will continue to be enhanced by this turn of events remains to be seen, and it will depend greatly on whether and how democratic and other progressive forces choose to participate in events at this critical juncture in Malaysian history. The sustained economic boom since 1986, the limited regional and ethnic inroads made by the opposition in the 1990 election, and the new possibilities thrown up by the UMNO leadership line-up after party elections in November 1993 may also serve to undermine efforts to develop the organizational coherence deemed so necessary to mounting a more formidable electoral challenge in the near future.

Nevertheless, despite their limitations and adverse implications for meaningful and participatory radical democracy, elections still seem to offer the only legitimate means for bringing about regime change at the national level. The attempt by the Labour Party of Malaya to organize an electoral boycott in the May 1969 elections—partly to protest the continued incarceration without trial of many of their leaders from the mid-1960s—failed miserably. Instead, the electorate moved strongly against the incumbent government, resulting in the ruling Alliance securing less than half the total votes cast, the weakest electoral mandate ever for the ruling coalition since the first ever federal election, in 1955.

Perhaps more important in the long run, the Labour Party thus relinquished its ambiguous position as the leading left-wing electoral party, enjoying the most support from the non-Malay masses, to the DAP, which had made a most unimpressive electoral debut in the 1964 elections despite the leadership of Singapore Prime Minister Lee Kuan Yew, when Singapore was still part of Malaysia.

To reject electoral means is to tie one's own arm behind one's back, unnecessarily limiting political options severely, especially when there are few other legitimate alternatives available. Instead, electoral participation may well be used to enhance the scope for further political involvement and to increase awareness of the severe political limitations of electoralism. To participate in elections does not necessarily mean that one's politics are merely electoralist. Not unlike war, elections may well be seen as politics by other means.

5

Malaysia:
Do elections make a difference?

HAROLD CROUCH

Elections are an established part of Malaysian political life. The first national election was held under colonial auspices in 1955, two years before Malaya (as it was before the formation of Malaysia in 1963) became independent in 1957. Following independence, successive national elections have been held without exception within the five-year period allowed by the constitution, although on one occasion polling was postponed in the East Malaysian states following the declaration of a state of emergency in response to postelection racial rioting in West Malaysia in 1969. Regular elections have been held not only at the national level but also at the state level in each of Malaysia's thirteen states.

But although elections have been held regularly in Malaysia, they have also been won regularly by the government. At the national level the governing coalition has not only retained office after each election, but except for a brief period between the holding of the 1969 election in West Malaysia and the postponed polling in East Malaysia, it has always enjoyed at least a two-thirds majority in parliament. Indeed, during much of the 1970s and 1980s the government held more than 80 percent of the seats. It has enjoyed similar success in most states, although it lost on several occasions in Kelantan and Sabah and on one occasion each in Trengganu and Penang.

In view of the ruling coalition's unbroken record of success, at least at the national level, it might be argued that elections in Malaysia are really no more than a ritual providing a cloak of legitimacy for what is really authoritarian rule. Elections allow critics to "let off a little steam" while giving the government a useful means of gauging the level of public

114

dissatisfaction. But elections are not intended to allow the voters to change the government.

There is, of course, some truth in such an interpretation. But elections have a deeper meaning and political significance in Malaysia. The opposition's prospects of defeating the government at the polls are indeed minimal, but this does not mean that the government can completely ignore popular demands. Moreover, the government does not set itself the target of merely winning elections but aims to secure two-thirds of the seats in the legislature, which enables it to change the constitution at will.[1] As shall be argued in this chapter, the electoral process in Malaysia does contribute in an important way to making the Malaysian government responsive, to some extent at least, to pressures from the community.

WHY DOES THE GOVERNMENT ALWAYS WIN?

The Malaysian electoral system has been organized in such a way that it would be difficult for the opposition to defeat the government. This is partly because of the nature of the parties in Malaysia's plural society. But it is also due to the specific provisions of the electoral system itself and to a range of authoritarian powers that the government has used to limit opposition.

Malaysian politics continues to be based in large part on ethnic identity. Elections are largely contests for ethnic support in which the ethnic parties in the ruling coalition compete with ethnic parties in the opposition. The core of the ruling coalition consists of three ethnic parties— the United Malays National Organization (UMNO), the Malaysian Chinese Association (MCA), and the Malaysian Indian Congress (MIC)—which purport to represent the interests of the Malay, Chinese, and Indian communities respectively. Since the early 1970s they have been joined by the Gerakan, a purportedly multiracial party, which is in fact overwhelmingly (although not exclusively) Chinese in composition, and various parties from East Malaysia.

The two main opposition parties are the Democratic Action Party (DAP), which gets almost all its support from the Chinese and Indian communities, and the Pan-Malaysian Islamic Party (PAS), whose mem-

---

[1]The constitution has been amended thirty-four times since 1957. Each amendment act usually contains many specific amendments.

bers and supporters are almost exclusively Malay. In the late 1980s a split within UMNO produced a new Malay opposition party, Semangat 46, but it performed poorly in the 1990 election and appears to have lost ground since. Several opposition parties have also appeared in Sabah and Sarawak in circumstances that are too complex to be discussed satisfactorily in this chapter.

The constituent parties of the ruling coalition—initially the Alliance but reconstituted as the Barisan Nasional (BN, National Front) in the early 1970s—contest elections as a single party. The BN nominates single candidates in each constituency who are then supported by the BN parties. In Malay areas, for example, the BN normally nominates Malay candidates who get the votes not only of UMNO voters but also MCA, MIC, and Gerakan supporters. On the other hand, in predominantly non-Malay areas, the BN nominates MCA, MIC, and Gerakan candidates who also get the votes of UMNO supporters.

One of the major weaknesses of the opposition has been its failure to form a similar multiethnic alliance against the BN. In elections before 1990, the two main opposition parties, the DAP and PAS, always contested elections separately, so that it was common for the BN to face both DAP and PAS opponents. The result was that BN candidates who failed to attract majority support from either the Malay or non-Malay communities could still win. For example, in a constituency where Malays made up 60 percent of the voters, a PAS candidate might win a majority of the Malay votes and a DAP candidate might win a majority of the non-Malay votes but the UMNO candidate could still win. Of the 60 percent of the voters who are Malay in this example, 35 percent might support PAS and only 25 percent support UMNO while, of the 40 percent who are non-Malay, 25 percent might support the DAP and only 15 percent support MCA, Gerakan, and MIC together. But with the MCA, Gerakan, and MIC supporters giving their votes to the UMNO candidate representing the BN, the BN would win the seat with 40 percent of the votes ahead of PAS with 35 percent and the DAP with 25 percent. In the same way non-Malay BN candidates could fail to obtain majority support within their own communities but still win the seat with the votes of UMNO supporters.

The BN constituent parties have often been portrayed as moderates on ethnic issues, while the opposition parties have been seen as extremists. Yet the attitudes expressed by members of the BN parties at party conventions and in private conversations are often no less extreme than those associated with the opposition parties. The difference appears to lie less in fundamental attitudes than in willingness to compromise on ethnic issues in the interests of political advantage. In the context of the ethnic divisions of Malaysian society, the ethnic parties of the BN have found that compromise and cooperation work. As the dominant party in the coalition, the compromises made by UMNO have, of course, been relatively minor compared with those forced on the non-Malay parties.

The opposition parties have naturally seen the compromises made by the government parties as opportunities to be exploited for their own electoral advantage. Both the Malay and non-Malay parties in the ruling coalition are vulnerable to charges of selling out to the other ethnic group and have been accused by the opposition parties of betraying the interests of their ethnic community. But, precisely because they take up the issue of ethnic betrayal, the Malay-based PAS and the non-Malay-based DAP find it very difficult to cooperate with each other.

So far the BN's approach has paid off electorally. While the BN parties have undoubtedly forgone votes, especially among non-Malays, because of their willingness to compromise ethnic aspirations, they have gained more from their ability to win cross-ethnic votes. This lesson was not entirely lost on the opposition parties, however. In the 1990 election, the two main opposition parties, now joined by the party of UMNO dissidents, Semangat 46, attempted to work out their own electoral alliance but only half succeeded. Both the DAP and PAS, which had built up their support in the past by condemning the ethnic compromises of the MCA and Gerakan on one side and UMNO on the other, found it difficult to join together in a formal alliance without undermining their own credibility among their existing supporters. But, realizing the electoral advantages of interethnic cooperation, they each joined separate alliances with the new Semangat 46. Despite their inability to form an unambiguous coalition, the main opposition parties were at least able to agree on nominating single opposition candidates in almost all the constituencies of Peninsular Malaysia. The result was a substantial increase in opposition representation in parliament and a spectacular victory for the PAS–Semangat 46 alliance in the overwhelmingly Malay state of Kelantan. The opposition's semialliance in 1990 depended, however, on the mediating role of Semangat 46. Since 1990 Semangat 46 has lost much ground, with the result that there is no certainty that the DAP and PAS will continue their electoral cooperation in the future.

The BN's continuing electoral success, however, is not a consequence of the communally based party system alone. The electoral system itself is skewed in such a way as to virtually guarantee victory for the dominant Malay party and its allies. The Malaysian constitution does not require that the number of voters in each constituency be roughly equal. On the contrary, the numbers in urban, predominantly non-Malay constituencies are normally much larger than in rural, predominantly Malay constituencies. At times the largest urban constituency has been as much as five times larger than the smallest rural constituency with the result in the 1980s that some 70 percent of the peninsular constituencies had Malay majorities, although Malays made up only 57 percent of the peninsular population. As long as UMNO remained the main Malay party, it was virtually assured of playing the dominant role in the government.

UMNO's battle with PAS and, in 1990, with Semangat 46 for the Malay vote is therefore crucial to the outcome of elections. Apart from the benefits flowing from its alliance with non-Malay parties in the BN, UMNO made the most of the advantages of incumbency to consolidate its support among Malay voters. The government machinery—especially the Information Ministry and Kemas (Community Development) workers—were regularly mobilized on behalf of UMNO during election campaigns, while UMNO leaders made it clear that development funds would be at risk in constituencies that voted for the opposition. Of central importance in tying Malay voters to UMNO was the party's patronage network, through which such incentives as commercial opportunities, government jobs, low-cost housing, access to land, agricultural inputs, and scholarships were awarded to faithful party supporters.

To a much lesser extent the non-Malay parties also dispensed patronage to Chinese and Indian supporters of the BN. Chinese businessmen were able to obtain licenses and contracts; Chinese and Indian primary schools received government grants; and children were able to obtain scholarships or at least loans to finance their studies.

The BN government has also used its authoritarian powers to create a political environment that has undermined, although not completely eliminated, opposition. The Internal Security Act has been used from time to time to detain opposition leaders, the Sedition Act limits the raising of ethnic complaints, the Official Secrets Act deters the use of intentional as well as unintentional leaks from government sources, and a number of laws and regulations impose limits on press freedom. Moreover, all the main newspapers are owned either by BN parties or by business groups close to them, while television and radio are in effect government monopolies (the private television channel being owned by a company controlled by UMNO). Ultimately, the government also has the constitutional power to declare a state of emergency if it sees fit. On two occasions, emergencies have been declared at the state level in order to overthrow opposition-controlled state governments, and the government's critics believed that an emergency at the national level could be declared—as it was in 1969 in the wake of racial rioting—if the BN's grip on the federal government were threatened.

It is hardly surprising, then, that despite Malaysia's formally democratic institutions, including regular elections, the federal government has never seriously faced the prospect of defeat. In elections since the formation of the BN shortly before the 1974 election, the ruling coalition's share of the popular vote has ranged between 53.4 percent and 60.7 percent while its shares of seats fell below 80 percent only once— in 1990 when, faced with the opposition's semialliance, it declined to 70 percent. Elections have thus served Malaysia's ruling coalition well.

GOVERNMENT RESPONSIVENESS TO ELECTORAL PRESSURES

Secure in office, the government seems to have little need to respond to electoral pressure. Even if a majority of the voters were to vote in favor of the opposition, the ethnic-based rivalries between the opposition parties, the gerrymandering of the electoral system, and the authoritarian powers at the government's disposal more or less ensure electoral victory for the government. The government coalition, therefore, does not appear to be under strong pressure to put forward policies to attract voters' support. It seems that it can normally win without making significant concessions to popular opinion.

But, in reality, the government is forced to take account of pressures from society that are channeled in part through the electoral system. In examining the ways in which popular pressures are felt in Malaysia, it is necessary to discuss the Malay and non-Malay communities separately.

MALAY PRESSURES

As noted above, the Malaysian electoral system is skewed heavily in favor of the Malay community. The Malay (and other *bumiputera* [indigenes]) proportion of the peninsula population, which rose from 51 percent in the late 1960s to an estimated 56.5 percent in the mid-1980s, has been increasingly overrepresented in parliament. In 1964 Malays made up a majority of voters in 59 (57 percent) of 104 peninsula constituencies, but this rose to 79 (69 percent) out of 114 after a redrawing of boundaries before the 1978 election and 92 (70 percent) out of 132 after another redrawing of boundaries before the 1986 election. This majority was reinforced by the overrepresentation of East Malaysia, where *bumiputera* politicians were expected to side with the *bumiputera*-dominated federal government. Although only 16.5 percent of the population lives in East Malaysia, the 48 East Malaysian constituencies in 1990 made up 27 percent of the seats in the federal parliament. It is clear, therefore, that any party able to win the overwhelming majority of Malay constituencies in the peninsula would almost certainly form the core of the federal government. Even if it lost all the non-Malay majority seats, it could still rule provided it won virtually all the Malay-majority seats and retained the support of the main *bumiputera* parties in East Malaysia. The battle for the Malay-majority seats, therefore, has always been crucial.

In practice, UMNO has always performed extremely well in the Malay-majority seats in the peninsula. Since the formation of the BN in 1974, the BN won all the Malay-majority seats in 1974 (when the main opposition party, PAS, was temporarily a member of the ruling coalition) and lost only five to PAS in both 1978 and 1982 and one in 1986. It was only in 1990, following a split in UMNO, that an alliance between PAS and the UMNO dissidents was able to wrest fifteen of the Malay-majority seats from the BN. The result has been that UMNO has normally not only won a substantial majority of seats in the peninsula but held close to half of all the seats in the national parliament—70 (45 percent) out of 154 in both 1978 and 1982, 83 (47 percent) out of 177 in 1986, although only 71 (39 percent) out of 180 in 1990.

UMNO's capacity to mobilize Malay voters behind the BN has also benefited its non-Malay coalition partners in constituencies where Malays constituted only minorities. Generally the non-Malay BN parties have been much more successful in constituencies with substantial numbers of Malay voters than in predominantly non-Malay constituencies. The dependence of the non-Malay government parties on Malay support mobilized by UMNO is shown by their usually weak performance in constituencies where Chinese voters made up a large majority of the voters. Thus, in 1978 the Chinese BN parties were able to win only two

Malaysia 121

of the fifteen parliamentary seats where Chinese made up more than 60 percent of the voters. In 1982 they did much better, winning eight of fourteen such seats, but in 1986 they lost all fifteen seats and in 1990 all fourteen seats in this category. Given the poor performance of the BN's Chinese-based parties in predominantly Chinese constituencies, UMNO not only helped its allies in seats where Malays constituted significant minorities but routinely bolstered its non-Malay coalition partners by placing a few of their candidates in Malay-majority seats.

The battle for the Malay vote was, until 1990, fought between UMNO and PAS, but in 1990 PAS was joined by the UMNO dissidents in Semangat 46. Leaving aside the 1974 election, when PAS was temporarily part of the government, support for PAS in the peninsula in the 1978, 1982, and 1986 elections ranged between 16.4 and 17.7 percent, whereas in 1990 the combined vote for PAS and Semangat 46 candidates rose to 25.2 percent. Malay support for PAS between 1978 and 1986 amounted to about 30 percent of the Malay votes in the peninsula (assuming that 55–57 percent of the voters were Malays).[2] Estimating Malay support for the main Malay opposition parties in 1990 is more difficult because it is likely that some of their voters were non-Malay supporters of the DAP, which was also allied with Semangat 46. The level of support for the Malay opposition varied regionally and was strongest in the north and northeast, especially in the state of Kelantan, where the PAS–Semangat 46 alliance won a spectacular victory at the state level in 1990.

The presence of substantial opposition within the Malay community has meant that UMNO could not take its preeminence for granted. As previously outlined, the UMNO-dominated government gerrymandered the electoral system, mobilized bureaucratic manpower and other facilities during elections, controlled the press, distributed bountiful patronage to its supporters, and occasionally detained opponents under the Internal Security Act. But it also sought popular support by implementing policies that brought direct benefits to the Malay community, or at least to significant parts of it. In the final analysis, UMNO needed the votes of Malay voters not only to remain in power but also to achieve the self-imposed goal of a two-thirds majority for the BN. It therefore presented policies that responded, in part, to Malay aspirations and interests.

[2]Malays made up 55.25 percent of the peninsular population in the 1980 census and increased to an estimated 56.5 percent by 1985. The results of the 1990 census had not been released by mid-1994.

The way in which the BN government has responded to the needs and wishes of significant segments of the Malay population can be seen in a number of areas. We will examine policies that can be plausibly attributed at least in part to UMNO's awareness of its need to continue to win support from Malay voters. Three major areas of responsiveness are rural development, the New Economic Policy, and Islamization.

RURAL DEVELOPMENT

In comparison with most Third World governments, the government of Malaysia has shown unusual interest in rural development. It can be plausibly argued that this interest in rural development is driven in large part by electoral considerations. The overwhelming majority of rural people are Malays, and the Malay-majority constituencies are largely rural.

The government devoted substantial resources to rural development. Through the Ministry of Rural Development (later National and Rural Development) it extended the supply of electricity and water to rural areas, built roads, provided public transport, made available health facilities, and assisted the development of small industries. The Ministry of Agriculture provided extension services to peasants and fishermen, while the Ministry of Education built new schools, both primary and secondary, throughout the country, and awarded scholarships to many Malay children. Most of these programs were directed toward Malays in the rural areas.

One of the most striking programs introduced to alleviate rural poverty was the government's massive land development scheme carried out by the Federal Land Development Authority (FELDA). Although established in 1956 at the end of the colonial era, FELDA expanded enormously after 1970. Under the FELDA program, land was cleared and prepared for rubber, palm oil, and some other crops and allocated to new settlers, who were almost all Malays. By 1970 some 20,700 families had been settled on ninety individual schemes, but by 1990 the number of families had grown to 116,293, involving about half a million people on 315 schemes.[3] Demand for places on FELDA land was very strong

---

[3]*Second Malaysia Plan 1971–1975* (Kuala Lumpur: Government Press, 1971), 125; *Utusan Malaysia*, April 2, 1990.

among poor rural Malays, who were often selected on the basis of their political loyalties.

Although the government's policies did not eliminate rural poverty, they undoubtedly brought benefits of one sort or another to a considerable number of Malay voters in rural constituencies. The official claim that the incidence of rural poverty fell from 58.7 percent in 1970 to 19.3 percent in 1990 need not be accepted without questioning, but it is supported by other, more concrete, social indicators. Thus, for example, by 1987, 88 percent of rural households were supplied with electricity compared with only 29 percent in 1970, and 73 percent had access to piped or potable water compared with 39 percent seventeen years earlier. During 1971–80, the number of rural health centers and clinics increased by 55 percent and by 1987, 63 percent of the rural population lived within five kilometers of a village clinic.[4] Moreover, by 1990 primary education was virtually universal, not only in urban centers, but also in rural areas, and a large number of Malay children from rural backgrounds were continuing their education at the secondary and tertiary levels.

It is plausible to argue that the UMNO-dominated government's interest in rural development is in large part a result of its need to maintain electoral support among the rural Malay population. Although Malays have become increasingly urbanized as the proportion of the *bumiputera* workforce engaged in agriculture declined from 62.3 percent in 1970 to 37.4 percent in 1990,[5] the weighting of the electoral system in favor of Malay-majority rural constituencies has meant that the government was forced to pay attention to the hopes and aspirations of Malay rural voters. By implementing policies attractive to Malay rural voters, the BN reaped electoral gains that were quite disproportionate to the resources expended.

THE NEW ECONOMIC POLICY

The responsiveness of UMNO to declining electoral support from the Malay community was shown most dramatically in the government's

---

[4]*Mid-term Review of the Fifth Malaysia Plan 1986–1990* (Kuala Lumpur: National Printing Department, 1989), 58–59; *Fourth Malaysia Plan 1981–1985* (Kuala Lumpur: National Printing Department, 1981), 43.

[5]*Fourth Malaysia Plan 1981–1985*, 59; *Second Outline Perspective Plan 1991–2000* (Kuala Lumpur: National Printing Department, 1991), 118.

response to its loss of seats and votes in the 1969 election and the rioting that followed it. During the late 1960s Malay dissatisfaction with the Malay-dominated government had increased as they demanded that the government take more vigorous measures to improve the economic position of the Malay community vis-à-vis the Chinese, who were seen to be dominant in commerce and industry. At the same time Malays were also demanding that the state identify itself unambiguously with the symbols of Malay political domination.

In the 1969 election the ruling Alliance (the predecessor of the BN) suffered a severe setback, winning only 66 of the 104 seats compared with 89 in 1964, while its share of the votes fell from 58.4 percent to 48.4 percent. Most of the losses—fifteen seats—were suffered by the non-Malay Alliance parties, but UMNO also lost eight seats. Of particular concern to UMNO was the rise of PAS (known then as PMIP), which won an increase of only three seats—from nine to twelve—but whose share of the votes rose from 14.5 percent to 23.8 percent. In the past, PAS had developed a strong base in the predominantly Malay states of the north and northeast—Kelantan, Trengganu, Kedah, and Perlis— but it seemed that the party was also beginning to attract urban support in the communally balanced states of the west and the south. The result was that not only did UMNO lose several seats to PAS in Malay areas, but UMNO was less able to deliver Malay votes to its non-Malay allies in predominantly non-Malay areas.[6]

Although the Alliance won the election, it was clear that UMNO was losing ground in its competition with the Malay opposition. The significance of the electoral trend against UMNO, however, was quickly surpassed by the impact of the racial rioting in Kuala Lumpur that followed the announcement of election results. Chinese-based opposition parties had defeated the Alliance at the state level in Penang and deprived it of its majorities in Perak and Selangor, where Kuala Lumpur is situated. In response to these Chinese victories, racial rioting broke out in Kuala Lumpur in which it was officially estimated that nearly 200 people, a large majority of whom were Chinese, were killed. In the wake of the rioting, the government declared a state of emergency and parliament was suspended for almost two years. The Malay-instigated rioting was seen by UMNO as a stark reinforcement of the message conveyed by

[6]See K. von Vorys, *Democracy without Consensus: Communalism and Political Stability* (Princeton: Princeton University Press, 1976), Chap. 12; R. K. Vasil, *The Malaysian General Election of 1969* (Kuala Lumpur: Oxford University Press, 1972).

the voting trend. The UMNO leaders believed that the party had lost ground because it had failed to meet the needs of the Malay community and had given too many concessions to non-Malays, especially the Chinese.

The government's response to the events of 1969 was partly authoritarian. Although parliament began to sit again in early 1971, the government retained its emergency powers, while various restrictive measures were introduced that strengthened the government against the opposition, as already outlined. Further, the ruling coalition was expanded to encompass former opposition parties including the Gerakan, which had won power in the state of Penang, and, after heavy pressure from the federal government, PAS, which formed the state government in Kelantan. But, in the long run, the UMNO leaders believed that it was necessary to take steps to win back and consolidate electoral support in the Malay community.

In 1971 the government launched its New Economic Policy (NEP), a program of positive discrimination in favor of the Malay community. The NEP aimed to bring the Malay community into the modern economy at all levels. Malays were given special assistance to go into business, and pressure was applied in various ways to force foreign and Chinese companies to make shares available to Malays. Malays were also given special opportunities in education. In secondary schools Malay students were advantaged by the gradual conversion of English-medium schools to Malay, while scholarships and quotas encouraged Malays to continue on to tertiary education. At the lower end of the spectrum, businesses were pressured to employ Malay workers. At the same time, the "Malayness" of the state was emphasized. Malay culture was promoted; the Malay language became the effective language of administration; and the Islamic religion was given great prominence.

As a consequence of these policies, Malay participation in the modern economy increased at an extraordinary rate. Foreign and Chinese enterprises were forced to accept Malay partners, while Malay businessmen, virtually all of whom had close ties with UMNO, became part of the business elite. Between 1970 and 1990 the Malay proportion of the workforce in middle-class occupations rose from 33.6 percent to 48.1 percent and the proportion of the Malay workforce in middle-class occupations rose from 12.9 percent to 27.0 percent.[7] Between 1970 and

[7]Calculated from *Fourth Malaysia Plan 1981–1985*, 59 and *Second Outline Perspective*

1988 the number of *bumiputeras* studying at Malaysian universities increased tenfold from 3,084 to 30,085 while another 14,531 were studying at overseas universities.[8] Virtually all Malay students at the tertiary level, both in Malaysia and overseas, were receiving government scholarships and many came from relatively humble rural families.

The NEP was introduced because the Malay-dominated government felt that its own Malay base of political support was being undermined. The Malay-instigated rioting of 1969 had dramatized a trend that had already revealed itself in the election results. Although the NEP in practice undoubtedly served the interests of some Malays—particularly those with UMNO connections—much more than others, it is also clear that a large part of the Malay community benefited in one way or another from the pro-Malay policies introduced after 1969.

ISLAMIZATION

During the 1970s, Malaysia, like many other Muslim countries at that time, experienced an Islamic religious revival. The worldwide Islamic revival may have been inspired in part by international developments such as the growing power of Muslim oil-producing countries and the Islamic revolution in Iran. In Malaysia, however, it seemed to be driven more by domestic developments, particularly the rapid changes in Malay society accompanying the implementation of the NEP. One of the consequences of the NEP was increased urbanization of young Malays who left their villages in search of employment or education in the modern sector. It was among these urban and often well-educated youth that Islamic revivalism had its strongest impact. The influence of the so-called *dakwah* movement was especially widespread among students at universities and other tertiary educational institutions. It has been suggested that newly urbanized Malays turned to religion as a way of overcoming the disorientation they experienced in their new environment. At the same time Islam became a badge of Malay identity for rural Malays finding themselves in close daily contact with non-Malays for the first time.[9]

Plan 1991–2000, 118. The 1970 figures refer to the peninsula alone while the 1990 figures refer to *bumiputeras* in the whole of Malaysia. The inclusion of East Malaysia in the later figures has the effect of slightly underestimating the increase.

[8] *Fourth Malaysia Plan 1981–1985*, 352; *Mid-term Review of the Fifth Malaysia Plan 1986–1990*, 277–78.

[9] For interpretations of Islamization in Malaysia, see J. Nagata, *The Reflowering of Ma-*

Whatever the explanation for the rise of Islamic revivalism in the late 1970s and early 1980s, it was quickly seen by UMNO leaders as a potential threat to their own political position. UMNO's leaders were, of course, practicing Muslims, but it could hardly be said that the Islamic faith provided the guiding philosophy for their political behavior. They were therefore vulnerable to the charge of neglecting Islam. The Islamic revival provided an opportunity for PAS to win over voters from UMNO, while UMNO's own membership itself was not uninfluenced by the Islamic revival and could sometimes be alienated by leaders who seemed lacking in religious commitment. The UMNO leaders, therefore, had good reason to reexamine the party's image in the light of the Islamic challenge.

In 1982 the government, now under the leadership of Dr. Mahathir Mohamad, launched its Islamization program. The prominent Muslim youth leader Anwar Ibrahim was recruited to UMNO shortly before the 1982 general election and quickly rose through the party and government hierarchy. In order to strengthen its Islamic credentials, the government established an Islamic Bank and the International Islamic University, both of which opened in July 1983. Courses on Islamic civilization were made compulsory for all university students. The government also launched a campaign to instill Islamic values—such as justice, honesty, and dedication—in public administration.

The government's Islamization program did not in fact lead to a significant Islamization of Malaysian life. Despite the existence of the Islamic bank, conventional banks continued to do business, and the new Islamic university co-existed with the old universities. Moreover, as adherents of other religions quickly pointed out, the Islamic values proclaimed by the government were hardly foreign to other religions and indeed were increasingly referred to by the government as universal human values.

Although the government's Islamization program was not especially far-reaching, it did, however, serve the purpose of identifying UMNO as a party representing Muslim interests, and it became more difficult for its critics in PAS to claim that UMNO was "doing nothing for Islam." It is unlikely that the UMNO-dominated government would have

laysian Islam (Vancouver: University of British Columbia Press, 1984); Chandra Muzaffar, *Islamic Resurgence in Malaysia* (Kuala Lumpur: Penerbit Fajar Bhakti, 1987); and Zainah Anwar, *Islamic Revivalism in Malaysia* (Kuala Lumpur: Pelanduk Publications, 1987).

felt the need to launch its Islamization program if it had not been faced
by the religious revival of the 1970s, which promised to provide a ready
source of votes for PAS. Confronted with a potential electoral threat,
UMNO moved quickly to preempt PAS in the struggle for Muslim votes.

NON-MALAY PRESSURES

The government was far less responsive to non-Malay than to Malay
electoral pressures. For UMNO, and therefore the BN, the Malay vote
was crucial. But this did not mean that Chinese and Indian voters could
be completely disregarded. First, in Malay-majority constituencies,
where Malay support was more or less evenly divided between UMNO
and PAS or even slightly in favor of PAS, non-Malay voters could provide the extra votes needed to ensure UMNO victories. And second, even
if UMNO won all the Malay-majority seats, it would still hold less than
a majority and need non-Malay allies in parliament. The BN therefore
had to balance its need to secure strong Malay support in Malay-
majority constituencies with its need to woo sufficient non-Malay support to tip the balance in favor of the BN in areas where the Malay vote
was fairly evenly divided.

It is not easy to get an accurate picture of non-Malay voting behavior.
Although the proportion of registered non-Malay voters is more or less
in line with the population statistics—the Chinese being slightly overrepresented and the Indians slightly underrepresented[10]—it seems that
non-Malay registered voters, especially Chinese, are less likely to exercise
their voting rights than Malays.[11] First, it is not unusual in Third World
countries for the turnout to be higher in rural areas than in urban areas.
Elections are usually an event for rural voters, who are also subject to
stronger pressures from local leaders compared to urban voters. In Malaysia, where rural voters are predominantly Malay, this means that Malay participation in voting is higher than among other communities.

[10]Sothi Rachagan, *Law and the Electoral Process in Malaysia* (Kuala Lumpur: Oxford
University Press, 1993), 113.
[11]For example, in the Federal Territory of Kuala Lumpur, which is entirely urban and
predominantly Chinese, the turnout in the 1990 election ranged between 62.1 and 71.3
percent, whereas in predominantly rural and Malay Terengganu, the turnout ranged
between 77.67 and 86.79 percent. However, in largely Chinese Penang, where the state
government faces a strong Chinese-based opposition, the turnout ranged from 74.33
percent to 80.76 percent. These figures, however, only suggest that there is a significant
difference between Chinese and Malay participation in voting. It is still impossible to
measure the difference accurately.

Second, many non-Malays believe (with good reason) that the electoral system, and indeed the whole political system, is biased against them. This sense of alienation leads, especially in the case of Chinese, to a strong vote for opposition parties, but it is also plausible to assume that a certain proportion do not bother to vote at all. The problem for the analyst, however, is that there seems to be no way of making an accurate estimate of the turnout in the three main communities.

It is commonly believed that as many as three-quarters of Indian voters, who made up 9.1 percent of the electorate in 1990, support the BN. The MIC, the Indian party in the BN, has traditionally mobilized Indian rural voters, especially plantation laborers, but it has had less success among urbanized Indian voters. Nevertheless, it seems that many Indian voters, conscious of their status as a small minority who are not even near to constituting a majority of voters in any constituency, fear that they can easily be ignored unless they are perceived as government supporters and thus vote for the BN.

Chinese voters, on the other hand, are more inclined to vote for the opposition. Chinese BN leaders often confess in private that the government usually expects to win only 35–40 percent of the Chinese votes. An examination of election results, however, suggests that while the majority of Chinese vote for the opposition, the government still attracts substantial Chinese support. During the 1970s and 1980s the main opposition party fighting for non-Malay interests, the DAP, usually won about 20 percent of the votes in the peninsula,[12] where Chinese made up between 34.5 and 36.8 percent of the registered voters. If we assume simply that the DAP vote was made up entirely of Chinese and that voter turnout among the Chinese was the same as for the other communities, then about 55 percent of Chinese voters must have voted for the DAP. But neither of these assumptions is valid. First, the DAP also obtains some non-Chinese votes. If we assume, fairly realistically, that one-quarter of Indian voters voted for the DAP, then we are left with about half of the Chinese voters supporting the DAP. Allowance should also be made for the small number of Malays in some areas, such as Perak, who vote for the DAP. On the other hand, if we vary the assumption about Chinese participation in elections, the level of Chinese

---

[12]The fall in the DAP vote in the peninsula to 17.6 percent in 1990 did not reflect a loss of electoral support but was a result of the DAP's alliance with Semangat 46 and some smaller parties. The DAP directed its supporters to vote for its allies in some constituencies.

support for the DAP will increase. For example, if the Chinese turnout were 10 percent less than the average, then the proportion of Chinese supporting the DAP would rise to about 55 percent, and so on. The lower the proportion of Chinese actually voting, the higher the proportion of Chinese votes won by the DAP. It could also probably be assumed that many nonvoters are in fact DAP sympathizers who think that the electoral system is so unfair that it is not worth their while to vote. In addition, some Chinese give their votes to tiny so-called mosquito parties and to independents.

The Chinese vote, of course, is not divided between government and opposition consistently throughout the peninsula. In preponderantly Chinese urban areas, Chinese are more strongly in favor of the opposition than in rural areas, where Chinese constitute fairly small minorities. In rural areas, Chinese often enjoy quite smooth relations with the Malay majority and are dependent on Malay officials for access to government facilities. They are reluctant to prejudice their ties with the Malay community by supporting what Malays see as the "anti-Malay" DAP. On the other hand, Chinese in the major urban centers often feel that they have nothing to lose—even if nothing but psychological satisfaction to gain—by supporting the opposition.

Paradoxically, the government's responsiveness to non-Malay, especially Chinese, concerns varies inversely with the strength of the MCA and the Gerakan in parliament. When the non-Malay BN parties do well in elections, UMNO feels less need to give concessions to non-Malay opinion. But when the non-Malay parties are strongly challenged by the DAP, the UMNO leaders feel compelled to take steps to win back at least a modicum of Chinese support. As a consequence, the electoral performance of the non-Malay BN parties follows a yo-yo pattern. The more seats the MCA and Gerakan win in an election, the fewer concessions they can extract from the government, with the result that they lose ground to the DAP in the next election, forcing the government to give new concessions to the non-Malays in order to win back voters to the BN in the election after that. Thus in 1974, following the MCA's catastrophe in 1969, the MCA and Gerakan did well, winning twenty-four out of thirty-one seats contested. In 1978 they fell back to twenty-one out of thirty-three but rose again to twenty-eight out of thirty-two in 1982, only to fall back to twenty-two out of forty-one in 1986. The pattern seems to have been broken, however, in the unique 1990 election, when the BN was faced by a semialliance of all the main opposition parties. In that year the MCA and Gerakan improved only slightly on their 1986 performance, winning one extra seat—although, as we shall see, the government made a special effort to attract Chinese voters.

In normal times, the government's response to Chinese interests is largely negative. It is a case less of the government's doing what Chinese want than of its not doing what Chinese do not want. The government resisted Malay demands, for example, to close Chinese primary schools or to increase the target for Malay share-holding under the NEP from 30 percent to 50 percent. Either measure might have led to a massive decline in Chinese votes for the government.

Occasionally, however, the government has responded to Chinese grievances by reversing earlier policies. During the 1970s the government took vigorous measures to increase the number of Malays studying in universities. In the mid-1960s only 30 percent of university students were Malays, but the imposition of quotas under the NEP led to a huge increase in the admission of Malays to university education. In 1977, 75 percent of new students in Malaysian universities were Malays, resulting in many better-qualified non-Malay students being excluded. Non-Malay frustration over access to higher education was one of the main issues in the 1978 election, which contributed to the non-Malay BN parties' loss of seats. Apparently feeling that the non-Malays had been pushed too far and, taking into account the electoral repercussions, the minister for education (an UMNO minister) reached an agreement with the MCA to increase the number of university places open to non-Malays by decreasing the Malay quota—in the context of rising overall enrollments—by two percent each year until a ratio of 55:45, roughly reflecting the racial balance in the country, would be achieved in the late 1980s.

The responsiveness of the government to non-Malay concerns increased dramatically after the split in UMNO in the late 1980s, when the new party of UMNO dissidents, Semangat 46, moved to form its own electoral arrangements with the DAP as well as PAS. In a by-election in Johor held in August 1988, one of the dissident UMNO leaders, Datuk Shahrir Samad, won a resounding victory over the official UMNO candidate in a constituency evenly divided between Malays and non-Malays. Shahrir's huge winning margin was due to the support he received from the DAP, which urged Chinese voters to support Shahrir as the lesser of two evils. In circumstances where the Malays seemed more or less evenly divided between UMNO and the UMNO dissidents,

Chinese voters suddenly found themselves objects of the government's blandishments during a series of by-elections before the 1990 general election.

The tone of the statements of UMNO leaders on issues important to the Chinese community changed drastically. UMNO leaders assured the Chinese that the government was committed to the preservation of Chinese primary schools, which received various government building grants, while certificates of an MCA-sponsored vocational college were suddenly recognized for purposes of government employment. Restrictions on visits to China were gradually liberalized, major concessions being announced just before an important by-election and during the month before the general election. Symbolizing UMNO's new line toward the Chinese, Dr. Mahathir personally opened a lion dance festival at the National Stadium two months before the general election. The Chinese lion dance had for many Malays epitomized the alien Chinese culture, and its performance had been subjected to all manner of restrictions. But with an election on the horizon in which Chinese votes would be unusually important, Mahathir, in an astounding speech, promised that his government would support multiculturalism, more or less echoing the demands made by Chinese spokesmen during the previous two decades.[13]

Unlike the government's appeals to Malay voters, who were not only promised but actually provided with substantial material benefits, the government's efforts to woo Chinese, and more generally non-Malay, votes usually involved largely symbolic concessions. Recognition of the lion dance and the removal of travel restrictions did not cost the government anything in terms of material resources, while the funds provided to Chinese schools were small. But they were significant concessions in a symbolic sense that made Chinese feel that their cultural identity was not being ignored. Other concessions to the Chinese, such as the lowering of the quota for Malays at universities and continuing opportunities open to Chinese businesses, however, did involve material resources, though fairly small ones in comparison with the resources showered on Malays.

The cost of giving concessions to the non-Malays was in fact not material but political. The UMNO leaders' dilemma was how to win over Chinese voters without alienating Malays. Malay support was the

[13]*New Straits Times*, August 22, 1990.

sine qua non of political success, but especially when the Malays were divided, some non-Malay support was required as well. Concessions given to the Chinese can usually be exploited by the Malay opposition as examples of the selling out of Malay interests, but in the particular circumstances of the 1990 election, when Semangat 46 had entered its own electoral arrangements with the DAP on one side and PAS on the other, the Malay opposition felt inhibited from doing so.

PRESSURES ARISING FROM PARTY ELECTIONS

Elections for national and state parliaments are not the only important elections in Malaysia. Often no less important, and sometimes more so, are elections within the political parties, especially the main components of the BN. Aspirants for party positions must be sensitive to sentiments within the community that their party purports to represent.

It is often said, only half jokingly, that Malaysia's real election is not the national election but the triennial election of UMNO's leadership. In normal times, UMNO reelects the prime minister as its president more or less automatically, the only exception being in 1987 when Dr. Mahathir defeated his challenger, Tengku Razaleigh, by a very narrow margin. But although the prime minister is almost never challenged for the party presidency, sharp contests have occurred on several occasions for the position of deputy president, and the battles for the three elected vice-presidencies and the party's supreme council are always hard fought. At lower levels in the party, contests for divisional posts, which often give the victor a good chance for a seat in the national or state parliament, also result in sharp rivalries.

In order to win in party elections, candidates must respond to grassroots sentiments. In the case of UMNO, this means that leaders must portray themselves as committed to the Malay cause. While the top party leadership is aware that there is a limit on how much the government can afford to alienate non-Malays, they have to be seen by ordinary UMNO members as champions of the Malay community. The sharper the contest, the more likely that the contestants will adopt avowedly pro-Malay positions; there are no votes for appeasing the Chinese in UMNO elections. Candidates for party posts at the local level also have to show themselves to be responsive to local demands for the usual rural development projects.

Party rivalries have been even more fierce in the MCA, Gerakan, and

MIC. In these cases, party leaders are faced with an unresolvable dilemma. As leaders of parties that are members of the UMNO-dominated
BN, they need to maintain good relations with the UMNO leaders by
presenting themselves as moderates on ethnic issues. But, as leaders of
communities that are to a considerable extent alienated from a government seen to favor Malays over non-Malays, they need to create an
image for themselves as fighters for their own communities' rights. As
long as these parties remain within the BN, their leaders must compromise on ethnic issues and thus lose legitimacy within their own parties,
so that sooner or later they are faced with serious challenges. Elections
in both the MCA and the MIC have regularly witnessed vicious struggles
between rival factions in which the challengers, especially in the MCA,
have accused incumbents of failing to stand up for non-Malay interests.
Similar struggles have also taken place in the Gerakan.

Internal party elections have thus reinforced the pressure on politicians
to be responsive to popular sentiments and interests. In party elections
responsiveness to ethnic sentiments is often the key to victory, although
other factors such as the endorsement of leaders, factional alignments,
and the buying of votes are also important.

CONCLUSION

If elections are seen as means by which citizens can change their government, elections in Malaysia do not make a difference at the national
level or in most of the states. The electoral system has been arranged in
such a way as to make the reelection of the government inevitable—at
least in normal circumstances—at the national level and in nearly all of
the states.

But elections have other functions as well. In the Malaysian case it
has been argued that elections play an important role in forcing the
government to take into account popular interests and sentiments. In
particular the government needs to be significantly responsive to the interests and sentiments of a large part of the Malay community in order
to attract sufficient electoral support to win most of the Malay-majority
seats. At the same time the government must avoid the total alienation
of non-Malays, whose votes are also necessary for electoral victory. But
the government is by no means fully responsive to popular demands.
While it responds to some popular pressures, the Malaysian government

continues to wield substantial authoritarian powers that allow it to repress or ignore others.

It could perhaps be argued that in the context of Malaysia's unique ethnic balance, the Malaysian government would have to take account of popular interests and sentiments even if elections were not held or were held in a very different way. Even an authoritarian Malaysian government would need to make sure that it retained substantial popular acceptance within the Malay community while, given the Chinese economic role, it would need to avoid excessive alienation of Chinese interests. But although this might be true, the electoral system has greatly facilitated the process and made the government responsive in a way that would be hard to imagine under unambiguously authoritarian rule.

For the ruling coalition elections have provided a convenient and economic means of retaining power. By relying primarily on the votes of heavily overrepresented rural Malays, the government can be assured of a comfortable majority of seats in parliament with a minimum expenditure of resources. Nevertheless, the holding of elections means that the government must make sure that the crucial voters do in fact vote for the government, which means, in turn, that it must respond in a significant way to the interests and sentiments of those voters.

6

Contested meanings of elections in the Philippines

BENEDICT J. TRIA KERKVLIET[1]

INTRODUCTION

What do elections mean in the Philippines? What purposes and whose purposes do they serve? Considering that the Philippines has a rather long history of incumbents' being defeated and their rivals' being elected and national and local governments routinely (except between the early 1970s and early 1980s) changing hands in accordance with ballot outcomes, one might expect that elections have a significant degree of democratic meaning.

Yet three prominent interpretations of Philippine politics, though differing in some important respects, argue that elections are really about matters having little to do with citizens weighing issues and candidate qualifications and freely choosing who is best qualified to serve the public. The patron-client, factional view of Philippine politics emphasizes that Philippine politics is about personal relations and networks linked by kinship, friendship, exchange of favors, influence, and money. These are most publicly manifested during elections. A second view, the patrimonial or elite-democracy interpretation, acknowledges the importance of patron-client relations but adds that the elites' use of intimidation, coercion, and violence is also widespread. And the system, despite having democratic-looking institutions, is essentially elites using their connec-

[1]I wish to thank Melinda Tria Kerkvliet for her notes on the *Manila Chronicle's* coverage of the 1969 elections and acknowledge her and the following people for reading a previous draft of this essay and making many helpful suggestions and criticisms: Jojo Abinalles, Bruce Cruikshank, Amando Doronila, Brian Fegan, John Girling, Pete Van Ness, and Peter Xenos.

tions, wealth, and force to control the country's resources. One lucrative resource for personal fortune is holding public office, which is why elites fight among themselves to get elected, manipulating voters and abusing the formal rules in the process. A third version, which might be labeled the neocolonial view, shares much of the second interpretation, but whereas the second sees Filipino elites as often able to manipulate foreign interests to their own advantage, the third sees foreign businesses and American military interests dominating the country, including the elites, who are in effect their clients. Elections are a way for foreign interests to control the country.

After looking at elections and related aspects of Philippine politics through the lenses of these three interpretations and indicating that there is evidence for each one, I want to argue that there are also expressions of democratic aspirations and values that do not nestle within the contours of these three views. I would like to highlight some evidence for this additional view in order to suggest two things: (1) The usual way of analyzing Philippine elections is not wrong but insufficient, and (2) a vital theme in Philippine politics is precisely that the meaning and purpose of elections are contested. Stated another way, without this additional understanding of Philippine politics, one misses a vibrant dynamic in the electoral process.

ELECTIONS ACCORDING TO COMMON INTERPRETATIONS

Since at least the nineteenth century, scholars argue, elections in the Philippines have been rituals without democratic purpose. Institutionalized by Spanish rulers as a way to select local officials from a tiny sector of the population deemed qualified, the election, writes Glenn May, "was seen to be not a ritual worthy of respect but rather a charade, silly and laughable." Municipal elections, he says, were "a marionette plan, where the puppets on the stage performed according to a script and the men behind the scenes pulled the strings."[2] Ruby Paredes argues that the earliest Filipino experience with electoral politics "was devoid of a populist ethic or democratic ideal," an attitude among those seeking public office that continues well into the twentieth century, she says, by

---

[2]Glenn May, "Civic Ritual and Political Reality: Municipal Elections in the Late Nineteenth Century," in Ruby R. Paredes, ed., *Philippine Colonial Democracy* (Quezon City: Ateneo de Manila University Press, 1989), 35–6.

which time Filipinos were socialized into a political system with American patrons at the apex even after formal independence in 1946.[3]

Early in the American colonial period the Philippine electorate was enlarged and, following the 1935 constitution, grew to include all men and women over the age of twenty-one (later the age was dropped to eighteen) who could read and write.[4] Also the number of offices for election has expanded from the initial mayorships and municipal councillors to barrio captains, village councils, provincial governorships, provincial councils, national legislatures (fluctuating between one and two houses), and the presidency and vice-presidency.

Elite Filipinos use these elective offices, scholars claim, to consolidate their fiefdoms. "Brothers, uncles, and cousins for the senior posts; sons and nephews for the junior ones. Here is the origin of the political dynasties," suggests one analyst, "which make Filipino politics so spectacularly different from those of any other country in Southeast Asia."[5] Prominent families—the Lacsons and Montelibanos of Negros, the Osmeñas and Duranos of Cebu, the Aquinos and Cojuangcos of Tarlac, the Josons and Diazes of Nueva Ecija, the Laurels of Batangas, the Dimaporos of Lanao, to name a few—often control several levels, a kind of corporate hold on public resources: mayorships and governorships, a congressional seat or two, a range of appointed provincial and national positions, and judgeships.[6]

The most renowned scholarly studies of the electoral process from the 1950s to 1972, the heyday of what Benedict Anderson calls "cacique democracy," argue that local elites organized their campaigns for office around extended family and patron-client networks cultivated for electoral purposes. The "foundation of political leadership," writes O. D.

---

[3]Ruby R. Paredes, "Introduction: The Paradox of Philippine Colonial Democracy," in ibid., 7, 11.

[4]Literacy rates in the late 1930s were about 53 percent for males and 37 percent for females (calculated from Philippines, Commission of the Census, *Census of the Philippines, 1939, Reports by Provinces for Census of Population*, Vol. 1 [Manila: Bureau of Printing, 1940]). I have not been able to locate records showing voter turnouts in elections between 1936 and 1940, but judging from elections in the 1940s, I would guess they are well over 50 percent.

[5]Benedict Anderson, "Cacique Democracy in the Philippines: Origins and Dreams," *New Left Review* 169 (1988): 12.

[6]Resil Mojares, *The Man Who Would Be President: Serging Osmena and Philippine Politics* (Cebu: Maria Cacao, 1986); Nick Joaquin, *The Aquinos of Tarlac: An Essay on History as Three Generations* (Mandaluyong: Cacho Hermanos, 1983); Isabelo Tinio Crisostomo, *Governor Eduardo L. Joson: The Gentle Lion of Nueva Ecija* (Quezon City: J. Kriz, 1989).

Corpuz, were "the contending factions or blocs in provincial politics, which, in turn, were based on the contending alliances in the towns. And the latter were made of the leading families."[7] More specifically, Carl Landé says, the

> typical local faction . . . is a loose combination of a number of . . . family constellations with a rather large and prosperous family constellation at its core and smaller or less prosperous ones at its periphery. Within each family constellation a strong web of kinship ties binds related families together into a cohesive group. Between the allied constellations of a faction, a smaller number of dyadic ties—more commonly ties of marriage, compadre ties, or ties of patronship and clientship rather than ties of blood—create a lesser bond. Family constellations work in alliance with one another for varying periods of time due to the need to create combinations large enough to compete with some prospect of success in local elections or in other community prestige contests.[8]

Alliances among family and patron-client clusters are loose, unstable, and often shift as one part jumps to join another in anticipation of greater chance of being allied with the winners and thereby getting more benefits.[9]

Political parties are essentially composed of numerous alliances among families and patron-client networks. Which families and factions are in which party fluctuates considerably, as does the number of parties (two major ones from 1946 until martial law in 1972, but also several minority parties; one major party during martial law until the early 1980s; and since then several parties, which are predicted to coalesce into two main ones). But their elements—those constellations of personalistic relations—and their fluid nature persist. During elections, parties per se provide little other than a label for candidates to run under. Candidates rely heavily on their own social networks, weaving together cascading tiers of client supporters, and supplement where necessary with money, material incentives, and promises. Local leaders tug on the lines of their clientalistic followings, hauling in votes for candidates for whom these leaders, in turn, are clients.[10]

[7]Onofre Corpuz, *The Philippines* (Englewood Cliffs, N.J.: Prentice Hall, 1965), 97.
[8]Carl Landé, *Leaders, Factions and Parties: The Structure of Philippine Politics* (New Haven: Southeast Asia Studies, Yale University Press, 1965), 17.
[9]Landé, *Leaders, Factions and Parties*; Remigio E. Agpalo, *The Political Elite and the People: A Study of Politics in Occidental Mindoro* (Manila: College of Public Administration, University of the Philippines, 1972); and Mary R. Hollnsteiner, *The Dynamics of Power in a Philippine Municipality* (Quezon City: Community Development Research Centre, University of the Philippines, 1963).
[10]In addition to works cited in note 9, see Carl Landé and Allan Cigler, "Social Cleavages

For the politicians, elections are about getting into office. The crucial thing is to win. Issues, to the extent they are addressed, are only window dressing for personal ambition. And the ambitious ones use lower offices as stepping-stones to higher ones.[11] Elite families and their anointed stand-ins compete to control public office, which winners can use to enhance their prestige and personal power, distribute favors to supporters, deny them to rivals, build a treasure chest for the next election campaign, use public positions to punish rivals and reward allies, and accumulate personal fortunes.

The office-for-profits feature is played down in the patron-client interpretation. But for the patrimonial/elite-democracy view, using public posts and resources for private gain is central to what the political system is all about. The higher the office, the more lucrative the returns to one's family and allies, though officials in prosperous provinces and cities can also do very well. National senate seats—and, of course, the presidency—are the most prized positions. Elections constitute a cover to obscure what the system is really all about: a device for the political elite to sort out who will feast in the public larder for a term or two and a way to make the masses feel a part of something from which they are actually left out.[12]

Many families parlayed large landholdings and other wealth to win

and Political Parties in the Post-Marcos Philippines," Final Report, for the U.S. Department of State's External Research Program and the University of Kansas, 1990; Arthur Shantz, "Political Parties: The Changing Foundations of Philippine Democracy" (Ph.D. dissertation, University of Michigan, 1972); and Hirufumi Ando, "Elections in the Philippines: Mass-Elite Interaction through the Electoral Process, 1946–1969" (Ph.D. dissertation, University of Michigan, 1971).

[11] A striking example is Sergio Osmeña Jr. of Cebu who was governor, mayor, congressman, and senator. As soon as he captured one office he began campaigning for the next (sometimes not even completing the term for the position he had), using the office's discretionary funds to help his new quest, until becoming the presidential nominee of the Liberal Party, running against Marcos in 1969. Resil Mojares's engaging account of Osmeña (*The Man Who Would Be President*) and accounts about him during the 1969 campaign (which I observed in Manila) suggest to me that the man had scarcely a shred of genuine concern for any public problem or issue.

[12] Anderson, "Cacique Democracy"; Paul Hutchcroft, "Oligarchs and Cronies in the Philippine State: The Politics of Patrimonial Plunder," *World Politics* 43 (April 1991): 414–50; A. R. Magno, *Power Without Form: Essays on the Filipino State and Politics* (Manila: Kalikasan, 1990), 70–92, 98–99. Arthur Williams, "Center, Bureaucracy, and Locality: Central-Local Relations in the Philippines" (Ph.D. dissertation, Cornell University, 1981), 50ff, argues that if indeed patron-client relations were central to the system, far more resources would trickle down to rural voters. Instead, most of the money to which politicians have access, legally and illegally, stays with them and within limited, elite circles.

public office, which in turn helped them to increase their economic opportunities and serve their class interests as landlords, sugar barons, and manufacturers. But there has been room in the expanding system of offices and the nature of the factional system for families of more modest financial means to win offices, which in turn often become avenues to wealth. Examples in post-Japanese occupation years are local leaders of guerrilla bands mobilizing their followings in order to be elected to municipal offices, then building from there.[13] Ramon Magsaysay, who rose to become the republic's third president (1953–7), is an example. Another is Eduardo Joson, who became governor of Nueva Ecija province in 1959 and remained in office for thirty years.

Personal networks are vital for stitching factions together but are insufficient and inefficient for winning offices in large electorates. Consequently, political machines have emerged. They became apparent in the 1950s and 1960s, and fell on hard times during the Marcos years, when *his* machine was the only game in the country, but have been resuscitated since the mid 1980s.[14] They are run by the politically skilled leaders of elite families, as well as by new men from less-wealthy and less well-known family backgrounds who have the required savvy for the age of mass electoral politics.[15] In order to compete for votes, scholars argue, personal connections are supplemented with political machines that provide immediate material rewards and inducements—not necessarily to voters directly, though there is evidence of that, but more often to key players in the provinces and municipalities who get their followers to vote for the machine's candidates. To win elections—now battles between political machines—it is imperative for politicians to come up with even more resources in order to stay in the game. This imperative,

---

[13]Ronald Edgerton developed this argument in "The Politics of Reconstruction in the Philippines, 1945–1948" (Ph.D. dissertation, University of Michigan, 1975).
[14]The revival of rival political machines since the demise of Marcos's is often cited in news coverage and commentary in the Philippines and abroad. For instance, see Conrado de Quiros, "A Triumph, Yes—but of What," *Philippine Daily Inquirer* May 16, 1992, p. 5; *Far Eastern Economic Review*, March 19, 1992, pp. 22–30.
[15]The term "new men" is from Kit Macado, who has done the most work on the evolution of Philippine political machines. See K. S. Macado, "Changing Aspects of Factionalism in Philippine Local Politics," *Asian Survey* 11 (December 1971): 1182–99; Macado, "Leadership and Organization in Philippine Local Politics" (Ph.D. dissertation, University of Washington, 1972), chap. 13; and Macado, "Changing Patterns of Leadership Recruitment in Philippine Local Politics," in Benedict J. Kerkvliet, ed., *Political Change in the Philippines: Studies of Local Politics Preceding Martial Law* (Honolulu: University of Hawaii Press, 1974), 77–129.

142   *Benedict J. Tria Kerkvliet*

some analysts argue, encourages incumbents to take even more from the public till, use more illegal schemes, and concentrate on pork barrel programs with scarcely a glance at policy issues.

So great was the need for ever larger campaign war chests by the 1960s that elections became huge drains on public coffers, aggravating the emerging economic turmoil. An often cited example is the 1969 presidential election, described as "essentially a battle of machines," pitting Senator Sergio Osmeña, Jr. against incumbent President Ferdinand Marcos.[16] To ensure victory, the Marcos machine outspent Osmeña's by an estimated 4,000 pesos per voter to 1, using money raided from the national treasury and printed by the mint.[17] His most brazen use of funds to entice blocks of votes was handing, often personally, 2,000 pesos to nearly every barrio captain in the nation, supposedly for village development but in fact for votes.[18]

Besides money, patron-client networks, and alliances, according to the patrimonial/elite-democracy interpretation, elections are won and lost by how effectively dominant families' minions and private armies intimidate voters, tamper with voting procedures, and use violence. While some studies find that violence and fraud are unusual and rarely affect outcomes,[19] others say that such nefarious methods have long been prominent features of electoral politics. The 1941 elections in Iloilo, concludes Alfred McCoy, "displayed all the negative attributes that so troubled postwar Philippine democracy—systematic fraud, armed thuggery as an electoral tactic, mass violence, and murder," while the national government, headed by President Quezon, did nothing; indeed, "Quezon himself showed little respect for the integrity of law."[20] In Leyte, one

[16]Mojares, *The Man Who Would Be President*, 126.
[17]Osmena's campaign spent an estimated two pesos per registered voter; Marcos's spent about 8,000 (Shantz, "Political Parties," 158, 162).
[18]After handing the money to barrio captains with elaborate pomp and ceremony, Marcos reportedly said to the throngs of villagers, "You have seen with your own eyes what I have done for you. I will ask on November 11 [election day] what small thing you have done for me" (quoted in Shantz, "Political Parties," 154). For analyses of machine politics and intraelite rivalries, see Thomas Nowak and Kay Snyder, "Clientalist Politics in the Philippines: Integration or Instability," *American Political Science Review* 68 (September 1974): 1147–70; Nowak and Snyder, in Kerkvliet, ed., *Political Change in the Philippines*, 153–241; and H. A. Averch, F. H. Denton, and J. E. Koehler, *The Matrix of Policy in the Philippines* (Princeton: Princeton University Press, 1971).
[19]Carl Landé, *Southern Tagalog Voting, 1946–1963: Political Behavior in a Philippine Region* (Dekalb: Center for Southeast Asian Studies, Northern Illinois University, 1973), 99; Shantz, "Political Parties," 145, 244, 286–9.
[20]Alfred McCoy, "Quezon's Commonwealth: The Emergence of Philippine Authoritarianism," in Paredes, ed., *Philippine Colonial Democracy*, 181.

researcher concluded, an election is basically "a personality and power contest between two politically identical candidates in which the little people are bought, terrorized, and intimidated. [A] Philippine election [is] a rich man's civil war fought in the public marketplace."[21] Negros Occidental, the Ilocos region, Cebu, and Marawi are among those parts of the country where violence between rival candidates and their supporters has reportedly been endemic.[22] Politicians often have bodyguards; many have their own armies (a major campaign expense in itself), which were dismantled or went underground during the 1970s martial law years but have since been revived. Scholars generally agree that the 1949 national election was very likely won by Quirino by means of padded electoral rolls, fraudulent tallies, threats, and widespread physical violence. Some claim Marcos stole the 1969 election by similar means, and certainly his opponent thought so, though Osmeña's own record on such matters was so notorious that his protests were hardly credible.[23] Massive cheating, fraud, and some violence by Marcos and his machine in the 1986 election provoked tumultuous protests.

When elections become too ugly, a neocolonial interpretation sees the Americans stepping in to refurbish the democratic image they would like the Philippines to have. Two striking examples, according to this reading, were the 1951 and 1953 elections. The United States government, alarmed about the alleged threat of communism—the Huk rebellion ranging in central Luzon and possibly spreading—and dismayed at the incompetent and corrupt President Quirino and his government, decided to replace Quirino with someone more able and popular. That

[21]Eugene Gibbs, "Family and Politics: A Study of a Filipino Middle Class Family" (Ph.D. dissertation, Claremont Graduate School, 1971), 127.

[22]Mojares, *The Man Who Would Be President*, 54–5 on Cebu; G. Carter Bentley, "People Power and After in the Islamic City of Marawi," in Benedict J. Tria Kerkvliet and Resil Mojares, eds., *From Marcos to Aquino: Local Perspectives on Political Transition in the Philippines* (Honolulu: University of Hawaii Press, 1992), 36–58 on Marawi; Alfred McCoy, "The Restoration of Planter Power in La Carlota City" in ibid., 105–42 on Negros Occidental before and after the Marcos years. Jorge R. Coquia (*The Philippine Presidential Election of 1953* [Manila: Philippine Education Foundation, 1955], 37–8) writes that the governor of Negros Occidental in the late 1940s and early 1950s financed his notorious private army from gambling dens sponsored by municipal mayors who collected protection money (*tong*) for that purpose. When the Philippine army forces were sent there to police the polls in the 1951 elections, they were surprised to find that this private army was better equipped than they were.

[23]Several observers have noticed that losers often cry foul. Shantz, "Political Parties," whose study emphasizes the 1969 election, draws attention to numerous incidents of coercion and vote-padding but seems not to think it was one-sided or that it significantly affected the outcome. *Manila Chronicle* accounts before and after that election do not put much stock in Osmena's claim.

man was Ramon Magsaysay, "an American boy." And to do that U.S. government agents needed to clean up the election process—or at least skew it to Magsaysay's favor. Hence, they created the National Movement for Free Elections (NAMFREL), which is given major credit for making the 1951 congressional elections and especially the 1953 presidential contest (where Magsaysay defeated Quirino) remarkably clean.[24]

According to the neocolonial interpretation, the U.S. government's meddling in Philippine elections, though not usually so extensive as in the 1951 and 1953 elections, is endemic. United States military and business interests have persistently influenced, even determined, who will be candidates, especially for the presidency, and how the election process will be handled. The purpose of elections themselves, according to this reading, is to help camouflage the continued control of the United States, World Bank, International Monetary Fund, and other capitalist interests over the Philippine polity and economy and give a semblance of legitimacy to that political system and to the particular governments that these foreign interests favor.[25] Marcos's martial law eliminated Congress, elections, and other democratic trappings, with the approval, endorsement, and possibly encouragement from key U.S. interests.[26] But

[24]Stephen R. Shalom, *The United States and the Philippines: A Study of Neocolonialism* (Philadelphia: Institute for the Study of Human Issues, 1981), 86–93; Raymond Bonner, *Waltzing with a Dictator: The Marcoses and the Making of American Policy* (New York: Times Books, 1987), 39–40, 408; Renato Constantino and Letizia Constantino, *The Philippines: The Continuing Past* (Quezon City: The Foundation for Nationalist Studies, 1978), 232–62; Ma Aurora Carbonell-Catilo, et al., *Manipulated Elections* (Quezon City: np, 1985), 26, 55. CIA people involved claim responsibility for both NAMFREL and Ramon Magsaysay—first as secretary of defense and later, in 1953, the successful challenger for the presidency against Quirino. See Joseph B. Smith, *Portrait of a Cold Warrior* (New York: Putnam's, 1976), 101–14, an account by a CIA agent who worked in the Philippines during the 1950s. Edward Lansdale (*In the Midst of Wars: An American's Mission to Southeast Asia* [New York: Harper and Row, 1972], chaps. 3, 6, 8), one of Smith's colleagues in Manila, sees himself as having helped to turn Congressman Magsaysay into President Magsaysay, though he gives more credit to the man than Smith does. Lansdale does not discuss the role of the United States in NAMFREL but does hint that it germinated from a seed planted by him and other Americans.
[25]This has also been the analysis of several political organizations, especially the country's two communist parties.
[26]Robert B. Stauffer, *The Philippines Under Marcos: Failure of Transitional Developmentalism* (Sydney: Transnational Corporations Research Project, University of Sydney, 1986), 1–5; Alex B. Brillantes, Jr., *Dictatorship and Martial Law: Philippine Authoritarianism in 1972* (Quezon City: Great Books, 1987), 115–8. A patrimonial/elite-democracy analysis of Marcos's imposing martial law is that, by ignoring the rule to which elites had agreed that one could not be president for more than two terms, Marcos was taking the next logical step in the evolution of familial, factional, machine politics: He was setting himself up as the country's supreme patron and preparing the way for

later Marcos established a national legislature, lifted martial law in 1981, and held numerous elections in part because of pressure by U.S. government and business interests seeking to reestablish the appearance of democratic processes in the Philippines.[27]

So far I have been discussing mainly what elections mean to politicians and others active in campaigns. What about voters? What do elections mean to them? Studies indicate a multiplicity of meanings, even within the same person. Many Filipinos see elections as the best available way to decide who will hold office. They prefer that method, despite its faults, over alternatives such as appointment from on high and violent struggle. At the same time, people are frequently cynical especially about national and provincial elections, seeing them essentially as contests among elites who have minimal interest in the electorate except when running for office. Then candidates will promise anything, but once elected they rarely deliver. Politicians use public office basically for their own personal gain. In other words, voters often see through the democratic exterior of the political system and are disgusted with the way things actually work.[28]

Voters also often have an instrumental approach toward elections, seeing the process as an opportunity to get something for themselves and their families. One could view this as a sign of democracy stirring in the body politic. If voters regard elections as a way to influence public officials, then elections may provide a process for them to participate in and affect the business of government.[29] But an election can also be a manifestation of voters who are said to be unconcerned about issues or have no expectation of getting some longer-term return for their vote and who seek mainly to extract what they can, preferably on the spot, by participating in a nominal way to please a relative or friend, extracting personal favors from candidates, selling their votes, or in other ways working the system.[30]

Elections also can be means for fulfilling clientele obligations, not only

his family to succeed him. And in the process, Marcos incarcerated, incapacitated, and murdered rivals and destroyed their political machines.

[27] Shalom, *United States and the Philippines*, 177–82; Stauffer, *Philippines Under Marcos*, 181; and David Wurfel, *Filipino Politics: Development and Decay* (Ithaca: Cornell University Press, 1988), 235–45 passim.

[28] This is one theme in studies from several parts of the country. See Kerkvliet and Mojares, eds., *From Marcos to Aquino*.

[29] Landé, *Leaders, Factions and Parties*, 116.

[30] See chapters in Kerkvliet and Mojares, eds., *From Marcos to Aquino*; also Ando, "Elections in the Philippines," 147, 149; and Landé, *Leaders, Factions and Parties*, 62, 68.

by voting but also by campaigning for candidates supported by one's patron and calling on family members and close friends to do the same. In this way, the client strengthens the bonds with her or his patron, and perpetuates the relationship.[31] Regionalism can also motivate citizens to become involved in elections when a candidate from one's own region is running against someone from elsewhere. Common language and other shared cultural attributes, it is said, predispose a person to vote for, even campaign for, the candidate from one's own region.[32]

Arguably much in Philippine society underpins the ritualistic, self-seeking, personalistic, and narrow, materialistic attitude of voters.[33] Family ties and obligations are the strongest social institution; next come other close personal relations. Both engender obligations and duties to particular people rather than to organizations, political parties, and certainly not to class-based associations or to society or the public at large. Secondly, prevalent voter orientations are a result of Philippine political culture characterized by poverty, pessimism, despair, and conservatism. That goes a long way, Resil Mojares concludes, to explain why voters seek "short-term gains and benefits for oneself, one's family, or small group, rather than one's class or nation" and why Philippine politics consists largely of "quick returns, personalistic leadership, and visible impact-projects."[34] The cumulative results of such "destructive, immiserizing" political practices are "orchestrated 'mandates' rather than genuine participation, manipulation of needs and rewards rather than

---

[31]Landé, *Leaders, Factions and Parties*; Agpalo, *The Political Elite and the People*; Hollnsteiner, *Dynamics of Power*; and Benedict J. Kerkvliet, *Everyday Politics in the Philippines: Class and Status Relations in a Central Luzon Village* (Berkeley: University of California Press, 1990), 219–30.

[32]Ando, "Elections in the Philippines," 77–80, 89; Landé, *Southern Tagalog Voting*, 73–98; Lande and Cigler, "Social Cleavage," 38, 41. Shantz ("Political Parties," 275) argues that apparent ethno-linguistic voting is really, instead, a complex manifestation of allegiances and values going back to the primacy of family in Philippine politics.

[33]In 1963, prominent newspaper columnist Indalecio Soliongco wrote in disgust that the daily news "during the campaign about ward healers and politicians in office selling themselves and their followers for a negotiated or dictated fee is the best indication of the sheep-like quality of the Filipino voter." Only in the Philippines, he complains, is a political leader "capable of making the completely undemocratic promise that he can deliver so many number of votes on demand . . . , that the landlord or the rich provincial merchant can substantiate his fealty to the highest ruler, not only by cash but also by the votes of his tenants or subalterns." Although "this traffic in votes is not as rampant as it was ten years ago . . . as long as these vestiges remain, Philippine democracy cannot be said to have reached a viable stage. And certainly . . . the political sophistication of the Filipino voter is an insult" (Renato Constantino, ed., *Soliongco Today: A Contemporary from the Past* [Quezon City: Foundation for Nationalist Studies, 1981], 123).

[34]Mojares, *The Man Who Would Be President*, 159.

a process of democratic 'bargaining,' the perpetuation of 'false consciousness' instead of purposive political education, and a continuing powerlessness of the people instead of empowerment through politics."[35]

ANOTHER READING

Although the prevalent interpretations of Philippine electoral politics have considerable merit, they leave out a great deal as well. I want to highlight three particular features and then elaborate on a broader, fourth matter.

Elections, especially before and after the martial law period (1972 to the early 1980s), have helped to legitimate the state, individual office holders, and the transitions from one government to another.[36] Having served these purposes, elections may very well have spared the Philippines the strife and turmoil that plagues other political systems in which the process for deciding who should hold office or establish governments is unclear or variable.

Second, motivations for why people vote and for whom are often more complex than what the prevailing syntheses portray. Although patron-client ties and factional affiliations are common considerations for many people, there is also evidence that these often do not effectively mobilize voters. This appears to be a recent phenomenon in some areas but of much longer duration in others. Assessing how effective such personalistic ties are may be a function of perspective. Politicians often emphasize them, but voters' explanations for why they voted as they did are frequently much more intricate. Such complexities are suggested in some quantitative data analyses.[37] They are more clearly seen in results of local studies, which reveal that while kinship and patron-client ties are factors considered when deliberating whom to vote for, people—even the same people—also weigh other considerations, including class interests. And though an instrumental attitude toward elections is often pronounced, moral and related deliberations also are important.[38]

[35]Ibid., 161–2.
[36]This argument features in Wurfel's multifaceted analysis, *Filipino Politics*, 37–8, 399.
[37]Landé and Cigler find some evidence suggesting class interests are important for rural voters in some areas. "Social Cleavage," 37, 40, 52, 59.
[38]The variety and complexity are conveyed in several chapters of Kerkvliet and Mojares, eds., *From Marcos to Aquino*. See, for example, those by Turner, Mojares, Blanc-Szanton, Eder, Pinches, Kerkvliet, Pertierra, and Zialcita. Also see Willem Wolters, *Politics, Patronage and Class Conflict in Central Luzon* (The Hague: Institute of Social Studies, 1983), chap. 3.

A related third feature concerns the argument that issues are rarely if ever important in Philippine elections. Yet social, economic, and political issues are often real concerns for voters and for candidates. This is not only true in campaigns for national offices but for local elections as well.[39] Cesar Climaco was elected mayor of Zamboanga City in 1980 largely because he ran "on an explicitly anti-Marcos, anti–martial law platform,"[40] a position that also helped other candidates for local government in Mindanao to win that year. The 1970 election of delegates for the 1971 constitutional convention was electrified by issues regarding the structure of government, the Marcos administration, and U.S. military bases, among others.[41] Campaigns including vigorous debate on issues go back at least to the late 1930s. Candidates for municipal offices in central Luzon in 1937 and 1940 and for congressional seats in 1946 often disagreed about agricultural tenancy arrangements, workers' conditions, social justice, and Philippine-American relations.

Beyond these complexities, the fourth point to emphasize is a theme in electoral history since at least the 1930s: contending claims and views about elections. It is true that for many participants and observers alike elections are about "guns, goons, and gold"; personal and factional rivalries within the elite to capture the spoils of public office; and narrow instrumental and materialistic objectives on the part of both politicians and voters. But frequently at odds with these understandings and uses of elections are Filipinos who try to make elections be about legitimacy, fairness, and democratic processes. Elections themselves, therefore, become a struggle about what is the meaning and purpose of elections.

My point is hinted at by Mojares, who indicates that the political culture is more complicated and variegated than the themes he emphasizes in his analysis of Osmena's political life.[42] Intellectuals, workers, farmers, and others disaffected with common political practices have, he notes, sometimes tried to push the system in a more democratic direction. This merits more attention than we analysts usually give. And elec-

[39]Issues in the 1986 presidential election have been highlighted in Steven Rood, "Perspectives on the Electoral Behavior of Baguio City (Philippines): Voters in a Transition Era," *Journal of Southeast Asian Studies* 22 (March 1991), 86–108; and Kerkvliet and Mojares, eds., *From Marcos to Aquino*. Another example would be the 1969 presidential campaign in which, according to my observations at the time and my reading of the *Manila Chronicle*'s coverage, Marcos and Osmena did represent different stances on various issues.
[40]Mark Turner, "Politics During the Transition in Zamboanga City 1984–1988," in Kerkvliet and Mojares, eds., *From Marcos to Aquino*, 15.
[41]Wurfel, *Filipino Politics*, 109; Petronilo Bn. Daroy, "On the Eve of Dictatorship and Revolution," in Aurora Javate-de Dios et al., eds., *Dictatorship and Revolution: Roots of People's Power* (Metro Manila: Conspectus, 1988), 4, 7.
[42]*The Man Who Would Be President*, 155–6, 160.

tions have been one of the important arenas in which such pushing has occurred.

Quite possibly, this happens in all elections, even if only in small, unorganized ways or in places that do not get national publicity. Here are three examples, each for a different level of office. In the 1969 congressional elections, candidates who had lost the vote tally for the contested seat in Batanes province protested that the winner had employed armed men to terrorize and coerce voters and polling station clerks. The winner, of course, denied the allegations, and newspaper columnists believed him.[43] When an official investigation began, eighteen Batanes teachers who had served as voting clerks stepped forward, defying threats against their lives, and testified that indeed armed men had forced them to endorse falsified tally sheets and other fraudulent voting procedures. Their testimony and subsequent evidence that came to light led to the criminal charges against the winner and the proclamation of one of the losing candidates as the real winner.[44]

In the 1988 gubernatorial election in Ilocos Norte, the reportedly very popular candidate Rodolfo Fariñas was nevertheless thought to have little chance of defeating Manuela Ablan, even though she was widely disliked in part because her family had smuggled in huge quantities of garlic from Taiwan, causing havoc for the local garlic industry. The Ablan family was expected to use its hold over certain mayors, military officers, and policemen to take the governorship one way or another. But a volunteer movement "to keep watch over the polls in all precincts" made the counting and reporting process honest, allowing Fariñas to win.[45]

In 1982 the nation held elections for village heads, the first in ten years and the first local elections since Marcos had lifted martial law the year before. Many villagers in San Ricardo (Talavera, Nueva Ecija) had long waited for this election, by which they hoped the incumbent, Fidel Lorenzo, would be replaced with someone better even though they knew that Lorenzo had the upper hand because he was backed by the municipal branch of Marcos's Kilusang Bagong Lipunan (New Society Movement) political party.[46] Using some of this political muscle, Lorenzo maneuvered to prevent a potential opponent from filing candidacy pa-

[43]*Manila Chronicle*, November 25, 1969, p. 15; November 28, 1969, p. 18.
[44]*Manila Chronicle*, December 18, 1969, p. 14; December 22, 1969, p. 1; January 1, 1970, p. 12; January 21, 1970, p. 1; February 3, 1970, p. 1.
[45]Fernando N. Zialcita, "Perspectives on Legitimacy in Ilocos Norte," in Kerkvliet and Mojares, eds., *From Marcos to Aquino*, 281–2.
[46]Fidel Lorenzo is a fictitious name.

pers, thereby assuring his reelection. His deed disgusted not only those who had long complained about his poor leadership but also many people who had previously supported him. To show their contempt, two-thirds of the registered voters either boycotted the election or voted for the person whose candidacy had been foiled.[47]

These small examples reveal people trying to preserve or create some integrity and honesty in elections and to turn them into expressions of actual sentiments or evaluations of candidates and issues. In so trying, they engage and oppose those who have different, often sinister understandings of what elections are about. From time to time, these conflicting views of elections burst onto the national scene as major confrontations.

Such occasions earlier this century were a series of provincial elections in Pampanga in the late 1930s and congressional elections in central Luzon in April 1946. Earlier I mentioned these to illustrate the importance of issues in some elections. These elections were also highly charged debates over the kind of elections the Philippines should have. People and organizations supporting the Popular Front (PF) party in Pampanga in 1937 and 1940 and the Democratic Alliance (DA) party in central Luzon in 1946 seemed to be making three main arguments at odds with the dominant powers' use of elections.[48]

One was that there should be an alternative to the dominant political parties (the Nacionalista and, later, Liberal parties). The PF and the DA in central Luzon were strongly oriented toward the peasantry and agricultural workers, and many of these two parties' provincial and municipal leaders and candidates for office were of these classes. Leaders and other activists in the parties made concerted efforts to represent villagers' interests, organize among them, and campaign for their votes. These parties were trying to be different in organization and purpose from the Nacionalista Party and (in 1946) Liberal Party, which the PF

[47]Kerkvliet, *Everyday Politics*, 233–4.
[48]The Popular Front was primarily a provincial alliance of several peasant and worker-oriented organizations, the most influential being the local socialist party. The Democratic Alliance (DA) was a national umbrella for organizations and individuals who had opposed the Japanese occupation, wanted to remove from office those who had collaborated with the Japanese, and believed elections should be a process for people across the social spectrum to express views and create a more democratic country. The next three paragraphs draw on material I have analyzed more fully elsewhere: Kerkvliet, "Peasant Rebellion in the Philippines" (Ph.D. dissertation, University of Wisconsin, 1972), 139–45, 409–31, 493–5; and Kerkvliet, *The Huk Rebellion* (Berkeley: University of California Press, 1977), 125–6, 133–51.

and the DA in central Luzon saw as organizations of and for landlords, *compradores*, and other privileged and dominant interests.

Second, leaders and participants in these challenger parties frequently criticized those who used intimidation, money, and other such inducements to get votes, and they pressed for honest electoral processes. During mayoral and gubernatorial campaigns in Pampanga in December 1940, PF supporters demanded that landlords allow their tenants to decide for themselves whom to vote for and stop threatening tenants with eviction if they did not vote as the landlords instructed. They also criticized Nacionalista Party incumbents who were reportedly trying to buy votes and using their offices to collect fees in order to accumulate campaign funds. Perhaps for the first time in Philippine history, voters formed parades and marches that pleaded for clean elections.[49] In 1946, the demands for fair elections were more frequent and urgent as repression had spread and become more violent. Already one prominent issue in the campaign was the repression and violence against people who had been in the Hukbalahap (an anti-Japanese guerrilla organization) and members of the Pambansang Kaisahan ng mga Magbubukid, a vibrant peasant organization in the region. As the campaign evolved, landowners' armed men and the government's military police frequently charged into DA rallies and fired at audiences. They broke up DA meetings, ransacked DA offices, and killed several party leaders, including one provincial president. DA and non-DA people alike appealed to local and national government authorities to stop the rampage, often to little avail.[50] The repression scared many people away; several DA members and leaders left the campaign and quit the party. But many more persisted, determined to make the election something besides a battle of brute force.

The third statement PF and DA supporters were making is that those candidates who win fairly seemed be awarded the office to which they were elected. Although this may seem obvious, it was not widely appreciated in many powerful circles for whom the outcomes were serious threats to their positions and interests. In 1937, PF candidates were elected mayor in two Pampanga municipalities. In one of these, six of the eight municipal council seats were also won by PF candidates (in-

---

[49]See report in the *Tribune* (Manila), December 6, 1940, p. 11.
[50]After the election, Secretary Alfredo Montelibano, head of the department of interior, which was responsible for the military police, admitted to the DA president, Jesus Barrera, that he had no control over the police. *Manila Chronicle*, May 19, 1946, p. 1.

cluding three peasants—one a woman—two tailors, and a law student).
In December 1940, PF candidates were elected mayor in those two municipalities plus seven more, a total of nine of the province's twenty-one.
At least six of these mayors had long been active in provincial and regional peasant organizations. Also elected were several PF vice-mayors and council members, including all councillors in three of the largest municipalities. Moreover, the party's candidate for governor, Pedro Abad Santos, nearly beat the incumbent, Sotero Baluyut of the Nacionalista Party. Accustomed to controlling municipal governments, landlords and others now began to devise ways to deprive the PF victors of their government posts, a process of harassment that continued until the Japanese army invaded and took over the country. Governor Baluyut led the way, liberally using his authority to suspend the mayors and if necessary vice-mayors to get someone in the office to his liking. He also put municipal police under his jurisdiction, then had these police team up with landlords' armed gangs to harass peasants and create other trouble.

In the 1946 election, despite this violence against the DA, the party's candidates won all six of the congressional seats they sought in four central Luzon provinces. All of the congressmen-elect had been Hukbalahap leaders or otherwise active in the agrarian movement. It was a profound victory for the region's peasantry and for the those who saw elections as a way for the relatively powerless to develop a political voice and have their interests taken seriously. That victory and the DA's vibrancy so deeply threatened the political and economic elite, including perhaps the Americans who still held the country as a colony, that the House of Representatives' leadership and newly elected President Manuel Roxas devised a way to refuse to seat these six (along with one additional congressman-elect from Bulacan province who was sympathetic with them). The national government also escalated the repression in central Luzon against dissenters, peasant leaders, and Hukbalahap veterans. The cumulative effect was that thousands of people were pushed into the Huk rebellion, which began in August 1946.

Because of the repression of the DA and other factors, no third party emerged in subsequent years to continue the underclass- and cause-oriented direction of the PF and DA. But the next four elections—1947, 1949, 1951, and 1953—can be seen as a protracted struggle over the election process itself. The 1947 elections for congressional seats and local offices and especially the 1949 elections, featuring the presidential contest between incumbent Elpidio Quirino (Liberal Party) and rival Jose

Laurel (Nacionalista Party), were probably the most foul and sordid in the country's history. Incumbents brazenly used their offices, the police, and especially the Philippine constabulary to muscle and finagle their way to reelection. They routinely terrorized and bought off challengers' election inspectors, heavily padded registration lists in many precincts, established polling stations wherever it was most convenient for their side and their manipulation of the count, and pistol-whipped those who stood in their way. People on one side often intimidated, beat, or shot opponents, supporters of opponents, and even people simply listening to opponents' speeches. Fraud and violence were particularly pronounced in several provinces. In Negros Occidental, for instance, the Commission on Elections, investigating reports of rampant violence and other shenanigans, advised Quirino's government a few days before the November 1949 balloting that "clean, orderly, and honest elections cannot be held."[51] But the elections went ahead and were horribly undemocratic, despite the efforts of some, including Catholic church leaders, to safeguard the process. People in Nueva Ecija associate both elections with blood. Some recall seeing "bobbing in the river" the heads of people Quirino's men and the Philippine constabulary had killed because they had opposed Quirino or other Liberal Party candidates. Individuals who attempted to assure accurate tallying in municipal halls were often beaten up. Two analysts who later examined those elections across the country concluded, "The experiences . . . dating back [to] 1947 have been on the sad side. Political leaders have not hesitated to commit frauds, coercion or terrorism. As a result, even now, there is widespread belief that the presidential election in 1949 did not reflect the choice of qualified voters." Had it not been for "violence, fraud and coercion, or terrorism," they continued, "Jose P. Laurel would have been an easy victor."[52]

By 1951, people braced themselves for even worse elections despite the new laws and procedures designed to eliminate some of the most obvious opportunities for manipulating the counting and reporting process. The military also had been reorganized, and the new secretary of defense, Ramon Magsaysay (appointed in 1950), had vowed that sol-

[51] Cited in Coquia, *Philippine Presidential Election of 1953*, 113. For additional depictions of the 1947 and 1949 elections, see ibid., 35–7, 111–4; Jose V. Abueva, *Ramon Magsaysay: A Political Biography* (Manila: Solidaridad, 1971), 139–41; Frances L. Starner, *Magsaysay and the Philippine Peasantry* (Berkeley: University of California Press, 1961), 60, 65–6, 252; and Kerkvliet, *Huk Rebellion*, 205, 211. I am also relying on reports in the *Manila Chronicle*, September-November 1947 and 1949.
[52] Enrique Fernando and Emma Quizumbing Fernando, "The Revised Election Code," *Philippine Law Journal* 28 (1953): 813. Cited in Coquia, *Philippine Presidential Election of 1953*, 114.

diers would protect voters rather than politicians. Nevertheless, many people remained skeptical. Some organizations decided to boycott the elections and urged more to do likewise.

Other people, however, went the opposite direction, throwing themselves into a struggle to prevent a repeat of 1947 and 1949. They reported to officials and the press cases of intimidation and violence, insisted on protecting polling stations against manipulation, monitored the counting of votes, publicized names of candidates and others who violated the rules, guarded ballot boxes, and often stood their ground against armed men and authorities who tried to scare them off. These widespread activities, coupled with improved media coverage and electoral reforms, contributed to making the 1951 and 1953 elections far cleaner than before.

Although efforts like these had been made before, in 1951 and 1953 they were far more numerous, were much better organized, practically spanned the nation, and were notably successful. The best-known among the many organizations pressing for honest elections was the NAMFREL, established in mid-1951. Even many remote villages had NAMFREL chapters to help make the voting, tallying, and reporting that year surprisingly fair and peaceful. These effects were repeated in 1953, when even more people got involved in NAMFREL to democratize the election process. In both years, numerous other organizations also became involved. Among them were the League of Women Voters of the Philippines, which had begun in 1934 (first to get women the right to vote and then to improve the election process) and whose members had been among those who had been harassed in earlier elections for objecting to nefarious practices. Among additional organizations were the Civil Liberties Union of the Philippines, College Editors Guild, Federation of Free Workers, National Federation of Tenants and Farmers, Philippine Association of University Professors, Philippine Lawyers Association, Student Council Association of the Philippines, and numerous Catholic and Protestant churches.

As pointed out earlier, some analysts have said that NAMFREL was an American creation and thus, they suggest, it was not an expression of genuine Filipino concerns. But there are several problems with this view. First, whether NAMFREL was merely putty in the hands of the CIA cannot be determined with available evidence. Even assuming NAMFREL was initiated by the CIA, it may not have continued to be. Filipinos may have taken it over. Second, many other organizations, not claimed by the CIA, were involved in the struggle. So even without NAMFREL there might well have been a movement to make elections more than a contest of physical and monetary clout. A third problem is the implication that the CIA need only snap its fingers, throw money around, get a clandestine group of Americans to twist their minds around the problem of how "we make a president"[53] who is liked and legitimate, and, bingo, success. Yet the same was tried elsewhere, notably Vietnam, even by several of the same men, and failed miserably. Time and place count for a lot. Something significant was going on in the Philippines. And to understand that, one must at minimum understand the seething discontent across the country with the way previous elections had been conducted and with Quirino and his government. Joseph Smith and Raymond Bonner, two authors who most prominently depict NAMFREL as American, completely ignore this.[54] Hence, such accounts exaggerate the importance of a few Americans and U.S. funding and miss the political context, as well as the role of Filipinos pressing to infuse democratic content into electoral politics. NAMFREL may have served some Americans' interests, but it also articulated the concerns of tens of thousands of Filipinos.

Both 1951 and 1953 show the determination across a wide spectrum of the population to make elections a major issue. Would elections be, as in the 1940s, largely a democratic facade behind which people are coerced, intimidated, and abused, and ballots are treated cavalierly? Or would there be substance to democratic appearances? Put simply, would the country live up to the rhetoric, which nearly every leader espoused but so few practiced, of free, open, honest elections? NAMFREL, the League of Women Voters, and many other organizations and individuals were pressing for a "yes" answer to these last two questions.

In 1986, a similar crisis over elections reached its peak, loosely referred to as the people-power revolution, which forced Ferdinand Marcos's authoritarian regime to buckle. I would not claim that this event—televised worldwide—was only about the meaning and purpose of

[53]This is the title of Smith's chapter on the period in *Portrait of a Cold Warrior.*
[54]Ibid. and Bonner, *Waltzing with a Dictator.* Lansdale (*In the Midst of Wars,* 28, 89) at least mentions that the fraudulent 1949 election had riled many Filipinos, though he says nothing about the anger provoked by the dismissal of DA congressmen-elect in 1946 or the dismal 1947 elections. Constantino and Constantino (*The Philippines,* chaps. 7–9) discuss the 1946 and 1949 election fiascos but do not connect them to the 1951 and 1953 movement for clean elections. Shalom (*United States and the Philippines*) only mentions the dismissal of the DA congressmen-elect and certain negative aspects of elections in the 1940s.

elections. The dynamics of that year and the events leading up to it were complex and their significance multifaceted. A credible argument could be made that 1986 represented a confrontation between competing clusters of elites—the Marcos clique opposed by elite leaders coalesced by their determination to stop the Marcos dynasty and joined in the final hours by prominent Marcos supporters who defected.[55] And as indicated earlier, certainly for many Filipinos, the election was about economic and political issues. Clientalism, factionalism, personal relations, regionalism, and other factors also influenced many people's votes and understanding of what the election was about.

These lines of analysis, however revealing, leave out a vital dynamic. For millions of Filipinos the 1985–6 campaign was also a struggle to make elections an expression of people's views and desires for their country. They were determined to bring the voting process in line with the rhetoric that elections should be free of coercion, intimidation, cheating, and fraud. They sought to make this election a method by which the majority could decide what person and what kind of government was best for the country. The differences between Marcos and Aquino and what they represented were striking, certainly more so than in most national elections in the Philippines (or elsewhere, come to think of it). Closely related, there were strong feelings across a wide spectrum of the country that the government had to change, lest already terrible conditions become much worse and, especially, lest civil war, already pronounced in numerous areas, spread and tens of thousands more conclude that violence was the only remaining option for changing the government. Or, an equally unpleasant alternative, the military could forcefully topple the Marcos government and establish a military regime. For millions of anxious Filipinos, the 1986 election was the best chance, perhaps the last chance, to change peacefully (for the better, they hoped) who rules and how.[56]

[55]Symbolic of this elite alliance in opposition to the Marcos regime were the Facilitator Group, Convenor Group, and Potential Standard Bearers—together a kind of "Who's Who" of the business and political elite *not* holding national government office—that emerged in 1984 and merged later that year and out of which in 1985 came the candidacies of Corazon Aquino and Salvador Laurel (Ma. Serena I. Diokno, "Unity and Struggle," in Javate-de Dios, et al., eds., *Dictatorship and Revolution*, 152–5).
[56]A sense of this mood is conveyed in an interview with Cecilia Munoz Palma, a former Supreme Court justice who was active in political organizations opposing Marcos (Paulynn P. Sicam, "Interview: Cecilia Munoz Palma," *National Midweek* ([December 11, 1985, p. 9]). Also see Ruben Canoy, *The Counterfeit Revolution: Martial Law in the Philippines* (Manila: Philippine Editions, 1980), 248–50. Many people I met in 1985 in Manila and rural areas were terribly worried about the spreading civil war and hoped

Between 1972, when Marcos declared martial law, and 1985, there had been five national referendums, two elections for local officials, two elections for *Batasang Pambansa* (National Assembly) representatives, and a presidential election (in 1981). Typically, government officials manipulated them to suit the regime, and winners were only or mainly from the president's political party even if considerable cheating were required to assure that they won. Intimidation and violence were common, and often voters had no choice of candidates.[57] The Marcos regime had mocked the concept of election more than any government since Quirino's in 1949.[58]

This practice contributed, I think, to growing indignation against Marcos and his government. Initially, during martial law, there was considerable support, or at least benefit of the doubt, for Marcos and his new form of government. Filipinos were promised reduced poverty, improved living standards for all, national economic development, the elimination of corruption, social and political peace, and a democratic revolution from the top. Large sectors of society got none of these promised benefits; indeed, they got the opposite.[59] Adding insult to injury, Marcos, his wife, children, and cohorts mocked people's intelligence, believing they could persist indefinitely to say one thing while doing the reverse, including holding democratic elections that clearly were not.

A catalyst for bringing into public view the growing disdain and moral revulsion against the Marcos regime was Ninoy Aquino's assassination. Across the nation, Filipinos mourned Aquino, whom many now regarded as another martyr for freedom from oppression.[60] In death, Aquino had overpowered Marcos. The crowds—hundreds of thousands

that a peaceful election would reverse that trend. The importance of the election and the seriousness with which many ordinary citizens regarded it are conveyed in a marvelous film directed by Gary Kildea (*Valencia Diary*, 1992) about villagers in Bukidnon province.

[57]Carbonell-Catilo, et al., *Manipulated Elections*, chap. 3; Raul P. de Guzman, "Towards Redemocratization of the Political System," in Raul P. de Guzman and Mila Reforma, eds., *Government and Politics in the Philippines* (Singapore: Oxford University Press, 1988), 16; Roberto D. Tiglao, "The Consolidation of the Dictatorship," in Javate-de Dios, et al., eds., *Dictatorship and Revolution*, 28–9.

[58]For an analysis of why the martial-law regime wanted the semblance of elections, see Mark Turner, "Authoritarian Rule and the Dilemma of Legitimacy: The Case of President Marcos of the Philippines," *Pacific Review* 4 (1990): 349–62.

[59]This has been fairly well documented across a variety of issues. For a recent study of the economy, see James Boyce, *The Philippines: The Political Economy of Growth and Impoverishment in the Marcos Era* (Honolulu: University of Hawaii Press, 1993).

[60]Reynaldo E. Ileto, "The Past in the Present Crisis," in R. J. May and Francisco Nemenzo, eds., *The Philippines After Marcos* (Sydney: Croom Helm, 1985), 7–16.

of people viewing his body, carrying him to his grave with placards
bearing his name and likeness together with those of other murdered
opponents of the regime—could not be contained by the police, by Marcos, by anyone but themselves. From this explosion came numerous organizations and tumultuous demonstrations in 1984–5 against the
regime and, significantly, *for* elections.

A key question for many Filipinos was: Would the 1986 election be
another Marcos-style one or would it be more democratic? And would
people tolerate having another Marcos-style election, or would they in-
sist on something more credible? Many strongly argued that it would
certainly be another Marcos-controlled and -manipulated election, which
his organization was well versed in pulling off. To participate would
mean becoming accomplices in the fraud and also, some especially on
the political left argued, boost the Marcos regime's standing in the Philippines. Boycott was the only decent choice.[61] Similar arguments had
been made against voting in previous elections during the Marcos years,
which tens of thousands, maybe millions, of Filipinos did boycott.[62]

But there had also been in previous elections significant efforts to challenge the Marcos machine's control over the process. One was the Batasang Pambansa election in April 1978, especially in Metro Manila. A
slate of 21 candidates, including Ninoy Aquino, of the newly formed
Laskas ng Bayan (LABAN) party waged as vigorous a campaign as martial law obstacles allowed (for example, Aquino campaigned from his
prison cell). I was in Manila at the time and was amazed that, despite
widespread cynicism and the fact that many people voted for the Marcos
slate, millions of voters had actually supported LABAN. They were so
numerous that the government, in order to make sure that none of the
LABAN candidates won, had to resort to clumsy illegal methods, like
literally threatening to shoot Commission on Elections (COMELEC) poll
watchers objecting to Marcos partisans who threw out ballots and replaced them with others to their liking. When thousands marched in

[61]See statements from the National Democratic Front and the *Bagong Alyansang Maz-
kabayan* in Javate-de Dios, et al., eds., *Dictatorship and Revolution*, 681–75, and the
Nationalist Alliance for Justice, Freedom, and Democracy (Philippine Education Project,
n.d.).
[62]Reportedly about 50 percent of registered voters opted not to vote in the 1981 presidential election in which Marcos was hard pressed to find someone who would run
against him (Carbonell-Catilo, et al., *Manipulated Elections*, 77). Arguments by individuals and groups favoring boycott during various referendums and elections during the
Marcos era appear in *Pahayag* (Honolulu), January 1973, August 1973, February 1975,
and April 1975; *Development Forum* (Manila), March 1978, 5ff. Also see Diokno, "Unity and Struggle," in Javate-de Dios, et al., eds., *Dictatorship and Revolution*,
151–2.

protest, police dispersed the demonstrators with tear gas and bullets, arrested opposition leaders, and drove others underground and into exile.

Another challenge was the attempt to turn the 1984 Batasang Pambansa election into a fair one. Locally many efforts to guard against ballot stealing and stuffing sprang up; nationally the NAMFREL alliance was revived.[63] Several candidates and their supporters tried to offer a clear alternative to Marcos's party slate. An example was Evelio Javier's effort in Antique province. Javier had been elected governor of the province just before martial law, campaigning as much for the governorship as for an election without "guns, goons, and gold." He won, despite his rival resorting to those very tactics. His 1984 campaign was similar: He opposed both the Marcos government and intimidation, violence, vote buying, cheating, and so forth. He relied heavily on volunteers to contribute time, food, placards, and money. Reportedly, the "enthusiastic participation of the people from all sectors—farmers, businessmen, vendors, housewives, grandparents, youth and children . . . was unprecedented."[64] Violence—including the slaying of several Javier campaigners—fraud, and other illegal tactics by opponents prevented Javier from winning the count. Two years later, his petition to have the election results annulled was endorsed by the Supreme Court, vindicating him and his campaign. By then, however, Javier himself had been murdered.

On February 11, 1986, Javier was shot 24 times in Antique's capital city, reportedly by a masked Philippine Constabulary (PC) officer and five other men. They killed him apparently because he was trying to prevent fraudulent results from being reported.[65] He had, as commentators said, literally given his life at a time when millions of Filipinos were staking their lives, trying to replace a Marcos-style election with a more democratic one and by that means eject Marcos himself. The most dramatic confrontation was the multitude of people putting their bodies in front of army tanks along the EDSA highway in Metro Manila. But there were hundreds of less publicized encounters between citizens trying to protect registration lists, ballot boxes, and tally sheets from others seeking to alter and destroy them.[66] Besides NAMFREL's half a million

[63]This NAMFREL is the National Citizens Movement for Free Elections: same acronym but a slightly different name from the 1950s NAMFREL, though the concept is the same.
[64]Luzvininda G. Tancangco, "Towards New Politics in the Philippines: Evelio Javier's Impossible Dream" (typescript, n. d.), p. 7.
[65]See reports in the *Philippine Daily Inquirer*, beginning February 12, 1986.
[66]Kaa Byington, *Bantay ng Bayan: Stories from the NAMFREL Crusade 1984–1986* (Manila: Bookmark, 1988). Despite their efforts, most observers and analysts agree, the

160   *Benedict J. Tria Kerkvliet*

volunteers across the country, many other organizations' members were active. And numerous people unaffiliated with these efforts got involved. Even in the COMELEC itself, employees objected to the cheating they saw; the most conspicuous incident was thirty computer operators in COMELEC's headquarters deciding to walk out in protest against counterfeit results.[67]

Two Filipinos, who had for years been active in anti–martial law and anti-Marcos struggles and, like many in their situation, were highly skeptical of elections and had considered boycotting the 1986 one, nevertheless opted instead for what was referred to as "critical participation." Seeing how people threw themselves into trying to make the election authentic was a real eye-opener. They wrote:

The whole experience . . . has been a humbling one for organizers like us. In the scenario building efforts, the external factors were all predicted but the people's response was not foreseen. I think it is because we [organizers] get lost in our agenda and fail to listen to our own people and heed the signs, the mode of political participation they are most comfortable in—the non-violent way.

The [political] revolution has clearly advanced the struggle of the Filipinos for a more just and democratic society; it has given people a sharp and refreshing sense of the oft quoted cliché—sovereignty belongs to the people—for in the end, it boils down to one thing—we refused to be duped once more, to be dictated upon and to have the truth mangled.[68]

Many observers have noticed that the ballooning hopes inflated by the heady people-power atmosphere of 1986 have since been punctured by political machines, personalistic factionalism, patron-client ties, old elite-family prominence, vote buying, ballot tampering, and violence in the 1988, 1990, and 1992 elections. But efforts to give more democratic substance to elections—and the political system generally—do persist. The 1992 presidential election, for example, offers some evidence. Miriam Defensor Santiago, many commentators said, could not win or even

cheating by the Marcos side was significant (particularly by altering results at the precinct, municipality, provincial, or city levels)—a perception that helped to provoke millions to defy soldiers and tanks. See, for instance, Romeo L. Manlapaz, *The Mathematics of Deception: A Study of the 1986 Presidential Election Tallies* (Quezon City: Third World Studies Center, University of the Philippines, 1986).
[67]For an account of the Commission on Elections (COMELEC) computer operators' protest, see Linda Kapunan, "Why the COMELEC tabulators walked out," *Philippine Daily Inquirer*, February 15 and 17, 1986. Unlike 1951 and 1953, the NAMFREL of 1984 and 1986 was not a partner with COMELEC but a rival or watchdog over COMELEC. NAMFREL even had its own nationwide computer system linked to its tabulation headquarters in Metro Manila. Funding came from contributions and, according to Bonner (*Waltzing with a Dictator*, 408–9), the United States Agency for International Development.
[68]Author's correspondence from Dinky and Hec Soliman, March 11, 1986.

come close because she had no political machine, relatively little money, and no national standing. Yet nearly 20 percent of the electorate voted for her, putting her second in the contest among seven candidates. Her major campaign promise was that, if elected, she would work vigorously against corruption—a pledge that resonated well with her record as a corruption-fighting public servant. Edging her out for first place was Fidel Ramos, who also was not predicted to win because his campaign organization and patronage machinery were relatively weak. Like Defensor Santiago, Ramos was widely regarded as an honest person.[69] So, the two top vote-getters—representing over 40 percent of the electorate—though underdogs in the eyes of many observers, apparently had considerable appeal in part, at least, because they were *not* typical Filipino politicians.

SPECULATIONS

If the democratic sense of proper elections, elaborated in the previous discussion, is strong and persistent, why is it often compromised and swamped by other motivations and purposes? If many Filipinos really want elections to convey people's preferences about issues, character and quality of candidates, and the like, why then are other purposes and meanings also at work? I am not sure of the reasons. And no doubt the explanations are complex and require considerably more thought and investigation than I am able to present now. I merely suggest a number of possibilities.

First, though, I must stress that the issues and the candidates' abilities often do rise above other considerations and features during Philippine elections. Previous sections have highlighted occasions when democratic values played prominent roles in outcomes. And if one scans the recent landscape of nationally elected officials, one sees Senators Jose Diokno, Jovito Salonga, and Lorenzo Tañada, among others, whose campaigns, while not devoid of distasteful practices, were generally respectable and upright. These politicians attracted genuine support and enthusiasm for their stances on issues, their character, and their reputations as decent and fair public servants. There are hundreds of others like them in various levels of elected office.

Now for the question at hand. One answer might be that pragmatic

---

[69]For examples of preelection assessments of the candidates' chances, see *Far Eastern Economic Review*, March 19, 1992, pp. 22–9, and *Asiaweek*, April 3, 1992, pp. 9–13.

considerations, even necessities, can enter voters' deliberations on how to vote and whom to support or oppose. And those reasons can cause people to set aside or give lower priority to their assessments of candidates' stances on issues, reputations, and so on. This probably happens in many countries but may be particularly frequent in those like the Philippines in which a large proportion of the people are economically poor, even desperate.

Another cluster of explanations concerns the Philippine state, which is rather weak in many respects, including its administrative infrastructure for implementing policies and enforcing laws. This has two implications for elections. First, the election process itself is often violated and abused, and the culprits are rarely prosecuted. The Philippines has laws that should assure a reasonably fair, honest voting and counting procedure. Yet the mechanisms for enforcing those laws, investigating alleged violations, and arresting and convicting guilty people are frequently starved of resources and are badly run. Such a system may be especially overburdened by the frequency and large number of elections for so many public offices extending from village to national levels. In this context, fraud grows. Luzvininda Tancangco makes an interesting argument that standards of leadership among various classes of Filipinos emphasize outstanding personal traits, high moral qualities, and service to the community.[70] Often such people do emerge as winners in village elections. But because of "corruption of the process" at higher levels, there has often been a "gap between what they [the voters] believed in and the qualities of elected leaders." And that corruption, she says, is linked to political machines and "electoral fraud."[71] Were the state more capable of running fair elections, perhaps the gap Tancangco identifies would be narrower and political machines less pernicious.

The second implication for elections of a weak state apparatus is that any tacit agreement regarding issues made between voters and the winning candidate is extremely difficult to keep even by a public servant who has the best intentions. The agreement might be that the elected person will champion in office the programs and issues on which he or she campaigned and won. If the politician is able to get the appropriate laws or policies enacted, implementation may never occur. The programs might be smothered by lack of resources and inertia or be scuttled and

---

[70]Luzvininda G. Tancangco, *The Anatomy of Electoral Fraud: Concrete Bases for Electoral Reforms* (Manila: MJAGM, 1992).
[71]Ibid., 11, 12.

undermined by opponents who have clout within strategic parts of the bureaucracy. As Ben Anderson suggests in his chapter in this book, the state apparatus has little autonomy from powerful elite individuals and families who use their influence and control over policy-making institutions, administrative agencies, and the electoral process itself to further their relatively narrow self-interests.

One antidote to this situation is for civic organizations and investigative journalists to push to give more democratic substance to elections and other parts of the political system. Encouraging in this regard in the 1990s are the numerous nongovernmental organizations with positions on major issues and vocal constituents that have gravitated toward electoral politics. Organizations like the new Institute for Popular Democracy are trying to bring together so-called left and middle forces to make political institutions, including elections, more open to nonelite voices and interests. A promising fresh avenue is the local development councils stipulated by the 1991 Local Government Code, one-fourth of whose membership must be representatives from nongovernmental organizations. Within the political left, which has in recent decades generally disparaged elections, strong arguments are being made for plunging into efforts to reform the electoral process, campaign for selected candidates, and form new political parties—activities that would be familiar to activists in the Popular Front, Socialist Party, and Democratic Alliance of the 1930s and 1940s.[72]

What do elections do? Elections in the Philippines have, as I have argued, multiple meanings, often simultaneously. They bestow legitimacy on those holding public office and, cumulatively, on the political system itself. They are also a process by which elites rotate among themselves access to public coffers, and a time for calling in political debts and exercising political muscle, including financial and physical force. They are avenues for foreigners to look after their interests. Elections may drape the cloak of democracy over a polity that may be no more democratic than the Ayatollah is Roman Catholic. But importantly, elections also invite people to pull away that camouflage. They provide an opportunity to debate and contemplate issues, including the meaning and purpose of elections themselves. And they are struggles to give substance to Philippine democracy.

[72] A taste of this current discussion can be savored in two issues of *Kasarinlan* 1992 (third and fourth quarters).

7

Elections in Burma/Myanmar:
For whom and why?

R. H. TAYLOR

The idea of formal elections for the holding of government office has
been a regular feature of Burmese politics for three-quarters of a century.
Since 1922, elections have been presented by those in power as the most
appropriate means of choosing at least some of the leading figures in the
central government, as well as in lower levels of administration. More
recently, elections have been advanced by the opponents of the ruling
military as the only way to establish a legitimate government. The am-
biguity associated with the purpose of elections—are elections to serve
the interests of those in power or those out of power?—has been as
much a source of political conflict as the elections themselves.

The limited study of Burmese politics has provided little detailed in-
sight into electoral behavior. Except for the elections of the 1950s and
that of 1960, no Burmese election has taken place under the scrutiny of
social scientists, although the press in the 1930s, as well as in the 1950s,
was in a better position to comment independently on the process than
has been the case since the 1960 national election. The most recent election, that of May 1990, has probably evoked the greatest amount of
foreign commentary, not only because of the dramatic circumstances
under which it was held but also because of the inability of the victors
to gain significant influence, let alone power, in the aftermath. Several
other elections had particular importance for one reason or another, at
least at the time of their occurrence.

COLONIAL ELECTIONS

The first major election, held in 1922,[1] was a consequence of the introduction of a limited franchise in what was called Burma proper[2] for a legislative council. That electoral politics on a broad scale was introduced into Burma by the British so early in the century was largely a historical consequence of the kingdom's being made a province of British India in 1886. Tutelary democracy, leading to dominion status within the empire, became the basis of Britain's plans for the political future of India at both the provincial and national levels early in the century. Shared power between elected Indian politicians and nonelected administrators, or dyarchy, became the first step in tutelage, following the involvement of Indian troops in World War I, the drive for expanded suffrage in Britain, and the evolution of British Indian policy designed to attach the Indian political elite to Britain, thereby avoiding the development of a broad-based and antiimperialist nationalist movement. In the evolutionary vision of British politicians, Indian politicians would gradually "learn to govern" through the "state frame" of administration that the empire had put in place the previous century. Burma was a recipient of this policy by default. Whereas India had begun to develop political parties and had an established political class before these changes were introduced, parties and politicians in Burma developed largely as a result of the stimulus of the promise of elections.

The partially elected 1922 Legislative Council in Burma was similar to that established in the other provinces of British India at about the same time following the extension of the electoral principle to India under the dyarchy or Minto-Morley reforms. Though Burmese nationalists had protested the initial exclusion of their country from these political reforms, when the elections took place a vigorous boycott was organized and less than 7 percent of the electorate turned out on polling day. Election boycotts became a major tactic of popular nationalist politicians in the 1920s, and this was reflected in the low turnout in subsequent years—just over 16 percent in 1925 and still a mere 18 percent in 1928.[3]

[1]There had been elections for urban councils in the nineteenth century, but the franchise was largely restricted to European residents.
[2]That is, the directly administered regions where the overwhelming majority of the population lived. Excluded from these early elections were the so-called frontier areas and the Shan and Kayah States.
[3]At about the same time, the government introduced elections to circle boards at district

Was the low turnout largely the consequence of the boycott campaigns? Cady has suggested that few wanted to vote,[4] perhaps because
of the novelty, the remoteness of the eventual outcome, and a lack of
awareness of the electoral process. The majority of Burmese, then as
now, lived in villages without politically independent institutionalized
links to the world of the Rangoon-based politicians other than by word
of mouth and the very occasional newspaper or pamphlet. The concept
of a government responsible to the people through the mechanism of
the periodic popular choice of remote rulers and lawmakers was un-
known to most of the population prior to the 1920s. The most successful
nationalist organizers and pamphleteers in the villages in the 1920s pred-
icated their appeals on notions of the nature of good indigenous
monarchical government, not on a demand for self-government and independence in the modern democratic mode.[5]

From the point of view of the British colonial authorities, elections
were highly desirable because they created an interest for people in the
colonial political order. But who did participate in the elections, and
why? One group who urged participation was the urban politicians from
the more prosperous Burmese middle class who, like their counterparts
in India, were the product of British economic and administrative policies and who saw in elections a safe route, first to influence and security
and eventually to power.[6] They consequently fell out with those boycotting politicians in the nationalist movement, who remained in closer
contact with the village, and radical groups, which were in opposition
to both the colonial authorities and their version of modernity. Another
group that participated actively in the elections of the 1920s was the
Karen Christians.[7] To them, like the new urban, middle-class Burmese
men, elections were part of a process of inclusion in the structures of
the colonial state that had created group and individual advantages not
available under the previous monarchical order.

The elections of 1925 and 1928 were perceived as more satisfactory,

and township levels. They were equally, if not more, unpopular with the population. Of
the 2,700 boards to be filled, in nearly 600 no candidate stood and in another 800 only
one candidate ran. John F. Cady, A History of Modern Burma (Ithaca: Cornell University
Press, 1958), 263–5.
[4]Cady, History of Modern Burma, 244.
[5]Patricia Herbert, The Hsaya San Rebellion (1930–1932) Reappraised (Melbourne: Monash University Centre of Southeast Asian Studies Working Paper No. 27, 1982).
[6]See Robert H. Taylor, The State in Burma (London: C. Hurst, 1988), 162–88.
[7]The group even won two general (that is, non-Karen–designated) constituencies. Cady,
History of Modern Burma, 245.

compared with that of 1922, by the colonial authorities because not only were a few more people willing to vote, but also more politicians were willing to participate in the political process. The party game came to take on a life of its own and to dominate increasingly the feuds and disputes of the urban political classes. It was the party game, the formation of parties and the alliances and feuds of the party leaders, not the elections themselves, that dominated the colonial press. Thus, when the Hsaya San peasants' rebellion began in 1930, the nationalist political elite and the Rangoon and Mandalay press not only had no role in the revolt, they were largely unaware of the political ferment that lay behind it. This was not, however, to mean that they ignored the lessons of the upheaval of that year. Indeed, in future years politicians began to pay more attention to rural interests, while also being aware of urban demands. Politicians also became more aware of the utility of the organizational support of Burmese university students who, because of the rural origins of many and their prestige in their home districts, could generate support for candidates at election time.

TRANSITIONAL ELECTIONS

If there was an issue at stake in the elections of the 1920s, it was the electoral process itself—whether the people should be drawn into the political web created by the colonial masters. The election of 1932, however, appeared to be different because it posed a substantive policy question of the kind expected in democratic politics—whether Burma should remain a province of India after the introduction of the forthcoming Government of India Act (1935). The 1935 act held out the promise of a greater degree of self-government under the British for India and Burma and their politicians than did the existing dyarchical order. But the intention of the British to separate Burma from India led to speculation that Burma would be excluded from these constitutional advances, just as Burma had been initially omitted from the Minto-Morley reforms. Though there was apparently never any serious intention by the British to deny Burma the same measure of reforms offered India, this fear, underlined by British intentions a decade earlier, was promoted by politicians. The politicians, in turn, came under the sway of Indian business interests that relied on their intimate ties with Burma to maintain the ease of labor and capital flows. And although it was generally believed that the majority of Burmese favored Burma's becoming a separate political entity in order to limit Indian immigration and capital domination, those favoring Burma's remaining part of India won the election, 529,127 to 293,042.[8] The heat of the issue and the money that poured into the campaigning led to a voter turnout of 40 percent. But the outcome of the election had little influence on the shaping of British policy. Burma was separated from India and no Burmese politician who had fought against that decision subsequently protested this denial of the people's will. Rather, having achieved office and influence through the dyarchical electoral system, they prepared themselves to participate in the more substantial party game offered by the reformed constitutional order.

That opportunity came in the last election held before the preindependence vote of 1947, the 1936 election, which resulted in a participation rate of 52 percent. In this election a number of political leaders who had emerged in the party games of the 1920s continued on, while being joined by newer figures. The appeal of the boycott had largely waned by now, and even the youngest and most radical of the nationalist groups, the Dobama Asiayone (We Burmans Association) formed the Komin Kochin (Own King, Own Kind) party with the ostensible purpose of getting elected in order to wreck the constitutional order from within.

It is striking that in a mere fifteen years, in colonial circumstances, which we would now see as essentially illegitimate on a number of grounds, the electoral process became accepted as not only important but necessary. The 1936 election was for a House of Representatives that, like the old Legislative Council, heavily overrepresented urban areas. The election was not, however, cast in terms of a national election because the residents of the frontier areas did not vote and were not represented in the new legislature. The principle of communal and special interest representation was not only maintained but extended. There were seventy-seven general rural constituencies, fourteen general urban constituencies, twelve Karen rural constituencies, eight Indian urban constituencies, and one constituency each for Anglo-Burmans, Europeans, Rangoon Indian Labour, Rangoon Non-Indian Labour, Oil-Fields Indian Labour, Oil-Fields Non-Indian Labour, the Burmese Chamber of Commerce, the Burma Indian Chamber of Commerce, the Nattukottai Chettyars Association, the Burma Chamber of Commerce, the Rangoon Trades Association, the Chinese Chamber of Commerce, and Rangoon University.[9]

[8]Telegram, Governor of Burma to Secretary of State for India, November 29, 1932. India Office Library and Records, Burma Office File P&J (B) 1.
[9]Though the participation rate in this election was about 52 percent, this varied with the

The second elections under the 1937 Government of Burma Act were to have been held by November 1941 but were postponed in circumstances similar to those that surround the role of elections in many states where electoral politics have not yet become routine. Early in 1941, U Saw,[10] the premier, indicated to Sir Reginald Dorman-Smith, the governor, that the Cabinet of Ministers, along with most members of the House of Representatives, wished the election to be postponed for at least a year. Though Saw said he was confident that his own party would win any election, his coalition colleagues had convinced him "that it would be unwise to hold a general election owing to [the] danger that Government would be forced to take repressive actions against extremist politicians and that this would not only produce conditions unfavourable to moderates but might also lead to serious disorder."[11] The alleged danger that so-called extremists, in opposition to the responsible—that is, cooperative—ministers (in this case, respectively, those out of power and those in power and then working with the British colonial governor), would dominate the election presages later arguments about the alleged dangers of communists and other leftists winning power through elections, not only in Burma, but elsewhere as well.

The governor, in conjunction with the Secretary of State for Burma, rejected this initial proposal from the Burmese cabinet, but six months later, after legislation had been passed in the British Parliament allowing for the postponement of elections in India and Burma for the duration of World War II and twelve months thereafter, the elected Burmese Ministers once more proposed postponing the 1941 elections. Rehearsing the arguments of January, Premier Saw told the governor he felt certain that the opposition in any election campaign would "undoubtedly adopt an anti-British and an anti-war attitude," making them "liable to arrest under [the] Defence of Burma Rules." If that were the opposition's platform, Saw suggested that his party would be forced to adopt the same stance; in fact, his supporters might feel the need to "outbid" the op-

type of constituency. General Burmese urban constituencies had a participation rate of 57 percent, while rural Karen constituencies had a participation rate of only 46 percent, and Indian urban constituencies had a rate of 60 percent. Data on the election is available in Gangha Singh, *Burma Parliamentary Companion* (Rangoon: British Burma Press [Rangoon Gazette Limited], 1940), 341–61.

[10]Saw was the most electorally popular politician in prewar Burma. He was hanged after independence for having been involved in the conspiracy to assassinate General Aung San and other members of the preindependence cabinet in July 1947. See R. H. Taylor, "Politics in Late Colonial Burma: The Case of U Saw," *Modern Asian Studies* 10, no. 2 (April 1976): 161–94.

[11]Telegram, Governor of Burma to Secretary of State for Burma, January 17, 1941. Burma File 10/41.

position at this game. Although Saw would not object to arresting his political opponents, as he in fact did in the following months, he knew that the opposition would then use the additional attack of "political repression" in the campaign. To this argument there would be no defense.[12]

Opposition leaders from Mandalay had already protested to the governor that Saw was using his legal powers to suppress the opposition. Although the governor had assured them that he would see that democratic rights were protected, Saw also wanted to make clear that there was "a strong Government in Office which will not (hesitate) to use its powers in order to maintain law and order."[13] Although Saw continued to tell the governor that he and his party were confident they could win an election, Saw also lost no opportunity to warn of the dangers of an election campaign. Directly and indirectly through the grapevine of the government, the premier put to the governor various proposals to deflect arguments about political repression by his government if an election were held. One called for the governor to make clear that the arrests during the campaign were made not on ministry orders but at the behest of the Defense Department under the governor's control. Another proposition was that the premier resign for the election campaign period while the governor ruled directly. Whatever the effects of a vigorously nationalist campaign coupled with harsh government suppression, Saw pointed out to the governor that the Japanese would use the resulting conditions in their anti-British propaganda.

Despite these arguments, and while conceding the force of the premier's arguments, the governor still wished to hold elections in November 1941. Not wanting to place his favored candidate in the difficult position of enforcing the law during a campaign, he sought an alternative to using the Defense Department under his control to order the arrest of opposition candidates or to governing directly himself. Either tactic would have violated the constitutional principles then prevailing. But, in an inspired moment, presaging Burmese politics in 1958, the governor hit upon a compromise, proposing that if Saw resigned for the duration of the campaign, after the dissolution of the house, he would appoint a nonpolitical, caretaker cabinet.[14]

---

[12]Telegram, Governor of Burma to Secretary of State for Burma, June 5, 1941. Burma File 10/41.
[13]Ibid.
[14]Ibid.

Actually, however, Premier Saw was loath to abandon the prerogatives of office during any campaign period. He indicated to the governor that on the dissolution of the house he would "be prepared to remain in office till after the General Election and . . . be ready to shoulder responsibility of enforcing law and order during the election."[15] Saw apparently did not favor the idea of a nonpolitical interim government, because it would have been "likely to prejudice his position in the country" as well as to have a negative effect on political opinion in Britain.[16] In one sense, all of this discussion was academic, as after the outbreak of the war in the Pacific, the election was not held. But the story provides a candid account of the concerns that arise in the minds of politicians as they calculate the advantages and disadvantages of repressing their opponents in an election.

The 1947 election was the first to be countrywide. Called as part of the process of Britain's granting independence to a democratic government, the election was held under conditions that were far from peaceful. In a number of areas the army was deployed in advance of the polls to establish order. "Operation Flush," in which troops under the command of Lt. Col. Ne Win were sent to the communist-dominated Yenangyaung oil fields, is an example of how a military campaign was used to establish conditions favorable to the holding of elections. The Anti-Fascist People's Freedom League (AFPFL) coalition, which had reached agreement with Britain on holding elections as a step toward independence and was sharing power with the departing colonial authorities, supported these campaigns against their former allies who had been expelled from the nationalist front.

As was noted, the electoral principle had previously been reserved to Burma proper, the directly ruled territories where the majority of the people resided. Under the electoral rules established for the 1947 election, 210 members of a 255-member constituent assembly were elected from this area. An additional 45 members were elected from what was referred to as the former frontier areas, which had remained under the nominal rule of indigenous Sawbwas, Duwas, and other authorities recognized by the colonial state. The expansion of the election and the representative principle had the effect of drawing the frontier area elites into direct and regular communication with the political elite in Ran-

[15]Ibid.
[16]Ibid.

goon, thus both underscoring the unity of the country within the borders previously drawn by the British and concentrating power in Rangoon.

The AFPFL, under U Nu, who had succeeded the assassinated General Aung San as acting premier, was victorious—winning with allied organizations all but seven seats, which were won by independent communists. As in the elections of the 1920s, there were groups that advocated electoral boycott. One was the Burma Communist Party, which argued that the independence agreement reached with the British by the AFPFL would not lead to genuine democracy; the other was the Karen National Union (KNU), whose Christian leaders recognized that under the new dispensation, their privileged place in colonial Burma would soon end, even though only they and Eurasians could maintain their own designated constituencies, all of the Indian and special-interest seats having been abolished at the insistence of the AFPFL.

Despite the fundamental importance of this election for determining the legitimacy of the postcolonial state and government, none of the readily available published sources provides any statistics on the participation rate of the electorate. The published records provide only an incomplete picture. There were ninety-one noncommunal seats (those not ethnically designated) available in the election. In fifty-six constituencies, there were no opposition candidates to the AFPFL, which returned two members for each. Preliminary and incomplete returns from thirty-two of the thirty-five contested constituencies showed a participation rate of 49.8 percent, down from the officially given prewar rate of 50.2 percent. The slightly lower rate was explained in terms of the instability then existing in the country. No published figures are available for the former frontier areas that were experiencing their first elections.[17] The final results for the ninety-one noncommunal constituencies revealed that the percentage of voters was 46.7 percent of the registered voters, with a return of 47.1 percent in rural seats and 42.2 percent in urban seats. The turnout rate was lowest in Rangoon: 34.1, 36.2, and 34.2 percent in the three contested areas.[18]

[17]Telegram, P. G. E. Nash to Sir Gilbert Laithwaite, April 30, 1947 (IOR: M/4/2677), reprinted in Hugh Tinker, ed., Burma: The Struggle for Independence 1944–1948, Vol. 2 (London: HMSO, 1984), 498–500.
[18]I am indebted to Kei Nemoto for this information from his unfinished Ph.D. thesis, Tokyo University of Foreign Studies.

POSTINDEPENDENCE ELECTIONS

The first elections held after independence, in 1951, were conducted in three stages because of the internal disorder that further disrupted the government after the British left. The turnout was less than 20 percent, with only 1.5 million voters out of an electorate of 8 million. This was the lowest turnout since the boycotts of the 1920s and followed in the wake of a decade of national mobilization for independence. The AFPFL won 60 percent of the votes and 147 of the 250 seats in the legislature.

One can but speculate on the reasons for such a low turnout. One may have been the uncertain security situation in the country. The military had to take control of many areas before government officials could conduct the ballot. Voters may have been intimidated. Some may have boycotted the polls in the belief that a vote was futile because the parties and candidates of their choice were excluded from the election. None of the underground insurgent groups, particularly the communists and KNU, participated in these and subsequent elections. Whatever the reason, a 20 percent turnout through which the government won the support of about 12 percent of the electorate was hardly a ringing endorsement of either the government or the electoral system. If elections provide legitimacy for governments, the 1951 election in Burma provided a mere fig leaf.

The second national election in independent Burma took place in 1956. By then political conditions were much more stable, and the turnout was about twice as high as in 1951. The support for the AFPFL slipped, however, to 48 percent of the vote.[19] The cause may have been the greater organizational coherence of the opposition parties or the larger turnout itself. With the decline in the fortunes of the underground opposition, voting may have been seen as the only means of registering disenchantment with the government and its leaders. Whatever the case, the opposition, despite being better organized than in 1951, won only 48 seats, allowing the AFPFL a secure majority of 173.

Burma's last multiparty election until 1990 occurred in 1960. The

---

[19]Maung Maung, *Burma and General Ne Win* (New York: Asia Publishing House, 1969), 226–7; Josef Silverstein, *Burma, Military Rule and the Politics of Stagnation* (Ithaca: Cornell University Press, 1977), 69.

campaign, coming during the final six months of the military "Caretaker Government," was dominated by a fight between two factions of the old ruling AFPFL. The result was a solid win for the former prime minister, U Nu, whose party took 57.2 percent of the vote in the divisions of the old Burma proper. The failure of U Nu's opposition, his former colleagues now organized as the Kyaw Nyein-Ba Swe AFPFL, was widely attributed to the unpopularity of the military caretaker government with which they were identified. Just as the 1956 vote registered an increased turnout over that of 1951, so the 1960 vote was 65 percent above that of 1956. Once more, despite the unfavorable circumstances under which the party game had been introduced, it appeared to have taken root. The winners and the losers began to draw up rules to ensure that the game would continue into the future on a basis that would ensure a free fight among themselves, while excluding those groups unwilling or unable to join in.[20]

The coup of March 1962 brought to an end the multiparty electoral system of postindependence Burma. In retrospect, though we know very little about these elections, they are now held up as models for the future of the country's politics. An assessment of their importance and meaning was made by a Burmese student of the party game in 1963:

Undoubtedly, Burma's three general elections were major achievements. It was a tremendous task to prepare election rolls and conduct elections. Complete accuracy in the rolls was not achieved but great care was taken to register every qualified voter. Much of the rural population was politically apathetic, yet, many voted in accordance with instructions—and material assistance—received from local party leaders. But it did not really matter because the AFPFL would have won anyway, for its was the best organised political institution in Burma. Further, the Opposition was hopelessly divided and was unable to produce any outstanding personality.[21]

The student notes, citing a foreign source, that "the methods employed during the elections were a far-cry from Western standards, [inasmuch as] there was shooting, kidnapping of candidates, intimidation, falsification, bribery and other tactics."[22] This description of electoral behav-

---

[20]See the discussion in Maung Maung, "The Role of Political Parties in Burma from Independence to the Coup D'etat of 2 March 1962" (M.A. thesis, Rangoon University, 1963), 55–9, 67–8.
[21]Ibid., 134.
[22]Ibid., citing H. C. Taussig, "Burma in the Positive," *Eastern World*, London, 10, no. 8 (June 1956): 16.

ior is very similar to accounts of elections and local leadership in the 1930s.[23]

The success of electoral politics in the 1950s must be seen within the context of the period. Following the upheavals of World War II, the anti–British colonial politics of the immediate postwar period, and the civil war that accompanied independence, local politicians, often referred to as *Bo*, had risen to positions of great authority in their regions. Many had their own private or pocket armies, often better armed than the government's military. The *Bo* came to dominate the local administrative structures, thwarting central planning edicts and creating powerful patronage networks, which could be used at the time of an election to ensure that they or their candidates were returned to power.[24] Much research remains to be done on this period, but what little is known suggests that force was more important than persuasion in the winning of elections in the 1950s and 1960. Indeed, while the success of U Nu's "Clean AFPFL" in the 1960 election may be interpreted as a victory against the military, which had backed the "Stable AFPFL," an alternative explanation is that the outcome was a victory of the local *Bo*, as well as the recognized leaders of the frontier areas, against an army that had spent much of the caretaker period attempting to undermine the independence of their private fiefdoms.

The only national referendum in the history of Burma occurred in January 1974, in a vote on the one-party constitution written by a government commission. In what the government hailed as a great success, but which was attacked as typical authoritarian tactics by critics, over 95 percent of the 14,760,000 eligible voters cast ballots. An overwhelming 90.19 percent favored the constitution. Despite the great effort the government had put into ensuring that the constitution was ratified by a huge majority, in the ethnically designated border areas support was less forthcoming: 66.44 percent in the Shan State, 77.69 percent in the Karen State, 86.09 percent in Arakan State, but 90.62 percent in the Mon State. Although the Arakan, Mon, and Karen States' populations had been familiar with electoral politics since the 1920s, elections had occurred in the Shan State only since 1947.[25]

After the introduction of the 1974 constitution, elections for the

---

[23]See C. J. Richards, *Burma Retrospect and Other Essays* (Winchester, England: Herbert Curnow, Cathedral Press, 1951), 62–6.
[24]Taylor, *State in Burma*, 266–9.
[25]*Guardian* (Rangoon), January 4, 1974.

Pyithu Hluttaw, or People's Council, occurred on four occasions, including the last in 1985. The electorate during that eleven-year period grew from 14 million to 18 million persons. Though occasionally an independent candidate stood against the ruling Burma Socialist Programme Party's (BSPP) nominee, these were one-party elections on the model then common in Eastern Europe and the former Soviet Union.

The election of 1990 grew out of the crisis which followed the collapse of the army-dominated, one-party socialist system established under the auspices of the 1974 constitution. During the crisis of 1988, as the old order gave way in the face of widespread public demonstrations, the promise of elections was held out during the one-month rule of the civilian president, Dr. Maung Maung, as an alternative to disorder in the streets and the renewal of military rule. This offer, considered a ruse for continued military dominance, was rejected by the "parliaments of the streets" and the politicians of the past who had reemerged to take advantage of the sudden political opening, as well as Daw Aung San Suu Kyi who was in the country tending her ailing mother, and the demonstrations increased. The army, a month later, clamped down hard and established the State Law and Order Restoration Council (SLORC) government in September. The SLORC, too, held out the promise of elections when conditions were suitable in its view.[26]

During the months preceding the 1990 elections, political activity was renewed with great vigor. As has occurred in several of the former one-party states of Eastern Europe, political parties multiplied with great rapidity. Politicians unseen for twenty-five years claimed once more to speak for the people, and many younger people who had never experienced competitive electoral politics entered the contest with exuberant expectations. In particular, the image of Daw Aung San Suu Kyi, cosmopolitan daughter of the assassinated General Aung San, untarnished by residence in Burma for most of her adult life, and speaking in the

[26]Since the election, critics of the military government in Yangon have advanced the argument that the army called the election as a means of revealing whom their leading opponents were in order to arrest and confine them. This view, while marvelously conspiratorial, fails to account for the apparent fact that both the leaders of the old BSPP and many others who ran in the election, such as former Brigadier Aung Gyi, were confident they would win. They were all wrong. There are no public opinion polls in Myanmar and, inasmuch as no one had experienced an election for thirty years, little means of understanding public opinion. I visited Yangon in the March prior to the May election. Meetings with representatives of a number of parties and journalists, both stringers and the official media, suggested that no one had a clear idea what the results would be.

idiom of parliamentary democracy, provided a focus for the belief that elections would rid the country of the mistakes of nearly thirty years of military domination.

These hopes were reflected in the highest participation rate of any competitive election in Burma's history: 72.59 percent of the 20,818,313 eligible voters turned out on election day. Voter turnout was highest in the more densely populated areas of the old Burma proper, where elections had been a feature of politics since the 1920s, but fell to about 66 percent in the Kachin and Mon States, and the mid-50 percent range in most other regions that made up the former frontier areas, except approximately 48 percent in the Shan State. While ninety-three parties fielded candidates, twenty-seven successfully won seats, the National League for Democracy (NLD), identified with its General Secretary, Daw Aung San Suu Kyi, being the most successful, winning 392 out of 485 seats with just slightly less than 60 percent of the vote. The descendant organization of the old BSPP, the National Unity Party, won a mere 10 seats while, together with its allies, gaining just over 25 percent of the vote. Ethnically designated parties from Rahkine (Arakan) and the former frontier areas won 70 seats with a total of about 12.5 percent of the total vote.[27] Faced with the prospect of a legislature filled with its opponents, the SLORC developed a program for drafting a new constitution that obviated the need to call the newly elected individuals together to draft an alternative constitution and form a government on their own until conditions were established to ensure a continued role for the military in government.[28]

The denial of power to the NLD, combined with the continued house arrest of Daw Aung San Suu Kyi, led to Burma's being an object of serious international political concern for the first time in decades. Capitalizing on the claim to legitimacy, which elections bestow, some of the elected individuals fled from Burma to the Thai border to form an alternative government, the National Coalition Government of the Union of Burma (NCGUB), in conjunction with long-standing insurgent groups, particularly the KNU. The fact that the NCGUB was willing to collaborate with the unelected, armed opponents of all Burmese govern-

[27]For details, see R. H. Taylor, "Myanmar 1990: New Era or Old?," in *Southeast Asian Affairs 1991* (Singapore: Institute of Southeast Asian Studies, 1991), 201–5.

[28]For a tentative discussion, in terms of the nature of political institutions in contemporary Myanmar, of the underlying reasons why the NLD was unable to use its electoral success to remove the army from power, see R. H. Taylor, "Burma's Ambiguous Breakthrough," *Journal of Democracy* I, 4 (Fall 1990): 62–71.

ments, elected and unelected since 1948, was used by the SLORC to question the patriotism of the NLD. The nationalist issue has been played in a number of ways by the SLORC, including raising doubts about the loyalties of Daw Aung San Suu Kyi because of her marriage to a British citizen and pointing out the support that the NCGUB receives from foreign sources, including governments and political organizations. Although this does little to change the minds of opponents of continued military rule outside Burma, the juxtaposing of the patriotism of the army, which dies for the nation, against the claims of the ballot box explains in part the success of the army in maintaining power in the face of the results of the elections.

The arrest of a number of leading and less well-known political opponents of the army both before and after the 1990 elections has also been an important element in the army's continued rule. In the long run, however, the military appears to hope that once normal conditions are established, elections will be possible as they are in Indonesia and other Southeast Asian countries where electoral politics has supported, rather than undermined, a leading role for the military in government. Economic development must be essential for such a strategy to be successful, but the international circumstances that allowed the Indonesian army to capitalize on suppressing its political opponents in the 1960s while establishing legitimacy though development do not pertain in the 1990s.

Nonetheless, the elections are not the only issues at stake. The major states in the international community have made it clear that unless their own interests are directly affected, they are unlikely to intervene in more than a symbolic manner to isolate or remove a government that negates the power of the ballot. In some cases, such as Algeria, the international community has positively welcomed, even if sotto voce, the denial of power to Islamic fundamentalists who were apparently able to win the national election of that country after Burma's 1990 election. More recently, little was done in the face of the annulled electoral contest in Nigeria. The frustration for those who oppose the continued rule of the military in Burma and who champion the ballot box as evidence for the lack of legitimacy of the SLORC is that Burma's lack of significant strategic or economic interest to the outside world means that although many governments are willing to support the publishing of innumerable newsletters, offer international prizes, and pass resolutions of condemnation in international forums, other values greater than an attachment to the ballot determine foreign policies.

BURMA'S ELECTORAL RECORD

What does this litany of electoral history tell us? The meaning of these elections cannot be found in government policies and programs. However you interpret the elections of the 1920s, they were not an endorsement for liberal-democratic government under colonial circumstances. The 1932 vote was a vote for Burma's remaining an Indian province; it did not. The 1936 election perhaps comes the closest of all of those in Burma's history to have the look of normalcy about it, and it led to the political success of the man hanged in 1947 for plotting the assassination of the national hero, General Aung San. The 1947 vote, though obviously a vote for independence, can also be interpreted as a measure to ensure that the non-communists came to power as the British left. It certainly had that result, and the outcome of the elections of the 1950s would support this interpretation as much as any other. U Nu's return to office in 1960 broke the support of the army for the ruling party, and set the stage for the 1962 coup. The elections of the BSPP era were not genuine elections in the sense of those that went before. And whereas most observers have argued that the 1990 election clearly was a mass demonstration of the people's will, it has not achieved a change in government.

If the elections of Burma have not achieved any significant policy or power shifts, nor significantly redirected the programs and personnel of the state, what have they shown us? Why have people bothered to hold them, participate in them, discuss them, and cause us to discuss them long after they occurred? Most obviously, because elections are events that happen. They generate records and commentary. They become a justification to support some individual's or group's preferences. For the student of political history, elections, along with wars, revolutions, and coups, provide the divisions in history that allow us to distinguish one epoch from another. Little may have changed, but we think things should have or might have.

Perhaps more fundamentally, however, these elections tell us something about the development of the polity of Burma/Myanmar in the twentieth century. The people involved in them were being incorporated into the rituals and principles of the modern state. This process was uneven, often unintended, and has had contradictory and incomplete consequences.

What does it take to hold an election? People, obviously. But not just any people; only the people who are deemed to belong to the community

R. H. Taylor

that is to be governed by the consequence of the election. Therefore
electoral rolls and roles have to be established and before that rules for
who is eligible to be on those rolls and fulfill those roles. Elections are
a bureaucratic representation of the imagined community that forms the
basis for the modern nation-state.[29] The clearest of rules in elections
almost everywhere is that foreigners cannot vote[30] and that only citizens
at the age of maturity and of sound mind are allowed to vote. The link
between elections and immigration is not merely one concerning the
gaining of citizenship in largely immigrant societies such as the United
States and Australia, but also one arising as an electoral issue when
foreigners are seen to be taking jobs and opportunities away from those
individuals already having the right to vote.

In this regard it is interesting to contrast the principles of the elections
in Burma in the 1920s with those since independence. The electoral rules
of colonial Burma clearly did not view elections as events that provided
an opportunity for the people (a united community of equal citizens) to
come together to choose its rulers. Rather, elections were events that
underlined the lack of a common egalitarian community in the colony.
The elections from 1922 to 1936 were for seats in a legislative body on
a communal and/or functional basis: There were seats reserved for Europeans, Anglo-Indians, Indians, Karens, business organizations, and the
university, as well as the general people, divided between more heavily
valued urban and less important rural votes. Even after the British and
AFPFL had reached an agreement on British withdrawal, communal representation was maintained for Karens and Anglo-Burmese.

Moreover, for the indigenous majority, the right to vote was initially
linked to the ownership of property and the payment of taxes until
1947.[31] In other ways, however, the rules were remarkably liberal for

---

[29]The imagery and idea is obviously taken from Benedict Anderson, *Imagined Communities*, 2d ed. (London: Verso, 1991).

[30]The only exception I have experienced is Great Britain, where Commonwealth citizens
and Irish citizens are enfranchised. This says something about the antiquity of the British
state. In recent years the principle that noncitizens can vote and stand in elections for
members of the European Parliament in other European Community countries has been
established.

[31]"The suffrage for the forty-four general rural constituencies created in 1922 was based
on the payment of the direct capitation or *thathameda* taxes, averaging around 5 rupees
per household. Voters must be at least eighteen years of age. There was no sex disqual-
ification, although 85 percent of the female voters qualified by paying the Upper Burma
thathameda tax. In the fourteen urban constituencies, the suffrage rolls were virtually
identical with the municipal election voting lists, which included persons paying taxes
on immovable property and others assessed an income tax of 4 rupees or more. In

their period, with eighteen recognized as the age of maturity and no formal disbarment for women.[32] But it is the absence of a common electoral system for all the residents of the country, and at the same time the right of foreigners and business interests to have special voting rights, that strikes us as odd in the world of the modern nation-state.

The electoral rules of colonial Burma provided a codified statement of the nature of the plural society that J. S. Furnivall so eloquently described in *Colonial Policy and Practice*.[33] Not only did the indigenous and foreign communities of colonial Burma not meet in the theater, place of worship, restaurant, or library, they did not even share the same ballot box. Inasmuch as one of the key demands of Burmese nationalists in the 1920s, '30s, and '40s was an end to free immigration, the formalized rights given to immigrants in the election rules could only have been one of the most glaring instances of the *iniquities* of colonial government.

The reformulation of the franchise rules to exclude noncitizens came simultaneously with the power to close off Indian immigration. First steps in this direction came in legislation passed by the post-1937 legislature but became a major issue of the AFPFL and its supporters in agreeing on the rules with the British administration for the 1947 election.

Since Burma's independence in 1948, citizenship laws, immigration restrictions, and electoral rules have been recast so as not merely to exclude the rights of foreigners to join in the community process of elections, but also to limit the rights of citizens whose ancestors entered the territory after it became a British colony. Although no eligible citizen is denied the right to vote, rules concerning the right to hold office and the quality of citizenship have been imposed. While this obviously rankles those who hold up the principle of human equality regardless of origins, these principles are in line with the nationalist principle applied in most of the world that the newest arrivals in a society are inherently different from, and have fewer rights than, had those who can claim

---

proportion to total population the urban centers were considerably over represented. The voters for the circle board [rural local government authorities] were predominantly rural, but they included also taxpayers of adjacent small urban centers, which were not yet recognized as municipalities." Cady, *History of Modern Burma*, 244.

[32]Women in Britain over the age of thirty had gained the franchise only four years before, in 1918. The franchise was not extended to women over twenty-one until 1928. It has been suggested that the liberal sex and age regulations for the franchise in Burma were intended to undermine the system (at least in the minds of the men over forty who wrote the legislation).

[33](Cambridge: Cambridge University Press, 1947; New York: New York University Press, 1956).

their ancestors arrived much earlier. Nationalism and indigenousness are two sides of the coin of electoral rights.

Citizenship and indigenousness are thus part of the electoral process, and the right or obligation to participate in elections is a badge and ritual of belonging to a common society. What do the postindependence elections of Burma tell us about the development of such a common society? National elections have been an aspiration of all Burmese nationalists, military or civilian, but have been opposed by all separatists and other special interests that seek to deny the sovereignty of Yangon over the periphery.

Electoral behavior underlined the contradictory notions in regard to egalitarianism in the 1947 constitution. The constitution recognized the principle of equality in elections to the lower house, but elections to the upper house were determined on an ethnic or regional basis. However, no longer were "foreign" persons—Indians, Anglo-Indians, and Europeans—given special privileges. Now these were extended to the populations living in the border or frontier areas that had been excluded from the principles of direct rule and electoral politics during the colonial period. That was altered under the 1974 constitution, and the removal of special electoral representation for the populations of the Shan and Kachin States may explain their less enthusiastic endorsement of the 1974 constitution in the referendum of that year.

The election of 1990 demonstrated a number of points. The high turnout indicated that the population took the event more seriously than they had previous multiparty elections. The areas with the longest experience of elections and the most developed means of communication had, as before, the highest participation rates. In the former frontier areas, identification with neither the national electoral process nor with nationally designated (as opposed to ethnically particularistic) parties was as strong. Having been excluded from national politics until the 1950s and 1960s, when these practices were introduced by the one-party government of the day, the positive advantages of participating in a national event may have seemed less significant. This behavior obviously also points to a weaker attachment to the national state on the part of these populations.

All this must seem obvious. But it is difficult to make much more of the easily available record of elections and related phenomena in Myanmar. Since the 1920s, the rulers of Burma/Myanmar, whether British or Burmese, whether civilian or military, have proffered elections as the solution to political problems of the Burmese people. Why they have done so is rarely asked. Elections have been held out as a panacea, but when the results, or expected results, have not been what those who offered the ballot sought, those in power have had no qualms about setting aside the outcome. It is those in power who have held elections and determined the consequences. Not until those out of power have the organizational means to contest them in a sustained and organized manner, both before and long after the polling day, will elections have much meaning in Myanmar.

8

◖━◗◖━◗◖━◗◖━◗◖━◗◖━◗◖━◗◖━◗◖━◗◖━◗◖━◗◖━◗◖━◗◖━◗◖━◗

Elections and democratization in Thailand

SUCHIT BUNBONGKARN

Elections in many countries are the basis of the process in which private citizens participate to influence government decisionmaking and the composition of the political leadership.[1] Electoral activity in Western democracies involves efforts by various political groups in competition for political power and position, as well as the exercise of the people's right to determine the outcome of elections. Elections are considered the conventional means of participation, and this routine behavior is shaped by the institutional channels of representative government.[2] In a routinized democracy, citizens do not have to risk their lives to participate in politics, and they do not have to take extraordinary actions in defiance of government channels to express their views. But in Thailand, parliamentary elections have not, until recently, been a process in which the people participated to choose their government and to influence its policies. In many instances, elections performed merely the symbolic function of ensuring the legitimacy of purportedly democratically chosen military governments. These elections were held to pacify the demands of liberal-civilian politicians for an expansion of political participation.

Since 1979, however, as a result of increasing political liberalization, elections have become a more significant element of the democratic process. Though interrupted by a military coup in 1991, parliamentary rule has become more firmly established. Political parties have assumed a

[1]For an analysis of political participation and electoral activity, see Samuel P. Huntington and Joan M. Nelson, *No Easy Choice: Political Participation in Developing Countries* (Cambridge, Mass.: Harvard University Press, 1977), 4–12.
[2]For a discussion of routine political participation in the Western democracies, see Kenneth Janda, Jeffrey M. Berry, and Jerry Goldman, *The Challenge of Democracy* (Boston: Houghton Mifflin, 1989), 4–12.

more powerful role while the military has been forced to retreat. The civilian bureaucracy's influence and political role have also been in decline. As a result of rapid economic growth, civil society has gained strength as the business community has expanded and its political influence has increased. Professional and societal groups have become more assertive and influential. Although the 1979 general election, the first after the 1976 coup, did not effect a change of government leadership, it ushered in a new period of more participatory politics. Subsequent elections gave greater legitimacy to the elected assembly, and after the 1988 election, the leader of the largest party in the lower house was chosen as prime minister.[3] The election of September 1992 reflected more clearly a competition for political power between two groups of political parties, and once more the leader of the party with the largest number of seats in the lower house, Chuan Leekpai of the Democrat Party, became prime minister.

Now that elections appear to have become more firmly established as an institution of Thai politics, a number of questions arise: To what extent do elections produce the circulation and renewal of elites? Do elections produce governments that represent the interests of the voters? How do elections assist efforts for greater democratization? This chapter addresses these questions. It analyzes the role of parliamentary elections in the democratization process, particularly since 1979, when the parliamentary form of government was reestablished.

ELECTIONS AND THE LEGITIMATION OF MILITARY RULE

Thailand had its first direct parliamentary election in 1937, five years after the absolute monarch was supplanted by constitutional government, the election of 1933 having been conducted on an indirect basis. Since 1933 Thailand has had seventeen parliamentary elections, one on an average of every 3.6 years, though not on any such regular basis. Of these seventeen elections, only those of 1946, 1975, 1976, and September 1992 were held in a democratic environment with the expectation of significant governmental change to follow. The others were designed to give legitimacy to military or military-dominated governments. The latter category of elections served to allow the military leaders to put

---

[3]The Chat Thai Party won the largest number of seats in the 1988 election, and General Chatachai Choonhavan, the party's leader and a member of parliament from Korat, was chosen after General Prem Tinsulinond declined to serve a further term as prime minister.

their own men in the elected House of Representatives, thus ensuring its support for their continued hold on power.

Although the military remained in control, they preferred to make their regimes appear legitimate. In appointing the prime minister, for example, the military usually sought the endorsement of parliament first. Thus, controlling parliament was vital to the military to ensure that their nominee would not be rejected. In addition, military control of parliament ensured the smooth passage of government legislation. It was common practice after 1946 for military leaders to set up an appointed legislative body to counterbalance the elected house. From 1932 to 1946, a unicameral legislature existed, but the 1932 coup leaders who dominated Thai politics during that period filled half the legislature with appointed members, most of whom were military officers and civil servants loyal to the coup group. The appointed members enjoyed the same rights and powers as the elected members.

Throughout the 1950s and 1960s, the military allowed limited political participation and occasional parliamentary elections, but elected members of parliament were still checked by appointed members. Half the legislature was appointed by the military government from 1952 to 1957. Following a decade with no parliamentary body in existence, a bicameral legislature was established from 1967 to 1971, and the military government appointed members of the Senate while the electorate voted directly for members of the lower house. The two-house system was reestablished in 1975 and 1979. The 1974 constitution had an upper house appointed by the king on the advice of the government before the 1975 election.

Nevertheless, control of the appointed legislators was insufficient to ensure the support of the National Assembly. During the period between 1932 and 1945, the government was defeated twice over important legislative issues, forcing two military prime ministers to resign. From 1948 to 1951, the elected house, which was dominated by the opposition, created a number of difficulties for Field Marshal Pibul Songkram's government. Thus, after 1952, the military leaders decided to exert more control over the elected house. In 1955, Prime Minister Field Marshal Pibul established the Serimanangasila Party, bringing into it leading military officers and civil servants, as well as a number of elected members of parliament. The same type of party, the United Thai People's Party, was established in 1968 by Marshal Thanom Kittikachorn. These parties were assigned to field promilitary candidates in the 1957 election. Fraud and a variety of forms of bribery were used to ensure their winning as many seats as possible. The most notorious fraud occurred in the Bangkok constituency where the Serimanangasila Party was determined to win seats at any cost.

The limited political participation provided by the elections of the 1950s and 1960s might be seen as safety valves, inasmuch as they allowed those unhappy with the status quo to express their views and grievances within a legal framework. The elections gave these individuals an opportunity to register their policies and to run for seats in parliament, but their influence on policy and elite circulation was minimal. The 1952 election did not produce any change of leadership as Pibul continued as prime minister. Likewise, after the election of 1969, Marshal Thanom was appointed prime minister, thus continuing in power, though he did not run in the election.[4] As a safety valve, the elections were pacifying instruments that induced antimilitary, civilian elements to work within the law and ultimately to accept the political domination of the military.

Nonetheless, the limited participation allowed in the 1950s and 1960s did produce consequences unfavorable for the military. Following the 1957 election, mass protests occurred in Bangkok because of dissatisfaction with electoral fraud in a number of constituencies. These protests precipitated the coup that ousted the government of Field Marshal Pibul. Marshal Sarit, the army chief and coup leader, secretly backed the protests in order to create a condition conducive to the replacement of Pibul and the defeat of his arch rival, Police Chief General Phao Sriyamond. In the end, though Sarit got his way, the conflict increased between civilian groups in Bangkok and the military because the new military government opposed the strengthening of democratic groups. A second election followed a year later, and when the civilian Democrats made significant gains, Sarit conducted a second coup, closing down electoral politics until 1969. Similarly, during and after the 1969 election, politicians were able to step up campaigns against military rule. Civilian members of parliament then thwarted the government's legislative program, including the budget bills, while heavily criticizing government policies. Thanom conducted a coup against his own government in 1971, and again political participation was suspended, this time until mass demonstrations in 1973.

[4]His United Thai People's Party won only 95 seats of the total of 218 in the 1969 election.

Suchit Bunbongkarn

Despite the ultimate frustration of aims, the elections of 1957 and 1969 did increase the political awareness of some parts of the electorate. The elections provided liberal politicians with an opportunity to campaign for greater political participation. These campaigns were often focused on antimilitary issues, including the demand for a full-fledged democracy and complete political freedom. By increasing the electorates' political awareness, civilian politicians hoped to erode the power base of the politicians-in-uniform, the military. Even these brief periods of electoral politics served to disseminate democratic ideas among the population.

THE ELECTORAL IMPACT OF THE TRANSITION TO DEMOCRACY

The establishment during the 1980s of parliamentary forms of politics has made elections more meaningful. Before, those who aspired to power had to go through the military's bureaucratic hierarchy. Those outside this structure rarely reached the top unless they developed close associations with military leaders. After 1979, as the parliamentary system became more stable, power seekers had to join a political party and run in an election to gain a cabinet post, the new ultimate political prize.

The present electoral system, though it has evolved since 1979, is based on that of the brief constitutional period in the years 1975–76. All provinces are divided into constituencies and the number of seats in each constituency ranges from one to three depending on the number of voters on the rolls. Thus a province which has three members or less has one constituency, making the constituency unit and the province identical.[5] Before World War II, a single-member constituency system was adopted, but it was replaced by multimember constituencies in 1946 and again revised under the 1975 constitution.

According to the present constitution, which was adopted in 1991, the total number of members of parliament, who can serve terms of up to four years, is fixed at 360.[6] The simple majority or plurality system

[5]Suchit Bunbongkarn, *Kan pattana tang kanmueng khong thai: patisamphan rawang tahan sataban tang kanmveng lae kanmesuanruam tang kanmueng khong prachachon* (Thai political development: The interaction between the military, political institutions and political participation) (Bangkok: Chulalongkorn University Press, 1991), 220–1.
[6]The present constitution was amended in 1995 to allow the number of MPs to increase in proportion to the increase in the number of voters.

of election is used. This means that those who are elected may not necessarily have received more than half the votes cast. Universal suffrage
has been adopted since 1932, with the restrictions imposed for age
(twenty is the age of eligibility), mental illness, serving in prison, or being
a member of the Buddhist monkhood. Gender, race, and economic status
have never been used as discriminating factors for determining the right
to vote.[7]

During the transitional period after 1979, the military remained a
powerful political force and played a decisive role in forming the government. Nevertheless, political parties, through their contesting of elections and roles in the legislature, began to exert increasing influence.
Following the 1976 coup, the coup group that eventually promulgated a new constitution in 1978 allowed for political liberalization and democratization in response to persistent demands by several
liberal political groups, including one faction of the armed forces.[8]
The 1978 constitution established a bicameral legislature, with a
lower house elected directly by the people and a senate appointed
by the prime minister. During the first four years after the introduction of the constitution, the senate had the same authority as the
elected house in overseeing the executive. Government officers, including those in the armed forces, were allowed to hold political offices
concurrently.

After the 1979 election, General Kriangsak Chamanand, the coup
leader, continued as prime minister with the support of the military. In
setting up his cabinet, Kriangsak paid no attention to the influence of
the elected house. Major parliamentary parties were not invited to join
the cabinet. He relied almost entirely on the military-dominated senate.
When the military shifted its support to General Prem Tinasulanond
some months later, Kriangsak had no choice except to resign. General
Prem succeeded him as prime minister and invited the major parties to
join his cabinet to ensure majority support in the elected house. The

---

[7]The exception to these rules occurred at the time of the 1979 election when Thai citizens
whose fathers were aliens were not entitled to vote unless they had completed secondary
education, served in the armed forces, or resided in the country for at least ten years.
These rules were revoked in 1980.
[8]This faction was known as the "Young Turks." For a discussion of their role during this
period, see Suchit Bunbongkarn, "Political Institutions and Process," in Somakdi Xuto,
ed., *Government and Politics of Thailand* (Singapore: Oxford University Press, 1987), 72.

Social Action Party, which controlled 82 of the total of 301 seats, the Democrats with 32 seats, and some minor parties agreed to join Prem's cabinet.

The elections of 1983 and 1986 did nothing to change the pattern General Prem had established. He continued as prime minister with the support of the mainstream of the armed forces and the major political parties. Although General Prem was no longer the army chief and the power of the senate was reduced to enacting legislation, the elected parliamentarians continued to support the general. They believed that their political influence and legitimacy, though increasing, was not sufficiently strong to force the military to withdraw completely from politics.

Nevertheless, these two elections, like that of 1979, allowed access for new elite groups, particularly from the business elites and local leadership, to top political posts. Many of these individuals were also leading figures in the political parties. They ran in the elections and were appointed cabinet members. Because of the rising democratic mood, the elections were providing legitimacy to the elected politicians, enabling them to assume more important political roles.

THE IMPACT OF ELECTIONS ON THE CIRCULATION OF ELITES

The elections of 1988, as well as those of March and September 1992, demonstrated the increasing strength of elected politicians and the further decline of the influence of the bureaucratic and military elites. They gave full legitimacy to political parties and elected parliamentarians, allowing them to control state power. This development was possible because of the growing strength of civil society. Thai social groups, particularly the business community, gained force in the late 1980s as political parties and the elected House of Representatives acquired more political legitimacy. The antimilitary and anti-Prem groups were more vocal in the 1988 election and gained more support from the urban, educated electorate, which believed that it was time for the military to step down and allow parliament to determine who governed. Because of this development, General Prem declined an invitation to remain as prime minister after the election, paving the way for General Chatichai Choonhavan, the leader of the largest party in parliament, to lead the government. This marked another important step in democratic development as an elected member of the house was appointed prime minister.

The March 1992 election reflected the continuing strength of antimilitary groups. This election was held after the military junta that took power following a coup against the Chatichai government in 1991 had promised political liberalization within one year. When it turned out that the military wanted to continue its political control after the election by naming army chief General Suchinda Kraprayoon prime minister, the prodemocracy groups launched strong protests that led to a violent crackdown by the military government.[9] This brutal suppression in turn produced a disastrous consequence for Suchinda's regime. It angered the people and led to more widespread protests, resulting in the king's intervention and Suchinda's resignation.

The subsequent election, the second of the year, was held in September in a democratic environment and determined who would form the government. The parties contesting the election were divided into two groups. The so-called angel or prodemocracy parties had participated in the antimilitary protests. The other military-aligned parties had joined the Suchinda cabinet. The election results favored the angel parties, the Democrats winning 79 seats and the New Aspiration Party, 51 seats. General Chamlong Srimuang's Palang Dham Party, predicted by one poll to capture the most seats, won only 47, and the Solidarity Party won 8.[10] Altogether, the angel parties won a small majority of 185 seats in the 360-seat parliament, just enough to form a new coalition government. Chuan Leekpai, the leader of the Democrat Party and a long-time parliamentarian from the south, was appointed prime minister.

The above developments show that the antimilitary group was efficient in exploiting the prevailing democratic mood, and the elections achieved their aim. But the group, like the promilitary parties, was dominated by wealthy political leaders who were becoming a new ruling elite that had begun to use elections to keep themselves in power.

VOTER MOBILIZATION, VOTE BUYING, AND MONEY POLITICS

It is widely accepted that elections are important for democracy in that they institutionalize mass participation in the governing process. To have a democracy, the people must participate in politics, and participation in elections is perhaps the most important form of this participation. To

[9]Suchit Bunbongkarn, "Thailand 1992," *Asian Survey* 33, no. 2 (February 1993): 220.
[10]*Rathasapha Sarn* 40, no. 3 (September 1992): 5.

make elections more meaningful and compatible with democracy, they should reflect the interests of the voters. In the case of Thailand, the last three elections were most important, but their outcomes did not reflect the voters' political awareness. The results reflected only a wide gap between democratic idealism and actual practices. The mobilization of voters through buying and patronage were common features of these elections.

One problem of the elections was the low level of voters' political awareness. This explains the use of vote buying as a means of political mobilization. From the first election in 1933 to the most recent in September 1992, the average rate of voter participation has been about 40 percent. But since 1986 the rate of voter turnout has increased to approximately 60 percent. (See Table 8.1.) If we compare Thailand with other major democracies in Asia, such as Japan and India, in the period between 1969 and 1988, Thailand has the lowest average voter turnout at 51 percent, whereas Japan and India achieved average voter turnouts of 71 percent and 59 percent respectively.[11] But if we include the voter participation rate in the two 1992 elections, Thailand is at the same level as India and approaches Japan with a turnout rate of 60 percent.

From Table 8.1 it can be seen that, contrary to many assumptions, voter turnout does not correspond with economic and social changes. The turnout rate was below 50 percent both before and after World War II, even though Thailand changed a great deal socially and economically after the war. The participation rate did not begin to rise until 1988, when the democratic mood was growing.

In Western democracies, the tendency to vote is strongly related to socioeconomic status. People with more education, higher incomes, and white-collar or professional occupations tend to be more aware of the impact of politics, to know what to do to influence the government, and to have a sense of political efficacy. They are therefore more likely to vote than are people of lower socioeconomic status.[12] But what has happened in Thailand is in strong contrast to this pattern of behavior. The rate of voter turnout in Bangkok, the most highly developed and most modern city in the country, was the lowest relative to the rest of the country in many elections. In the 1952, 1957, 1969, 1979, 1983, 1986, and the two 1992 elections, the voter turnout in Bangkok was the lowest

[11]Janda, Berry, and Goldman, eds., *Challenge of Democracy*, 248.
[12]Ibid., 249–51.

Table 8.1. *Voter turnout in general elections, 1933–92*

Date	MPs elected	Electorate	Votes cast	Turnout %	Highest turnout (provinces)	%	Lowest turnout (provinces)	%
11/15/33	78	4,278,231	1,773,532	41.45	Petchburi	78.82	Maehongson	17.71
11/7/37	91	6,123,239	2,462,536	40.22	Nakornnayok	80.50	Maehongson	22.24
11/12/38	91	6,310,172	2,210,332	35.03	Nakornnayok	67.36	Trang	16.28
1/6/46	96	6,431,827	2,091,827	32.52	Burirum	54.65	Suphan	13.40
1/29/48	99	7,176,891	2,117,464	29.95	Ranong	58.69	Paknam	15.68
2/26/52	123	7,602,591	2,961,291	38.95	Saraburi	77.78	Bangkok	23.30
2/26/57	160	9,859,039	5,668,566	57.50	Saraburi	93.30	Suphan	42.46
12/15/57	160	9,917,417	4,370,789	44.07	Ranong	73.00	Udon	29.92
2/10/69	219	14,820,180	7,285,832	49.16	Ranong	73.95	Bangkok	34.66
1/26/75	269	20,243,791	9,549,024	47.17	Phuket	67.88	Petchboon	32.18
4/4/76	279	20,623,430	9,072,629	43.99	Nakorn Panom	63.53	Petchboon	26.64
4/22/79	301	21,283,790	9,344,055	43.90	Yasothorn	77.11	Bangkok	22.56
4/18/83	324	24,224,470	12,295,339	50.76	Yasothorn	79.62	Bangkok	32.57
7/27/86	349	26,160,100	16,079,949	61.43	Chayaphum	85.15	Bangkok	38.13
7/24/88	359	26,658,638	16,944,931	63.56	Yasothorn	90.42	Samutsongkram	35.92
3/22/92	360	32,436,370	19,216,670	59.24	Mukdaharn	81.11	Bangkok	42.01
9/13/92	360	31,860,156	19,622,332	61.59	Mukdaharn	90.43	Bangkok	47.40

Source: Department of Local Administrations, Ministry of Interior

in the country (below 40 percent except in 1992, see Table 8.1), whereas the highest voter turnout was in the poor and less well-developed provinces.

How can we explain this? In research on voting behavior in Thailand, Bunbongkarn and Phongphaew have concluded that voter turnout in the less developed rural provinces is always high because of the mobilization activities of politicians in their areas.[13] Rural voters, most of whom have a low level of education and are poor and less aware of the impact of politics on their lives, can be easily mobilized to vote by local leaders, influential candidates, political parties, or government officials. These people cast their votes not because they are politically conscious but because they are encouraged or mobilized by other agents.

The motivation for mobilization varies depending on who is doing the mobilizing. In some elections, such as those of 1983 and 1986, the Ministry of Interior, which administers elections, instructed district officers to encourage voters to cast their ballots and to set a reward for the district that had the highest turnout. This encouraged district officers to do whatever possible to get people to vote. Many local leaders who were the major canvassers for candidates played a decisive role in getting votes for them. The patronage system, which is deeply rooted in many rural areas, facilitated this mobilization by local leaders. Because the rural voters are largely uninformed of the policies of the candidates, it is easy to win their votes through personal links. Lack of solid party links to the constituencies is another factor in mobilization. The parties themselves turn to local patrons for support in the election.

Vote buying is another method of voter mobilization in rural constituencies. It has become a common practice for candidates to give money to electors in exchange for their votes. Money is given through local leaders and canvassers, and once the voters have received money they feel obliged to vote as instructed. Vote buying is effective in areas where the party of the candidates' bases does not exist and the voters are politically apathetic and unaffiliated with any party.[14]

In Bangkok, where the voter turnout tends to be lower than in rural areas, other factors have been identified to explain this unexpected phenomenon. One is that Bangkok voters are immune to the prevailing

[13]Suchit Bunbongkarn and Pornsak Phongphaew, *Preutikam kanlongkha-nansiang khong khonthai* (Voting behavior of the Thai people) (Bangkok: Chulalongkorn University Press, 1984), 224–50.
[14]See "The Confessions of a Vote-Buyer," *Nation*, February 9, 1992.

mobilization methods in the countryside. In every election, government authorities, the parties, and their candidates use various methods to encourage Bangkok people to vote. These include public rallies and media campaigns, but these prove ineffective. The Bangkok voters, particularly those in the educated, middle-class stratum, are very independent and when they vote, do so on the basis of their own judgment. Not needing money that might come from vote selling, this stratum usually believes in democratic ideology. Others vote probably because they are supportive of a political party. Mobilization and vote buying are effective to get out the vote of only the lower-income groups.[15]

Since the average turnout in Bangkok elections is around 40 percent, there must be quite a number of those in the middle- and upper-middle-socioeconomic stratum who do not vote. What are other possible explanations for this? One is a lack of trust in politics and politicians. These people are not politically apathetic. They are quite aware of the impact of politics on their lives and communities, but they are pessimistic that the candidates will improve things for them. Some say that they do not vote because they would see no improvement after the election. Others say that all politicians are alike: They cannot be trusted, so there is no point in voting.[16]

Bangkok voters are close to the center of power and are knowledgeable about politics. The fact that a number of politicians are corrupt and have come to power for their personal gain reinforces the people's belief that politics is always corrupt, and no one can do anything about it. Another factor discouraging people from voting is the belief that the result will make no difference. In fact, of course, before 1988, this was true, inasmuch as there was no significant change in the government after elections. After 1988, however, this has not been the case, but change in people's attitudes takes longer to affect their behavior.

DIFFERENCES BETWEEN URBAN AND RURAL VOTING BEHAVIORS

Turnout rates alone do not indicate the quality of elections. The value of elections depends on not only the turnout rate but also the value of

---

[15]Bunbongkarn and Phongphaew, *Voting Behavior*, 224–5.
[16]Suchit Bunbongkarn and Pornsak Phongphaew, *Raingan kanvichai preutikam kanlong-kha-nonsiang khong khonthai* (A research report on voting behavior of the Thai people in the April 22, 1979 general election), typescript, Chulalongkorn University, 1982, 79–89.

the votes. Elections are institutional mechanisms that implement democracy by allowing citizens to choose their rulers and public policies. By participating in elections, do Thai citizens choose their government or do they merely want someone who can help them in time of trouble or hardship? The answer reflects the value or impact of elections in Thailand.

Here there is again a sharp distinction between urban and rural voters' motives in casting their ballots. Those educated, urban voters who are likely to participate in elections tend to do so because they think it is their duty and responsibility. They think that elections should be the process by which the government is chosen, not just the members of the House of Representatives.[17] This demonstrates that educated, urban voters want elections to have an impact on choosing the government, although they know that in many elections that impact does not occur. But rural voters, most of whom are of lower socioeconomic status, vote because they think it is their duty and are not concerned with the impact of the elections in choosing the government. They know that elections are held with the purpose of letting them select candidates to be their representatives, but they expect their representatives to work for their interests, which are parochial, such as building bridges and roads in their villages, raising the price of rice and other commodities, and providing electricity. The villagers are not interested in the role their representatives are playing or should play at the national level.[18]

Another difference in voting behavior between urban and rural electors has to do with voters' attitudes toward party attachment. Party identification is not strong among Thai voters and is nonexistent in most rural constituencies. The urban voters, particularly in Bangkok, tend to vote more for a party than for individuals, whereas the party attachment of the candidates, party policies, and national issues do not count at all to rural voters. The personal ties of the candidates with a constituency are also important. Many rural candidates change party affiliation several times but are still reelected.

Bangkok voters have tended to vote for a party-team since the inception of electoral politics. Voting for a split ticket rarely occurs. But party loyalty or alignment of Bangkok voters has shifted over time. For three decades from the 1950s, the majority of Bangkok voters supported the

---

[17]Bunbongkarn and Phongphaew, *Voting Behavior,* 229–30.
[18]Ibid., 229.

Table 8.2. *General-election results in Bangkok, 1976–92*

Party	Seats won	% of vote
Jan. 26, 1976, election		
Democrat	22	88.0
Chat Thai	2	8.0
Social Action	1	4.0
Total	25	100.0
April 22, 1979, election		
Prachakorn Thai	29	90.62
Social Action	2	6.25
Democrat	1	3.13
Others	—	—
Total	32	100.00
September 13, 1992, election		
Palang Dham	23	65.7
Democrat	9	15.7
Prachakorn Thai	2	5.7
Others	1	2.9
Total	35	100.0

Source: Department of Local Administration, Ministry of Interior.

Democrat Party. In the early 1980s, Bangkok voters turned to the Pra-charkorn Thai Party. Now the Palang Dham is the most popular party in Bangkok. (See Table 8.2.)

The shift in voting indicates that the Bangkok electors always take major political issues into account. When issues change, so do the voters' party allegiances. From 1950 to 1976, the Democrats won because voters wanted someone to stand up against the military. In 1979, when success by the Communist Party seemed imminent, they shifted to Prachakorn Thai because of its anticommunist position, and when they were disenchanted with the corrupt politics of the late 1980s, they shifted to the Palang Dham because of its allegedly clean-politics stand.

The contrast in the behavior of urban and rural voters in the September 1992 general election was sharpened when the urban electorate voted on the issue of democratization while rural voters still considered their local interests the most important factor in shaping their voting decisions. It is impossible for rural constituents to vote on party preference when there is no party in their constituency. Party organization and activities do not exist at the grass-roots level. The fact that candidates' campaigns often concentrate on their personal attributes and their contributions to the constituencies keeps the rural voters unaware of the importance of political parties. Perhaps the candidates themselves do not want to help develop party preference among their constituents to avoid the risk of losing support if they change party affiliation.

The differences in voting behavior discussed in the previous section present an interesting problem in the democratization process in Thailand. Since the majority of the voters who are rural residents do not, in casting their ballots, act with the intention of influencing government decisionmaking or government changes, they cannot be an effective force to check the performance of the parliamentarians and the government. Rural citizens are less concerned with the role their representatives play at the national level. In a democracy, not only the opposition in the parliament, but also the citizens or societal groups outside are expected to keep a check on government. But in Thailand, only Bangkok voters and residents of some other cities are politicized in this way, and thus interested in, and sometimes critical of, the performance of the government and the parliament. A number of societal and professional groups are active in exerting their influence in government decisionmaking, but most of them are urban-based. In many cases, negative reactions by Bangkok voters and these groups to the performance of the government and the parliamentarians have not been effective in influencing decisions because a number of key members of the government and the parliament came from rural constituencies. Consequently they do not worry about being unpopular in the capital city.

The Chatichai government (1988–91) is a case in point. During the three-year reign of this government, a number of cabinet members were allegedly corrupt and heavily criticized by the mass media, Bangkok voters, and some business groups. The prime targets of these attacks were key ministers such as Banhan Silapa-acha, Praman Adiresan, Montri Ponpanich, and Wattana Asawahem. The attacks failed to shake their position, because their power bases were in rural areas where the people were not concerned with what they had done in the national government. They continued to back their representatives as long as they were responsive to their rural needs. This came out clearly in the elections in March and September 1992. In the March election those representatives who were accused of corruption during the Chatichai administration and whose assets were frozen by the 1991 coup group won reelection. They came back again in the September election despite the fact that they had joined hands with the coup group itself to form a government and tacitly agreed with the brutal suppression of the prodemocracy demonstrators in May 1992.

Thailand is now witnessing a transfer of power from bureaucratic elites to political bosses, from the civil bureaucracy and the military to political parties, and from national political institutions to local authorities. Elections are replacing coups as a mechanism for institutionalizing access to power. It is a transfer of power from the bureaucratic forces to the nonbureaucratic ones whose base of power lies in the electorate. However, this does not mean that the people now have real power and influence. As reflected through elections, the electorate is manipulated in casting its votes. Local leaders, party bosses, and influential local business tycoons continue to maintain the patronage system in their areas. Economic growth and expansion of commercialization and industrialization in the provinces have provided them with a better chance to increase their wealth and influence. Before, these local business leaders or *jao poh* gave money to state officials in exchange for protection of their illicit businesses and the granting of large contracts for public transportation and communications. Now with the shift of power to political parties, some of them have set up political parties, run in elections, and become cabinet members.[19] Others have funded parties, given financial support to candidates, or helped them get out the vote. Some of them have maintained a solid power base in their provinces, and any candidates who want to get elected there must seek their help. Outstanding examples are Somchai Khunplum, better known as Kamnan Poh, a business tycoon from Cholburi, a major province on the eastern seaboard, and Sia Leng, a local business leader in a northeastern province.[20]

Elections have become the instruments by which the ruling elite maintain power. Unlike most Southeast Asian countries, the Thai ruling elites are split into various parties, and these parties, through elections, take turns in governing. Government or opposition parties' alliances are temporary and eventually break up after an election. The party leaders may differ in social and economic backgrounds, but they have one thing in

[19]The Chat Thai Party is one in which many *jao poh* have joined and held key positions. *Nation*, January 28, 1992.
[20]*Nation*, January 30, 1992 and February 1, 1992.

common: wealth. Because money is extensively used in elections, those candidates without strong financial support can hardly win. Although Thailand has a multiparty system, the major parties do not differ fundamentally in political and economic programs and ideological orientations. They are middle-of-the-road, capitalist, and pragmatic. Their political domination has encouraged the spread of money politics, which makes it very difficult for a left-wing party to emerge as a major party.

If the elections continue to be manipulated by these political bosses, should they be revoked? Some military leaders once have asserted that appointed legislators represent the people better than elections do. Elections were often discredited by coup leaders. They claimed that the elections never produced honest and stable civilian governments that worked in the people's interest. Nevertheless, elections are now indigenized and more accepted despite their shortcomings. What should be done is not to revoke them but to make them free and fair so that they represent the interest of the majority.

Several measures might be adopted to free elections from the manipulation of influential local leaders and party bosses. First, an independent election commission might be established to supervise and administer elections to cut down the influence of the political bosses. At the moment, the Ministry of Interior is responsible for election administration, but politicians who control the ministry can dominate this process. A poll watch committee has been set up to monitor election campaigns, but it is not effective enough to make elections free and fair.

Second, the political parties could be encouraged to develop links with the electorate to reduce their dependence on the local leaders at the time of elections. Party branches in constituencies could be developed to be mechanisms for political campaigning and recruitment. Third, political education could be given to rural voters on an ongoing basis to provide them with a proper understanding of the object of elections and their mechanisms, as well as to arouse political awareness. With steps such as these, the government would be more accountable to the people, thus making elections more important in the eyes of the electorate.

9

A tale of two democracies:
Conflicting perceptions of elections and
democracy in Thailand

ANEK LAOTHAMATAS

INTRODUCTION

For those who care for the big picture, studies of elections—particularly
those of the Western systems—often seem trivial because those studies
simply seem to report on the political behavior of the electorate, offer
profiles of the candidates and their platforms, or at best interpret the
outcome of particular elections. This has also been true of most studies
of Thai elections. But there are few places where studying elections can
be more fruitful than Thailand, for if properly focused, such an analysis
can provide a major explanation of the stasis or dynamism of the political system as a whole.

Thailand has an unfortunate record of cyclical alternation between
democracy and military authoritarianism, despite the fact that its first
democratic regime dates back as far as 1932, well ahead of most ex-
colonial nations. Most bewildering, by the time the last putsch was
launched on February 23, 1991, the number of coup attempts since 1932
had risen to seventeen, and thus exactly equaled the number of general
elections held over the same period. These intriguing statistics graphi-
cally represent the parity in strength between the democratic and authoritarian forces in the country's politics. Although the military has
now been pushed back to its barracks, having been disgraced by its
brutal suppression of the demonstrations of May 1992, the question
"When will the next coup occur?" is still very much in the mind of
everyone interested in Thai politics. How can one explain the persistence

201

of the entrenched position of the military in the political landscape in the face of a worldwide democratization trend and strong economic fundamentals at home?

Often it has been said that the answer lies in the absence of a social base for democracy. Until recently this was definitely true. Yet, events of the past two decades suggest that dynamic forces pushing for democracy have recently come of age. Long before the advent of people power in the Philippines, the Suu Kyi–led uprising in Burma, and the Tiananmen Square battle for democracy in China, hundreds of thousands of college students in Thailand in 1973 took to the streets and successfully unseated a military regime. During the 1980s, businessmen, middle-class professionals, and rural dwellers participated fairly actively in a budding form of electoral politics. And most recently, a worldwide television audience bore witness to the heroism of the Bangkok middle-class and working people who braved the water cannons and deadly bullets of the armed forces in the summer of 1992 to protest the attempted restoration of military government.

It can now be argued that the military domination of politics does not spring from the absence or weakness of social forces favorable to democratization. Rather, it is rooted in the conflicting expectations of elections, politicians, and democratic government itself of two major social forces—the urban, educated middle class and the rural farmers or peasants. For rural voters, democracy is a means to bring greater benefits and official attention to themselves and their villages. Voting in farming areas is not guided by political principles, policy issues, or what is perceived to be the national interest, all of which are regarded by urbanites as the only legitimate rationale for citizens casting their ballots in a democratic election. The ideal candidates for rural voters are those who visit them often, address their immediate grievances effectively, and bring numerous public works to their communities. Winning candidates are, in other words, those who manage to construct a workable patron-client network in the villages or those who meet the financial needs of the villagers in their day-to-day lives, including in the midst of election campaigns.

What is regarded by the middle class, rightly or wrongly, as shameful vote buying and perverted electoral behavior is rampant in Thai elections. More relevant to our point, the middle class firmly believes that electoral venalities result in the return of unqualified politicians to the corridors of power. Undoubtedly, in the middle-class mind, these politicians can give rise only to a corrupt and unqualified government. Before long, the elected government usually comes under heavy attack from the middle class and its allies or mentors, such as the mass media or academia. It is for this reason that, despite unfavorable political trends abroad, a military takeover is far from a thing of the past in Thailand. To grapple with the dilemma of the Thai democratization process, then, one has to seek help from a study of elections that is firmly placed in the larger context of political change: the purpose of this essay.

ELECTIONS AND RURAL VOTING BEHAVIOR

Because Thailand is a highly centralized parliamentary democracy, local elections are of little significance. General elections are what matter. By 1994, there have been nineteen general elections: the first in 1933 and the most recent in September 1992. Voting turnout has always been low, ranging from 30 to 40 percent in the period 1933–1957 to 40 to 50 percent in the past two decades. Parliamentarians have always been elected by a plurality, as opposed to an absolute majority or proportional representation. Presently, the electoral system is a combination of single-member and multiple- (two- or three-) member constituencies. As the overwhelming majority of the Thai population reside in villages, with even now almost 70 percent of the workforce farmers or peasants, voting in Thailand has been very much dominated by the rural electorate.

As in many other developing nations, party identification, public policy issues, and political ideology and principles have played a minimal role in rural elections.[1] However, although it is argued that voting in most developing societies is generally motivated to a large extent by ethnic or confessional allegiances, this is not the case in Thailand. This is because the country has fared much better than most in terms of social harmony or even homogeneity. Voting decisions in rural Thailand have been conditioned primarily by the prevailing relationships between patrons and clients. However, the penetration of electoral behavior by patron-client loyalties has, for several reasons, had little to do with direct cash payments to the voters until the last two decades.

---

[1] Two brief historical periods—one at the end of World War II, the other immediately after the October 1973 popular uprising—are exceptions to this general trend. During these two extraordinary periods, left-wing parties were relatively strong and campaigned actively, resulting in a rural voting pattern much more oriented to ideological and policy issues.

A major reason for this relatively recent development has been that elections were not the crucial vehicle to political power during the first four decades of democratization. Although overthrow of the absolute monarchy was undertaken in the name of democracy, Thai governments until the early 1970s were at best semidemocratic, at worst authoritarian. During much of the period between 1932 and 1957, the power of parliament was limited, and only half the members were popularly elected, with the other half appointed by the government. Even worse, the subsequent period, 1957 to 1973, except for a few years, saw fledgling democracy succumb to outright military rule, allowing no room for elections. Thus, until recently, for both power holders and contenders alike, garnering the support of rival factions within the military and civilian bureaucracy was more important than winning an election. Added to the point that parliament was too powerless to attract heavy investment in electioneering is the fact that the economy had not yet developed to the level where significant social and political transformations had taken place. Elections in the early years were run mainly by not-so-rich local politicians. It should be noted, as well, that poor transportation networks in the countryside also worked to prevent wealthy urban politicians from reaching remote areas. Finally, not until the last two decades did big businesses emerge that deemed running or funding elections indispensable to the advancement of their interests.

Sporadic incidents of "money-dumping" were first reported in the 1938 general election, when some candidates were found wooing voters with petty gifts such as groceries, health care items, liquor, and access to outdoor film shows. A few cases of direct cash payments to voters were reported for the first time in 1957. Overall, however, electoral venality did not figure prominently until the last two decades. Indeed, when corrupt electoral behavior first made the headlines at the national level, it was a case of government officials trying to stuff ballot boxes or cheat on vote counting. Fraudulent manipulations then were largely the exclusive domain of the government. The privatization of electoral cheating on a large scale came into being only after the opening of democratic politics in 1973.

Since 1973, parliament has become much more potent, despite occasional military interventions. Moreover, of the two houses of the legislature, the now entirely elected House of Representatives has, by and large, prevailed over the appointed Senate in importance and power. Meanwhile, unlike in the past, the military establishment has for the most part stopped running its own parties or supporting parties of its choice. Thus, officials monitoring elections have managed to remain impartial. All of these circumstances result in an electoral system highly prized and hotly contested. Equally important, the highway system of Thailand has become one of the best in Southeast Asia, reaching virtually all corners of the country. On top of that, decades of rapid economic growth have swollen the ranks of candidates for the elected house with legions of business tycoons from Bangkok and major regional cities. Electoral politics in the last two decades has become characterized by the lavish spending of money.

Extensive reports of vote buying, especially in the rural areas, began in the 1975 general election. The *Asia Yearbook* of 1976, echoing domestic press coverage of that election, recorded that among the less orthodox campaign tactics were "offering money, gifts, free meals, and even girls in return for votes."[2] However, it is generally agreed that direct cash payments to voters reached an alarming level for the first time in a by-election held in a northeastern province that was fiercely contested by two well-funded candidates—one of whom was a former prime minister, the other a former cabinet minister. Since 1983, legions of candidates have been reported by the media to the educated classes for their supposedly venal and scandalous vote-getting ploys.

Although hard figures about the pervasiveness of vote buying are hard to obtain, in a survey of voters in the 1986 general election, 5.2 percent of those in Bangkok reported the existence of the practice in their constituencies, while the corresponding figures for the provinces in the north, the northeast, the central plain, and the south were 25 percent, 27.7 percent, 14.7 percent, and 4.6 percent, respectively.[3] Surveys on candidates' assessment of vote buying yield similar findings. For example, when candidates were asked in survey taken by the Department of Local Administration during the 1983 election, "What do you think is the vote-getting measure most welcome by the voters?" 64.8 percent replied, "offering money and gifts," whereas 33.8 percent replied, "talk to them door-to-door," and only 9.7 percent replied, "making good public speeches."[4] Generally, a rural voter is offered a cash bribe amounting to the minimum wage he would have received in return for toiling a few days.

The popular view about the prevalence of direct cash payments to the

[2]*The Asia Yearbook* (Hong Kong: Far East Economic Review, 1976), 301.
[3]Sombat Chantornvong, *Luak Tang Wikrit* (Thai Elections in Crisis: Problems and Solutions) (Bangkok: Kobfai, 1993), 25.
[4]Ibid.

contrary, most careful researchers find that in most cases candidates pay for votes only through networks of their vote canvassers (*Hua Kanaen*). Vote canvassers in Thailand, in marked contrast to their counterparts in the West, are not party workers. They are, instead, local influentials such as village headmen, landlords, shopkeepers, and schoolteachers, who are personal supporters of candidates. A closer look at the way vote canvassers operate and the criteria actually employed by voters in choosing candidates suggests that trading votes for money is not entirely about elections. Nor is it an adequate factor to ensure the victory of a candidate.

It is impossible for politicians, incumbents in particular, to keep in close touch with voters all the time. Vote canvassers, on the other hand, are part and parcel of village life. They represent politicians in every village, addressing the grievances or problems of villagers. The services they perform are manifold, such as lending money or making donations to the needy, doing paperwork for those contacting government officials, giving legal or practical advice to those in trouble with law enforcement officers, and securing school or hospital admission in big towns for village children. There are many things the poor and insecure villagers can do in return for the favors they received from the canvassers. Yet, most relevant is that they may deliver a large bloc of votes for the candidates supported or endorsed by the canvassers who are their patrons.

In highlighting the influence on voters of these village-based patrons, we do not omit the use of violence in gaining people's votes. However, compared with the manipulation of clientalistic ties, physical intimidation has played a minimal role in recent Thai elections. Nor do we play down the personal role of the candidates. In fact, successful candidates must be able to create several groups of reliable canvassers and earnestly help them with financial or nonfinancial resources so that they in turn can help the needy villagers effectively. The personality and performance of the candidate also matter, especially when villagers have the luxury of being equally well connected to contending networks of vote canvassers. Most recent studies find that voters pick politicians who visit them regularly; who help them cope with difficult personal or family problems, often in collaboration with their canvassers; who regularly attend social functions at the village level; who make generous donations to neighborhood monasteries or schools; and who bring in public programs that generate jobs, money, and reputation for their villages and provinces. Conversely, rural voters care very little about the election platform of the candidates, their party affiliation, or their integrity or work as members of the house or of the cabinet.

Returning to the question most disturbing to the educated middle class, it is true that there are cash payments to villagers in return for their votes. However, the decision to buy votes is inextricably linked with the assessment of candidates by the status of their canvasser networks. My interviews with several candidates, successful and unsuccessful, suggest that there are some rich candidates from big towns who are aggressive vote buyers because, running for the first time, they suffer from a lack of preexisting canvasser networks.[5] Other old-time candidates pay for votes because their networks, while long in existence, are neither reliable nor effective. Still other candidates have to buy votes, in spite of their good networks, simply because their competitors, too, have effective networks and solid preelection performances. Finally, there are candidates who have to buy votes just for peace of mind, since other candidates—with or without preexisting networks—have spent prohibitively on vote buying. In brief, in most cases vote buying is employed as an imperfect substitute for, or supplement to, the building up of constituency support between elections with reliable canvasser networks.

Studies of the attitude of voters toward the practice of vote buying also substantiate the argument that giving cash bribes to villagers does not necessarily hold the key to victory. Voters have rejected incumbents despite their generous vote buying because they subsequently rarely visited the village or helped resolve problems. Voters in general do not appreciate those candidates who resort exclusively to money-dumping to get elected.[6] Also, although rural dwellers are willing to accept money from any candidates, they vote, in most cases, only for those who are also endorsed by their local patrons. It is a well-known fact among candidates that money given out by unpopular canvassers tends to be wasted.[7] However, it must be emphasized that rural voters have increasingly asked for cash payments from candidates who are deemed sincere, honest, and helpful. The point is that they do not regard taking money

---

[5]This concurs with the observation made by Pichai Kaosamran, et al., in *Karn Luak Tang Pattani Pi 2529* (The election in Pattani, 1986) (Bangkok: Foundation for Democracy and Development Studies, no date), 120. Those candidates who dump a lot of money are, often, those "stray dogs" (rich candidates from other places).
[6]Titinantana Vettivong, *Prutikam Lae Krabuankarn Ha Siang Kong Pu Samak Ti Mi Okat Dai Rub Luak Tang* [Campaigning Style of Front-running Candidates], M.A. essay, Thammasat University, Political Science, 1991.
[7]Sombat, *Thai Elections in Crisis*, 100.

from favored candidates as taking bribes and hence deserving of condemnation. Instead, they often reason, "What we have received is like getting some modest gifts upon purchasing quality merchandise."[8]

Clearly, current electoral practices in rural areas necessitate enormous funding. In addition to directly or indirectly buying voters, candidates have to make donations to local charities and finance the building or repair of infrastructure. Most burdensome is the astronomical sums of money paid to canvassers as work compensation, or, no less important, as resources through which the canvassers forge ties with potential voters. Career politicians with modest funds are therefore usually doomed to failure. The elected house and the cabinet alike have been overwhelmed in recent years by politicians who enjoy the strong support of the wealthy elite, or by politicians who have a solid financial base themselves. To be sure, the rural electorate has nothing but appreciation for the generosity of these politicians toward their villages. The urban middle class, however, is unhappy with the fact that a large number of politicians and their financiers are involved in illegal, organized crime–type businesses, or in enterprises that thrive on official permits, contracts, and concessions. For the middle-class public, electioneering degenerates into a convenient route for businesses to seek government protection or to plunder the coffers of the state.

However, as noted above, money is not the only thing needed to clinch an electoral victory. Winning candidates also need to stay close to the electorate in terms of taste, culture, and outlook. Thus, there is little room for victory by the favorite candidates of the middle class—highly educated and cosmopolitan candidates who are deft policymakers often fail to stay close enough to the voters in both a physical and a cultural sense. On the contrary, the candidates who are highly regarded by rural dwellers as reliable and understanding patrons often appear to the middle class as parochial in outlook, boorish in manner, and too uneducated to be competent lawmakers or cabinet members.

Thus, in the eyes of the middle class, democracy turns out to be the rule of the corrupt and the incompetent. Such a cynical perception of democracy has inevitably pushed the middle class into a dilemma. While they oppose authoritarian rule, they are not satisfied with the performance and integrity of elected governments. To understand fully the root

[8]Ibid., 171.

of the democratic impasse in Thailand, we must look at the middle
class's perception of politics as well as its place in Thai politics.

THE MIDDLE-CLASS ONSLAUGHT ON DEMOCRACY

By middle class is meant those socially situated between the wealthy
propertied classes and the poverty-stricken peasants, farmers, and workers. Put simply, they are city-based, middle-income persons employed in
managerial, executive, or technical positions in the private sector, as well
as self-employed professionals such as doctors, nurses, journalists, ar-
chitects, and lawyers. The root of this modern nonbureaucratic segment
of society can be traced back to the modernization efforts of the monarchy from last century, but it was only two decades ago that they became sizable and influential. The middle class made its presence felt in
1973 by rendering moral and financial support to the student-led uprising against the military that brought about first a civilian government
and then elections in 1975. This democratic period did not last long, as
it was soon badly shaken by a confrontation between the progressive
student movement and more conservative forces. In the face of this clash
a good many of the middle class, as described by Ben Anderson, turned
against the radical democratic vision of the students and embraced the
right wing, which vowed to bring back law and order.[9] In 1976, the top
of the military-officer corps—with the support and approval of the middle class—dealt a fatal blow to the fledgling democracy.

The post-1976 authoritarian period did not last longer than the post-
1973 democratic interregnum. Before long, people in most quarters,
particularly the urban middle class, became disgusted with the ultracon-
servatism and fanatical anticommunism of the reinstalled authoritarian
regime. In 1977 a group of moderate officers brought Thailand back to
the course of moderation. The same urban middle class that had felt
relieved upon hearing of the death of democracy in 1976 received with
relief the demise of an authoritarian regime a year later. The middle class
was uncertain which was the best way, democracy or authoritarianism.
As shown by the events of 1976–77, the middle class did not want to
live under military-authoritarian rule, but at the same time, was willing

[9]Ben Anderson, "Withdrawal Symptoms," *Bulletin of Concerned Asian Scholars* 10 (July–
September 1977), 13–30.

to allow military intervention as a means to remove a perceived threat from the Left.

After a period of transition, Thailand between 1978 and 1988 enjoyed a time of stabilized politics characterized by a viable power-sharing scheme between the military-bureaucratic elite on the one hand and elected politicians and nonbureaucratic forces on the other. To ensure political continuity, the ruling parties for eight years banded together behind Premier Prem Tinsulanonda, a retired army chief, well respected by the military. In return for his acceptance of the premiership, Prem— neither a party man nor an elected politician—was empowered to fill about one-fourth of the cabinet with his trusted aides, leaving the rest to the parties.

During this decade of semidemocracy, the middle class came to be even more prominent in size and political strength. In comparative perspective, among the five large nations of the Association of Southeast Asian Nations (ASEAN) at the opening of the 1980s, the relative size of the Thai middle class ranked fourth, after Singapore, Malaysia, and the Philippines. As Harold Crouch estimates, about 4.4 percent of the Thai population in 1980 belonged to the solid middle class (those classified as professionals, technicals, administratives, executives, or managerials); whereas the corresponding figures for Singapore, Malaysia, the Philippines, and Indonesia were 13.8 percent, 7 percent, 6.7 percent, and 3.2 percent, respectively.[10] However, by 1986 Thailand seemed to have surpassed the Philippines in this sense. Using the number of television sets, telephones, and cars per million population as indicators of the size of the middle class, Thailand ranked behind Singapore and Malaysia only. Of course, one may argue that the Philippines has been in steady decline over the last two decades; yet, the gap between Malaysia and Thailand from 1986 to 1991 seemed to have narrowed more so in all categories as well. (See Tables 9.1, 9.2, and 9.3.)

The stable politics and rapid economic growth of the 1980s were associated with a greater tolerance by the government of the assertive elements of civil society—business and the middle class in particular. This period also saw the spawning of a myriad of newly established media enterprises geared toward the growing consumer middle class. This, coupled with the newfound liberal stance of the state toward freedom of

---

[10]Harold Crouch, *Economic Change, Social Structure and the Political System in Southeast Asia* (Singapore: Institute of South East Asian Studies, 1985), 3.

Table 9.1. *Numbers of television sets, telephones, and cars per million population in the five major ASEAN nations, 1981*

	Singapore	Malaysia	Philippines	Thailand	Indonesia
Television sets	139,420	63,759	20,450	28,807	11,409
Telephones	292,500	31,772	9,039	8,693	3,921
Cars	63,573	48,703	9,808	6,481	4,362

Source: *Far Eastern Economic Review Asia Yearbook*, 1982.

Table 9.2. *Numbers of television sets, telephones, and cars per million population in the five major ASEAN nations, 1986*

	Singapore	Malaysia	Philippines	Thailand	Indonesia
Television sets	185,349	106,962	36,145	66,288	33,848
Telephones	415,385	59,494	15,181	13,068	4,925
Cars	85,107	87,975	6,267	17,803	5,862

Source: *Far Eastern Economic Review Asia Yearbook*, 1987.

Table 9.3. *Numbers of television sets, telephones, and cars per million population in the five major ASEAN nations, 1991*

	Singapore	Malaysia	Philippines	Thailand	Indonesia
Television sets	205,357	95,137	54,559	95,064[a]	50,584
Telephones	435,714	86,339	14,254	24,348	9,041
Cars	102,413	102,413	7,296	38,261	9,592

[a]Information for 1988.
Source: *Far Eastern Economic Review Asia Yearbook*, 1991.

the press, made the middle class major sources, as well as receivers, of media reports and opinions. The middle class, in alliance with the mass media, became strategic political actors, playing the role of public-opinion formers.

By the early 1980s the conservative wing of the middle class largely shed its concern about democracy falling prey to radical agitators. This was because the progressive movements in the towns and countryside, highly energetic in the mid-1970s, were forced to retreat into the background. For this reason, democracy might have been enthusiastically embraced by the entire middle class. This, however, was not the case. No sooner had the fear of democracy playing into the hands of the Left subsided than there loomed the threat that democracy would be trampled by demagogues and their local partners. Sections of the middle class became disillusioned with what they saw as the domination of the cabinet and parliament by corrupt and incompetent politicians who had bought their way to the pinnacle of power by vote buying in the rural constituencies. There were, however, segments of the middle class who did not share this adverse attitude toward electoral politics because they themselves became consummate politicians, managing to build reliable patron-client ties with the rural voters. The majority of the middle class, however, were of the view that democracy Thai-style was too flawed to produce a government possessing both integrity and competence.

Many of the more highly educated middle class were comforted by the belief that the existing system was not a full-blown democracy. Indeed, until mid 1989 the semidemocratic system was ruled by a military-technocratic alliance. Premier Prem in particular was widely noted for his personal integrity. The media and the middle class believed that, with Prem at the helm, corruption was bound to be limited from the top. Moreover, the frustration of having unqualified politicians in power was allayed by Prem's placing nonpartisan technocrats in key cabinet positions, as well as his generous delegation of decision-making authority to career officials at the Ministry of Finance, the National Economic and Social Development Board, and the Bank of Thailand.

When Prem stepped down in August 1989, he was succeeded by the elected Chatichai Choonhavan, leader of the Chat Thai Party. For the first time in more than a decade an entirely elected government took power. To some quarters of the middle class this was a cause for celebration; in other quarters there was grave and growing concern over the integrity and technical competence of the elected leaders. From the outset, members of Chatichai's cabinet were ridiculed for their scandal-prone behavior and, to a lesser extent, dubious administrative experience. An editorial in *Lak Tai*, a leading news magazine, boldly predicted that the new government would not last longer than eight months. The magazine also exposed a member of the cabinet who had been arrested for his involvement in illegal gambling dens; another cabinet member was charged with illegal logging; several others were suspected of re-

ceiving massive kickbacks for their delivery of lucrative official concessions or contracts to well-connected businessmen.[11]

Six months later, *Sayam Rath Weekly*, a magazine popular among the
urban educated, carried an article entitled, "Corruption: A Precondition
for a Coup."[12] The article featured opposition efforts to censure the
government for alleged corruption. By December 1989, more than a year
after the installation of the elected government, the negative mood of
the public escalated. *Sayam Rath Weekly* ran a front-page article entitled, "Corruption: A Bad Omen for the Chatichai Administration?" The
article claimed that even some cabinet members and leaders of the government coalition parties admitted that the prevailing criticism of the
integrity of high officials was not groundless.[13]

Distinguished intellectuals and academics, supposedly the mentors of
the middle class, also spoke out against corruption in interviews and
articles in the popular dailies and weeklies. Kukrit Pramoj, former prime
minister and respected intellectual, dealt the Chatichai government a
heavy blow when he sarcastically asked the government for a one-year
moratorium on corruption.[14] Likhit Dhiravegin, a leading scholar of
Thai politics at Thammasat University, dubbed the Chatichai government a "plutocracy," or worse than that, a "buffet cabinet," denoting
the free-for-all scrambling for kickbacks and commissions.[15] Pongpen
Sakuntapai, an expert on constitutional law at Chulalonkorn University,
went further, writing, "[These days] if we have no other alternative but
to choose between military authoritarianism and an elected government
headed by crooked businessmen-cum-politicians, then I would rather opt
for the former."[16]

On top of these scathing remarks were harsh critiques delivered by
nongovernmental-organization leaders, most of whom were from the
middle class. These reformers were not interested in exposing corruption.
Yet, they were depressed by what they saw as excessive pro-business,
pro-growth policies at the cost of excessive social and environmental
degradation. A social critic, Prawase Wasi, put it this way: "The heavy

[11]*Lak Tai*, August 25, 1988, 60.
[12]*Sayam Rath Weekly*, February 19–25, 1989.
[13]Ibid., December 17–23, 1989.
[14]Ibid.
[15]See his "Kharn Pattana Settakij Rabob Prachatippatai Rabob Ratchakarn Lae Kwam
Mankong Khong Chat Nai Nai Miti Bedsej," (The Economic Development, Democracy,
Bureaucracy, and National Security in the Total Perspective), *Warasarm Sangkomsat* (a
Chulalongkorn University journal), March-July 1990.
[16]*Ekalak*, October 12, 1990.

influx of businessmen into politics naturally makes the government
overly concerned with commerce and private businesses . . . and hardly
appreciative of the humanitarian, social and environmental sides of development."[17] Another middle-class onslaught by student activists oc-
cured late in 1990. Much publicized was the case of a Ramkamhaeng
University student setting himself on fire in October 1990. The ill-fated
student, together with scores of his colleagues, had demonstrated
against the Chatichai administration over the issue of corruption, and
he eventually made a suicide threat to corner the government into resignation. Later, in February 1991, just a few weeks before the Chatichai government was ousted in a coup, the Federation of Students of
Thailand held a series of sensational conferences on corruption with a
view to forcing Chatichai to address the widespread public distrust of
his government.

The mass media and the academic community were at one in seeing
a strong link between vote buying in rural areas and government corruption. In this view, either the need to finance vote buying necessitates
blatant corruption or, conversely, the taking of bribes from the private
sector or stealing from the coffers of the state once in power makes vote
buying worthwhile. Rural electoral behavior then became a subject of
press and academic attention. Newspapers and graduate theses went to
great lengths outlining a long list of vote-buying tactics and formulating
proposals to curb them. The middle-class notion that vote buying was
widespread in the countryside and that it was doing great harm to democracy was consistent with the decision in 1990 by the National Research Council to commission research on what was referred to as
deviant electoral behavior in Thailand.

For the media, the scholarly community, and their middle-class audience alike, electoral venality was to blame, not only for government
corruption and incompetence, but also for the rise of political inequality
in favor of the rich. Since it was almost impossible for qualified candidates with modest funds to clinch parliamentary seats, the middle class
reasoned, the system in the making was "the capitalist domination of
politics."[18] The urban middle class had come to the conclusion that an
election was at best an inadequate, at worst an invalid, source of regime

[17]*Sayam Rath Weekly*, August 20, 1989.
[18]Pornsak Pongpaew and Udom Piriyasingh, *Prutikam Karn Long 'Kanan Siang Luak Tang
Samachick Sapa Putan Rassadorn Ket Sam Changwat Konkaen* (Voting behavior: A
study of the general election of B. E. 2526, Khon Kaen Region) (Bangkok: National
Research Council, 1984), 189.

legitimacy because a great many voters were bribed and thus failed to exercise their rights with an independent and responsible judgment. In the eyes of the middle class, the citizens of Thailand, having been blatantly abused by the politicians as a vehicle for illegitimate power, were hardly "the sovereign of the state" as democratic theory would have them believe.[19] The politicians were seen not to be the representatives of the people, but merely successful vote buyers. Even a well-respected political scientist such as Khien Teerawit of Chulalongkorn University shared this condescending view of politicians. He wrote in a popular weekly, "Many leaders do things at whim, claiming that they have been popularly elected. These people have bought their way to power, have they not? Such being the case, is there any substantial difference between their way of power grabbing and the military seizure of power?"[20]

Apart from voicing their criticisms through the press and the academy, the middle class since the mid-1980s has registered its discontent through support of a political movement that promised to get rid of vote buying and corruption. In 1985 a new party, the Palang Dham, was launched by Chamlong Srimuang, a retired officer known for his exceptional integrity and devout Buddhist faith. Chamlong made his political debut in 1985, contending for the Bangkok governorship against candidates much better financed. Chamlong won an upset landslide victory through his solemn vow to "make politics virtuous." Chamlong's triumph was in a sense a middle-class protest against old-style politicians and a call for a new leadership more compatible with their values. In 1988 the Palang Dham contended in a general election for the first time and managed to win ten of thirty-seven seats in Bangkok. In 1989 Chamlong was reelected governor of Bangkok. The following year his party won an upset victory in a Bangkok by-election.

Middle-class opposition to scandalous elections and politics was in resonance with criticisms from the military of Thai-style democracy. From the early 1980s, military strategists had concluded that democracy had failed to take root in the country because of the greedy and irresponsible behavior of business-backed politicians. For the military leaders, politicians and political parties were simply business concerns in disguise. Early in 1983, the commander of the powerful Bangkok army division, in defending military efforts to halt the introduction of a new, party-based electoral system, admonished the public that the new system

---

[19]See Titinantana, "Campaigning Style," 59.
[20]*Sayam Rath Weekly,* November 18–24, 1990.

would work in favor of well-funded parties and politicians, and as a result, pave the way for so-called capitalists to march into parliament. The generals also had harsh words about the technical competence of politicians. To justify his demand for the retention of the authority of the government-appointed and military-dominated Senate beyond 1983, the commander-in-chief of the army said:

While [everywhere else] we have a great shortage of qualified persons, you have to admit that there are abundant human resources in the bureaucracy. [On the other hand], our politicians are still incompetent. How come we assign anyone [just because he is an elected politician] to a ministerial post overseeing the [more qualified] career officials? This is doomed to failure. Some [politicians] just do not have the qualifications needed for their jobs.[21]

In a keynote speech to high officials on the suppression of the communist movement, a strategist hailed as the brain of the army stated in the same vein:

Nowadays Thailand has two policies to solve national problems. There is the political party policy, proposed to the parliament by the government, and the policy of the National Army, the policy to defeat the communists. . . . But fact, reason, and theory prove that the National Army can solve national problems, namely to win over the CPT [Communist Party of Thailand], while the political party policy has not succeeded in solving any problems.[22]

These predominantly negative judgments of Thai democracy in the late 1980s were aggravated by disputes between the military command and the Chatichai administration. They first surfaced as conflicts between the armed forces and Chatichai's personal advisers. The crux of the issue was that the fiercely proud officers felt their dignity was being denied by being repeatedly criticized by disrespectful civilians. Mutual animosity increased when Premier Chatichai refused to dismiss from the cabinet an ardent critic of the military leadership. To add insult to injury, Chatichai reinstated an officer, a long-time foe of the incumbent military leadership, who had masterminded the last two failed coup attempts. Indignation alone, however, would not have resulted in the military's taking action against the government except for the solidarity among the leading generals who had graduated from the same class of the mil-

---

[21]Chalermkiat Piewnual, *Prachatippatai Bab Tai* (Democracy: Thai Style) (Bangkok: Thai Khadi Research Institute, 1990), 100–1.
[22]Chai-anan Samudavanija, "Democracy in Thailand," in Larry Diamond, Juan Linz, and S. M. Lipset, eds., *Democracy in Developing Countries: Asia* (Boulder: Lynne Reinner, 1989), 332.

itary academy. Miscalculation by Chatichai early in his administration had led him to appoint the so-called class five generals to all the top posts. The armed forces, not under a solid, well-coordinated command for several decades, were once again unified under a politically ambitious leadership.

To prepare for a head-on collision with the government, the military capitalized on the criticism by the middle class over the issue of vote buying and corruption. Military-controlled radio took up the anticorruption banner with enthusiasm, blaming not only the personalities but also the governance of the democratic system as the root of the problem. One general blasted politicians in a style reminiscent of leading academics:

Time and again you say you have been elected. You look down upon the appointees. Let me ask you: of the two parties—the elected and the appointed—who have been making trouble for the country? Further, in saying that you have been elected, could you swear to the gods, and to the press as well, that you have not bought votes?[23]

Frequently army-influenced radio commentaries called for a cabinet reshuffle or dismissal from the cabinet of those widely seen as crooks, mafiosi, and incompetents. At times the commentaries proposed structural changes, such as barring members of the House of Representatives from holding cabinet positions. The rationale behind the proposal was to discourage vote buying because the elected politicians would not be able to achieve executive positions with access to power and wealth. Public relations officers from army headquarters displayed thousands of letters urging the military to intervene and put an end to the problem of financial improprieties by the top politicians.

By the beginning of 1991 the situation was ripe for a putsch. The February 1991 coup met little, if any, resistance from the new institutions of civil society. The middle class, inadvertently in unison with the military, had prepared the nation for the demise of the Chatichai government. Though the coup may have been motivated by the illegitimate ambitions of key officers or by concerns shared by soldiers of all ranks about the corporate autonomy and interests of the military, what ensured the success of the coup was the middle classes' uneasiness with democracy. The middle class, while supportive of democracy as an ideal, was not at ease with the system in reality. Its fierce onslaught on the

[23]*Lak Tai*, November 12–18, 1990.

flaws of the system was taken by the military as a veiled request for a takeover of the government. Very few in the ranks of the middle class realized that they had in effect formed a pro-coup alliance with the military. The military leaders, on the other hand, seemed to be well aware of the existence of this informal alliance. Moreover, they held the strengthening of this alliance as pivotal to their successful handling of the postcoup situation.

THE MIDDLE CLASS AND THE RETURN OF DEMOCRACY

The junta admitted that the coup had pushed Thailand one step backward in terms of democratic aspiration but went on to defend its action as an indispensable means to put the future democratic house in order. While constitutionalism was temporarily abandoned, press censorship was not imposed, parties were not banned, and martial law was declared for only a few months. A special antigraft commission, with the power to freeze and seize assets, was established to investigate alleged corruption among top politicians. New ideas to curb vote buying and ensure the election of candidates acceptable to the middle class were advanced. Significant among these were proposals to abandon the system of dividing provinces into several small constituencies and instead to use entire provinces as constituencies; to require voters to cast their ballots for a single party slate; and to introduce proportional representation. Equally satisfying to the middle class was the junta's decision not to establish its own administration, but to install an interim government headed by Anand Panyarachun, a diplomat-turned-businessman noted for his ability and integrity.

All these steps made the coup leaders and their political program popular with the middle class. Several leading academics accepted an invitation from the military to draft a new constitution. Premier Anand's cabinet was hailed by the well educated and the business world as the best Thailand had ever had. A foreign journalist, echoing the euphoria of the Thai financial and business world, saw the February takeover as a "coup de technocrats" and described the new cabinet "a World Bank dream list."[24] Moreover, as promised by the junta, in less than a year Thailand was back on the road to democracy when another general election was called. Thousands among the middle-class ranks, with a

---

[24]Peter Janssen, "Coup de technocrats," *Asian Business* (April 1991): 16.

view to minimizing vote buying in the countryside, joined a government-sponsored poll watch committee. The committee made strenuous efforts to deter or suppress various forms of vote buying, including indirect ones such as offering free meals or gifts. The committee tried as well to instill among voters proper democratic principles for use when choosing a candidate. Villagers were repeatedly told that "to sell votes was to sell your own lives and your nation." At its extreme, the message conveyed to the country folk was that the only legitimate vote-getting act was to give public speeches, while the only proper voting consideration was the merit of the candidates' policies.

As was noted, the educated middle classes accepted military guardianship only as a means to stop democratic vices but not as an alternative government. Thus, the new constitution was examined closely to prevent the military from exploiting it to regain power after the next election. On the way to the election the junta leaders had to vow publicly several times not to assume power in the future. Despite these vows, the middle class regarded the resolve of the military to return to the barracks as at best ambivalent, at worst deceiving. Worrying to the middle class was that the new military-influenced constitution gave the junta-appointed Senate equal power with the House of Representatives. Moreover, a new party, Samakki Tham, was founded by trusted aides of the military. The new party was believed to have been established, along with the Senate, as a vehicle for the coup leaders to regain political control once the junta formally ceded power to the parliament. Ironically, the Samakki Tham Party was joined by a number of the patronage-oriented politicians of the Chatichai government who had only recently been removed from the list of corrupt politicians by the antigraft commission. The graft investigation, praised by the middle class at the outset, was now viewed as a military ploy to encourage old-style, corrupt politicians to join the junta at the next election.

To the middle class, confusion about the future of the generals became irritatingly clear by April 1992. The Samakki Tham Party was the largest party in the house after the March election. Together with several other patron-ridden parties, Samakki Tham formed a ruling coalition. Against the protests of the middle class and opposition parties, this coalition proceeded to nominate General Suchinda Kraprayoon, the head of the junta, for the premiership. To the dismay of the politically sophisticated public, Suchinda accepted the nomination in violation of his often-repeated vow never to do so. Suchinda's action triggered a deadly confrontation between the military and the middle class–led prodemocracy forces that forced the end of the military regime the next month. The military–middle class alliance to oppose patron politics had disintegrated by March. Intent on retaining power, the military turned to the politicians they had ousted in February 1991. In contrast to the middle class and their party leaders, the corruption-prone politicians chose to compromise with the military by allowing the generals to have a role in the postelection administration. Thus, by the end of March 1992, the middle class, true to its opposition to the patronage-ridden parties and their rural bases, turned against the military.

Following the ouster of the Suchinda government, new elections in a more democratic atmosphere were held in September. The politically conscious middle class reinvigorated its campaign for proper electoral behavior. Several middle-class groups, working closely with the poll watch committee, tried to mobilize villages to support qualified politicians. Vote selling or anything like it was condemned. In addition, the parties associated with Suchinda were stigmatized as satanic, while those on the prodemocracy side were hailed as angelic. But the rural electorate was largely unpersuaded, though the parties endorsed by the middle class gained a marginal victory. Several politicians clearly identified with the corruption of the Chatichai government were easily returned.

Although the middle class has been satisfied with the integrity of the postelection government, concerns arose about its competence and achievements soon after its inception. But should this situation change, a future temporary alliance between the middle class and the military cannot be ruled out. The Thai passage to democracy may not have ended.

RECONCILING TWO ASPIRATIONS:
A KEY TO DEMOCRATIZATION

Conventional wisdom has it that the democratization impasse in Thailand was caused by the endless quarrels between two political villains: the ambitious, dictatorial officers and the greedy, irresponsible politicians. While this line of thought contains elements of truth, the two villains do not operate in a political vacuum. Military leaders have found a base among the highly educated middle class, which holds electoral politics in low esteem. The politicians have risen to power through the support of the rural voters. In a more fundamental sense, then, the reason democracy failed to be firmly established over the past decade is to be found in the differing views and expectations of the middle class and the poor in the country over democracy, elections, and politicians.

For the rural electorate, democracy is valued not as an ideal, but as a mechanism to draw greater benefits from the political elite to themselves and their communities. To them, elections are very much local, not national, affairs, dealing with the exchange of votes for benefits of a non-policy type. Rural people do not regard their voting as separate from other sociocultural obligations. Rather, they feel obligated to use their votes as repayment to those who have been friendly, helpful, or generous in coping with daily difficulties while bringing progress and prosperity to their community. The rural voters do not expect abstract rewards such as laws, policies, or the public interest.

For the educated middle class, influenced by Western thought, democracy is a form of legitimate rule adopted by most civilized nations. Although it admits that democracy is rule by the people, the people should be knowledgeable and public-regarding. By knowledgeable, it means that voters must understand the implications of the policy positions of the candidates and use these as their criteria in casting their ballots. By public-regarding, the middle class means that voters should transcend personal or local interests. Voters must understand that elected politicians are representatives of the nation, as well as of their own constituencies. To the educated middle class, elections are means of recruiting honest and capable persons to serve as lawmakers and political executives, rather than a process through which voters get parochial and personal benefits. Voting decisions should be made independently of social, cultural, and especially financial obligations.

This gap in perceptions exists in societies other than Thailand. However, in Thailand this gap is linked to the frequent interruptions in the process of democratization. The issue hinges on the fact that a democratic system in Thailand allows the rural majority to choose the government. The middle class less determinately influences the composition of the house and cabinet. Yet the position of the middle class as a public-opinion former allows it to form a pro-coup alliance with the army and oust an elected government. Thus arises the paradox of contemporary Thai politics: Those who put a government into being and those who end its life are not the same people. Moreover, these two groups hold incompatible views of democracy. When the rural electorate chooses its candidates, it chooses patrons to look after its welfare and represent its communities. When the middle class evaluates the performance of the elected politicians, it looks for political executives or professional lawmakers who could operate effectively at the national level.

How can this paradox be resolved? Western-oriented, middle-class perceptions of a solution have been most frequently heard. Democracy is advanced as if there is only one proper version. The problem in Thailand is found in the "deviant" behavior of the rural electorate. The favorite solution is to "educate" the rural electorate with "proper" democratic norms so that it will vote for "qualified" individuals.

To discover a viable solution, however, it must be recognized that there can be several versions of democracy. The rural interpretation is as legitimate and rational as that of the urban middle class. In the first place, the rural electorate does not take financial inducements as the most important factor in its voting decision. Loyalty to local patrons is much more important, though money may strengthen this bond. But most of the money is expended between elections, maintaining established loyalties, not as a one-time bribe.[25]

Second, the rural electorate is not selfish or irresponsible toward the public interest. Candidates who advance the reputation and prosperity of their villages are always viewed in a good light. In the last two elections most candidates who garnered the largest number of votes were those noted for their ability to bring with them large budget allocations and public infrastructure projects. The middle class is certainly correct in saying that the champions of local interests may turn out to be villains at the national level. Yet, that is a different definition of the national interest; the urban middle class does not have a monopoly in defining the national interest.

To build a fortress for democracy, the middle class must bow to the popular mandate and never encourage military intervention again. It should, rather, form an alliance with the peasants or farmers. Such an alliance is conceivable, however, only if the middle class becomes reconciled to the democratic understanding and aspirations of the rural voters rather than trying to remake them. Above all, the middle class should realize that patronage-oriented voting is caused by the need of the rural poor to draw greater attention or benefits from the center to themselves. This goal should be accepted, while efforts are made to

---

[25]One of the few scholars to detect this was Nidhi Eosriwong, in "Suu Kai Siang Jing Ruu" (Is there really vote-buying and vote-selling?), *Matchichon Daily*, August 2, 1988, reprinted in *Cherng Ard Sangkom Tai* (*Footnote to Thai Society*) (Bangkok: Komol Keemtong Foundation, 1988).

change the means villagers employ to achieve it. Ideally, patron-client ties might be replaced by a more responsive and effective system of local government. On top of that, voters are to be convinced that principle- or policy-oriented voting brings them greater benefits than what they may get from local patrons.

To retain middle-class support for democracy, these people's desire for efficient and honest government must be acknowledged. Certain ideas floated by the junta or the middle-class public that were not im-plemented, such as constituency enlargement or proportional represen-tation, might be tried as a means to reduce the excessive influence of local patronage in elections. Finally, the middle class should be encour-aged to understand that democracy cannot be an ideal system as long as the huge socioeconomic gap between urban and rural areas persists. To realize fully its quest for a virtuous democracy, the middle class must actively support rural developments that will turn patronage-ridden vil-lages into small towns of middle-class farmers or well-paid workers.

10

The Cambodian elections of 1993: A case of power to the people?

KATE G. FRIESON

A veteran of Cambodian politics told a public rally in Phnom Penh in April 1993, "Cambodians have been eating the same soup for fourteen years. It's time to try another dish."[1] Enough voters agreed with him, 45 percent of the electorate, to vote out the incumbent Cambodian People's Party in favor of Funcinpec, a royalist party led by Prince Sihanouk's eldest son, Prince Ranariddh. Elections in Southeast Asia have rarely resulted in a change of government, but the national elections in Cambodia held in May 1993 were unique. This is because for the first time (earlier elections having been rigged) the votes of Cambodians were respected in United Nations–organized elections for the next government.

Obstacles to the elections were daunting: a legacy of twenty-two years of brutal war, autogenocide, and the massive destruction of almost all aspects of a civil society; the refusal of the well-armed and unforgiving Khmer Rouge faction to abide by the Paris Peace Agreements; armed banditry by soldiers; and organized suppression of the political opposition by the incumbent regime, which led to the death or injury of hundreds of persons in the months leading up to the elections.

In keeping with Southeast Asian patterns of social relations, patron-clientalism was also a formidable obstacle to voter autonomy and a challenge to the promise of the United Nations Transitional Authority in Cambodia (UNTAC) of free and fair elections. Political patrons used

---

[1] The speaker was In Tam, former deputy prime minister in the Lon Nol regime, presidential candidate in the 1972 elections, and leader of the Democratic Party.

the standard strategies to force obedience from their clients: payoffs, threats, violence, and promises. And the mushrooming of political parties meant that many new and competing patronage systems were established, creating a political environment that Cambodians often referred to as *smok smanh*, or tiresomely complex and confusing. In spite of these apparent constraints, and against almost all predictions, 90 percent of the Cambodian electorate turned out to vote in what was perhaps the most democratic election in Southeast Asian history. How can this be explained?

Any explanation must explore the issues of voter autonomy and patron-clientalism in relation to what can be described as the reemergence of a civil society in Cambodia. As UNTAC's mission transformed a one-party state into a multiparty political system, the relationship between state and society was considerably loosened, allowing the reemergence of independent social, political, and economic organizations, rudiments of a civil society. The positive and negative impacts of this development on political patronage and the range of responses by voters are discussed next, and then the meaning and consequences of the elections are considered.

BACKGROUND TO THE ELECTIONS: UNTAC AND THE PARIS PEACE AGREEMENT

After more than twenty years of war (1970–1991), the Agreement on a Comprehensive Political Settlement of the Cambodian Conflict, commonly known as the Paris Peace Agreement, was signed on October 23, 1991, by four Cambodian factions, their foreign backers—Vietnam, China, the United States, and Thailand—and seventeen other countries committed to supporting the establishment of a United Nations presence in Cambodia. The agreement was designed to secure peace in Cambodia through the establishment of UNTAC, with authority for civil administration, human rights, elections, civil police, the military, repatriation, and rehabilitation. Under the agreement, Cambodia's sovereignty was represented by the Supreme National Council (SNC), composed of representatives of the four political factions, under the chairmanship of Prince Norodom Sihanouk. In turn, the SNC delegated to UNTAC "all powers necessary" to implement the agreement. In practice this meant that UNTAC attempted to exercise direct control over the administrative structures of each of the four factions in the areas of foreign affairs, national defense, finance, public security, and information.

UNTAC's goal was to organize and hold free and fair elections to allow Cambodians to elect a constituent assembly, which in turn would draw up a new constitution, and then transform itself into a legislative assembly and government. Such a government was successfully formed in September 1993.

At the time of the Paris agreement, most of Cambodia was governed by the socialist regime led by Hun Sen and Chea Sim (known as the SoC or State of Cambodia), which had come to power in 1979 after the Vietnamese invasion had put an end to the murderous government of the Khmer Rouge. Throughout the 1980s, in opposition to their regime and their Vietnamese backers were three political factions that combined to form the Coalition Government of Democratic Kampuchea (CGDK) in 1982. The CGDK was based on the Thai-Cambodian border, supported by the United States, Thailand, and China, and composed of the Khmer Rouge, led by Pol Pot, militarily the strongest faction, but feared and hated by many Cambodians for its conduct during its rise to power; Funcinpec, a political and military movement to restore the monarchy of Prince Sihanouk, who had ruled Cambodia between 1953 and 1970; and the Khmer People's National Liberation Front, a faction-ridden group of older military and political leaders who had been prominent in the Khmer Republic of 1970–5, led by former prime minister Son Sann. These three factions fought against the Hun Sen government and the Vietnamese Army from 1982 until the signing of the Paris agreement.

The Paris agreement was reached after several years of brokered negotiations among the Cambodian factions. But at the end of the cold war in 1989, following the withdrawal of Vietnam's military forces from Cambodia and a protracted military stalemate between the armed forces of the SoC and the CGDK, the treaty was signed.

With the exception of the Khmer Rouge, all factions involved in the Paris agreement participated in the elections through their own political parties. Representing the SoC was the Cambodian People's Party (CPP) led by Hun Sen. The royalist Funcinpec was transformed into a political party known by the same name; the Khmer People's National Liberation Front split into two political wings, the Buddhist Liberal Democratic Party (BLDP), led by Son Sann, and the rival Liberal Democratic

Party (LDP), led by Son Sann's military associate Sak Sutsakhan. Joining these four main parties, sixteen other political parties competed in the elections. Ranariddh's Funcinpec won slightly more than 45 percent of the vote, edging out the CPP, with 37.75 percent of the vote, by 7.25 percent. The BLDP came in third with just over 3 percent of the vote. In terms of seats, Funcinpec won 58 out of 120; the CPP, 51; the BLDP, 10; and a breakaway group from Funcinpec, the Moulinaka Neak TaSou (Strugglers) for Freedom Party, received enough votes to win 1 seat.

Before 1993, elections played little part in determining who held power in Cambodia. They did not represent the *demos* in determining the *polis*. None was organized in what could be called a free and fair manner, nor did any result in a change of government. Rather, elections were a method of containing political opposition with the pretense of a contest for power. The first election, in 1946, was contested by two main parties and several independent candidates, and had an impressive 60 percent turnout of voters. The popular Democratic Party, which died out in the mid-1950s but resurfaced with In Tam as its leader in 1992, won fifty of sixty-seven seats in the Consultative Assembly. David Chandler wrote, "In this election, as in others over the next twenty years or so, many peasants voted as they were told to vote by people whom they habitually obeyed."[2] But real power was denied to the party since the Consultative Assembly was subservient to the French colonial government, enjoyed few connections with the economic elite, and was disdained by King Sihanouk. In the following election, held in 1951, the Democrats won fifty-five of seventy-eight seats. Incensed by their popularity, Sihanouk plotted a coup d'état with French support and assumed the premiership himself in 1952.

The next election, that of 1955, was part of the terms of the 1954 Geneva agreement on Indochina. Sihanouk formed a political movement called the Sangkum Reastre Niyum (People's Socialist Community) to compete with the other parties. After a violent campaign during which several opposition party workers were killed, their supporters harassed, and ballot boxes disappeared, Sihanouk's Sangkum candidates won most of the seats in the assembly.[3] The elections of 1958, 1962, and

---

[2]David Chandler, *A History of Cambodia*, 2d ed. (Boulder: Westview Press, 1993), 175.
[3]See David Chandler, *Brother Number One: A Political Biography of Pol Pot* (Boulder: Westview Press, 1992), 51.

1966 were similarly orchestrated events.[4] Sihanouk squashed his political opponents, some of whom ran to the maquis to join the Khmer Rouge communist movement, and ruled over the Cambodians, whom he called his children, until he was ousted from power in 1970. Only one election—that of 1972—took place without the involvement of Prince Sihanouk. In an equally rigged manner and with a voter turnout of merely 30 percent, General Lon Nol was confirmed in office.[5]

What, then, did elections really mean to the Cambodians who participated in them? For young and energetic organizers of political parties, the elections that took place before Cambodia regained independence from France were a legal framework through which to contest the authority of the monarchy and to negotiate what they believed were better terms of independence than the king was willing or able to deliver. For Cambodian peasants, who, then as now, formed the overwhelming majority of voters, the elections were not as much political events in which to participate as they were a type of ritual in which support for their patrons was given in exchange for security and protection through the promise of independence or monetary rewards.

The 1993 election departed from those of the past in three important ways. The first is that all stages of the election—from voter registration to counting the ballots—were organized and conducted by UN personnel and Cambodian staff under their direction. This did not prevent political hopefuls from trying to gain victory through fraudulent or unscrupulous means, but the United Nations tried to expose and neutralize such practices. Second, the election was designed as a political solution to the civil war. The massive voter turnout indicated how seriously Cambodians viewed the importance of their act. And the virtually fraud-free polls gave voters leverage over their patrons they had never had before: a secret ballot. Third, the election symbolized the transition from one-party rule to a pluralist political system. With politics no longer the exclusive sphere of the state, there was an explosive growth of political parties whose activities challenged existing power relations between state and society. All of these factors combined to give the electorate unprecedented authority in the outcome of the election.

---

[4]David Chandler, *The Tragedy of Cambodian History: Revolution, War and Politics since 1945* (New Haven: Yale University Press, 1991), 95–8, 120–2, 153–5.
[5]William Shawcross, *Sideshow: Nixon, Kissinger and the Destruction of Cambodia*, rev. ed. (New York: Simon and Schuster, 1987), 234. The voter turnout figure comes from Donald P. Whitaker, et al., *Area Handbook for the Khmer Republic (Cambodia)* (Washington, D.C.: American University, Foreign Area Studies Division, 1973), 199.

PATRONAGE, HIERARCHY, AND *KHSAE ROO-YIA'* (NETWORKS)

Patronage, the dyadic ties of exchange so central for understanding Cambodian social and political structures, includes ritual, economic, and political elements.[6] One entrée into the world of patronage is through the *bong p'on* (older kin–younger kin) relationship to which every Khmer belongs. Since almost all relationships in Cambodian society are hierarchical, a person's status in relation to others is determined by age and gender. The generic term for elder kin, *bong*, is always used in relation to its counterpart for younger kin, *p'on*. In its crudest form, the *bong p'on* relationship fits in with the standard concept of patronage, in that elders in Cambodian society are expected to look after their younger kin and protect them. In return, the younger kin provide services and labor to their elders. These relationships are not static but in a state of flux.

Alongside the *bong p'on* relationship, other hierarchical terms are used by Cambodians to define their social status in a hierarchy of relationships. Cambodian communities, whether urban or rural, are composed of what Eric Wolf has called "lopsided friendships," dyadic relations between people of unequal wealth, power, or access to power.[7] In Cambodian villages, typical patrons might be village elders who have ties to district and provincial government authorities, soldiers, bandits, teachers, merchants, and the most wealthy in the community. Although many relationships can be described accurately as patron-client, other hierarchical relationships do not fit the model. Buddhist monks, for example, are theoretically outside the patronage system since they do not expect to receive in return for what they give. Relating patronage and hierarchy, Judy Ledgerwood has written:

Khmer society is organized around followers attaching themselves to persons of higher status. These patrons then take care of their followers. The groups which form around individual patrons are not united as groups, but linked by personal ties to the individual patron. These relationships are constantly in a state of flux. People can change from one patron to another, or may use different patron

---

[6]See May Mayko Ebihara, "Svay, a Khmer Village in Cambodia" (Ph.D. dissertation, Columbia University, 1968); Eveline Poree Maspero, *Etudes sur les rites agraires des Cambodgiens*, 3 volumes (Paris: Mouton, 1962–1969); and Judy Ledgerwood, "Changing Khmer Conceptions of Gender: Women, Stories and the Social Order" (Ph.D. dissertation, Cornell University, 1990).

[7]Eric Wolf, "Kinship, Friendship, and Patron-Client Relations," in M. Banton, ed., *The Social Anthropology of Complex Societies* (London: Tavistock, 1966), 1–22.

contacts to accomplish different specific tasks. Similarly patrons may rise or fall depending on whether or not they can really provide the goods and services that their clients need.[8]

Previously, status and prestige, two essential elements of hierarchy, were defined by age, gender, and proximity to the monarchy.[9]

In its simplest terms, political hierarchy began with royalty and worked down through strata of government and military officials in geographical layers from the palace to the province, district, subdistrict, and village. Peasants constituted the lowest social stratum, along with unskilled laborers, fishermen, and craftsmen. The egalitarian characteristic of Cambodian villages in the 1950s and 1960s, which stemmed from a low land-person ratio and the fact that most peasants owned enough land for their subsistence, suggested that peasants had a measure of independence from their patrons. By the late 1960s, however, this had changed. The growth of capitalism, a rural economy financed by plantations, and a huge black market for rice exports to Vietnam combined to squeeze more peasant households off the land.[10] Traditional systems of political patronage broke down after 1970 when the monarchy ended, the Vietnam war spread to Cambodia, and the Khmer Rouge began fighting its way to power.[11] With the return of Prince Sihanouk to Cambodia in 1991 and the reinstatement of Buddhism as the state religion, pre-1970 markers and status came back into use.

The status-free society that Pol Pot sought to engineer after 1975 attempted to end all elements of patronage and hierarchy that defined social relationships in Cambodian society. People were told to change their use of language in order to eliminate hierarchically marked pronouns and terms of address, as well as references to royalty and the Buddhist *sangha* (monkhood).[12] The *angka* (organization), as the Com-

[8]Judy Ledgerwood, *Analysis of the Situation of Women in Cambodia* (Phnom Penh: UNICEF, 1992), 4.

[9]Wealth alone was no guarantee of prestige or high status, but increasingly became so after the monarchy ended in 1970, when military titles, a new marker of high status, could be bought.

[10]Hou Yuon, "The Peasantry of Kampuchea: Colonialism and Modernization," in Ben Kiernan and Chantou Boua, eds., *Peasants and Politics in Kampuchea 1942–1981* (Armonk, N.Y.: M. E. Sharpe, 1982), 69–86.

[11]Although many district and subdistrict officials switched their allegiance to Lon Nol after the coup, many feared for their lives at the hands of the royalist rural population. See Kate Frieson, "The Impact of Revolution on Cambodian Peasants" (Ph.D. dissertation, Monash University, 1991), 60–2.

[12]See John Marston, "Language Reform in Democratic Kampuchea" (M. A. thesis, University of Minnesota, 1985).

munist Party was known by its members, replaced all forms of authority from the old society, from parents to nuclear families, the monkhood, and the monarchy. The *angka* was not only the new patron, it was also the new parent. In reality, of course, old hierarchies and patrons were merely replaced by new ones.

Pol Pot's *angka* was replaced in 1979 by the party of the People's Republic of Kampuchea, the forerunner of the SoC, led by Hun Sen. Though not as cruel as the communists, the new authority penetrated deeply into the lives of the people. The party's cadre and secret police were well organized and watchful of acts of political disloyalty, especially contacts with resistance groups on the Thai-Cambodian border.

Regardless of regime type—monarchical, republican, communist, or socialist—there is a strong impulse toward a hierarchical system of social and political relationships with a big man manipulating various *khsae roo-yia'* or networks.[13] *Khsae roo-yia'* in politics operate along patronage lines in that clients are loyal to party leaders or party big men rather than to the party itself. Political leaders at all levels of the party network down to the village level try to maintain the loyalty of their supporters through a variety of means, depending on the needs of their clients. Party networks are hierarchical, with each patron responsible for a group of clients. To join a political party, for example, it is necessary to have a patron, someone who is already a member who will vouch for the new member and assist his or her political aspirations. Likewise, it is invariably the case that voters will not support a party to which they have no personal connections. Party leaders are patrons in the sense that, in return for the services rendered by clients in the upper echelons of the party, they promise to put their clients in positions whereby they are patrons to those lower in rank. Political parties can be viewed as being constructed from a series of related *khsae* or strings emanating from the top leadership and working down to the lowest rank at the village level. "If ones does not belong to a *khsae*," the saying goes, "it is impossible to do anything." This was abundantly clear after the election, when huge crowds of *khsae* members formed outside the offices of the winning Funcinpec party in Phnom Penh to try to cash in on their support by gaining a job in the new government. Those less well connected paid for the

---

[13]The following discussion is based on the author's observations during a thirteen-month period working for UNTAC.

opportunity to join a political network, hoping that their new patron would find them a position suitable to their rank.

It was within this political environment that UNTAC came to Cambodia promoting the idea of a free and fair election through the secret ballot and voter autonomy. Cambodians, however, had different perceptions of UNTAC.

THE NEW PATRON AND
THE REEMERGENCE OF CIVIL SOCIETY

When UNTAC arrived in March 1992, it was viewed by many Cambodians as possibly the richest patron in centuries, having a U.S.$2 billion budget at its disposal. Some people viewed UNTAC with reverence, quoting Buddhist scriptures that predicted "white elephants with blue hats" would enter the kingdom to end the long war and bring peace and prosperity. Blending the organization with its staff, people referred to UNTAC personnel as UNTACs.

At the time of the arrival of UNTAC, many Cambodians had high expectations of these UNTACs who drove around in large white cars and spent money freely. During a trip to the western edges of Siem Reap province, in a moderately wealthy subdistrict town, I introduced myself to a group of villagers at the local market. After smiling politely and listening deferentially, a women in her seventies blurted out, "So when are you going to fix this road?" "UNTAC is not here to fix roads," I replied, watching the old woman's face crinkle into confusion. Such exchanges occurred across the country. If these UNTACs were not going to build new roads and hospitals, treat the sick, educate the young, and pay teachers and soldiers, what were they going to do?

UNTAC became the new *angka* and thus a potentially powerful patron. But it took many months before the relationship between UNTACs and Cambodians was mutually understood. There were several reasons for this. UNTAC was seen by many as another familiar authority figure—a big, bad bully whose power was viewed as exploitative, burdensome, and feared. The disrespectful, reckless behavior of some UN personnel increased popular resentment against UNTAC as a group of freewheeling, fast-spending, prostitute-seeking soldiers and civilians. On the other hand, a certain amount of bad behavior is expected from authority figures. UNTACs' abuses were tolerated to a large extent because UNTAC was rich, and with the right connections, profit could be made from the new patron-client relationship. Also, many Cambodians hoped that UNTAC could bring peace to their shattered country, and they decided to wait until after the elections before making permanent judgments.

UNTAC, for its part, performed its role of patron well by employing hundreds of thousands of persons to be interpreters, drivers, office workers, mechanics, builders, and the like. UNTACs also rented houses and apartments and bought expensive goods in the markets, injecting millions of dollars into the economy. Housing prices soared, and many people got rich on the dividends.

But UNTAC's impact on the polity was perhaps more profound. It promised to hold free and fair elections. To help accomplish this goal, UNTAC encouraged the development of institutions, independent of the state, that would generate political debate and provide forums for public access to political ideas and activities. UNTAC, in effect, attempted to pry the state from the society long enough that institutions such as the national media association, human rights organizations, and the twenty registered political parties could take life and exist separately from the state. This process, imperfect as it was and strongly opposed by the SoC apparatus, reflected the forced reemergence of a civil society such as had not been in evidence since the early 1970s, if then.

The imposition of UNTAC's authority over the administrative structures of the SoC was one of the unique features of the UN mission in Cambodia. No other UN peacekeeping mission has attempted to intervene so deeply in the political life of a society. In some senses, UNTAC was the state, and its mandate was to encourage a multiparty political environment guided by fair play rules of conduct and equal access to the media.

UNTAC's administration was physically separate from that of the SoC, Funcinpec, and the BLDP within their zones. The Khmer Rouge never allowed UNTAC access to its areas. Eighteen thousand military and two thousand civilian UNTACs established their presence throughout the country and began the task of demobilizing soldiers, removing land mines, registering voters, conducting civil-education campaigns, patrolling the districts, and repatriating refugees. Civil administration, electoral, police, and military offices were set up in the provinces. Fifty thousand electoral workers were hired and trained to help organize and run the election, working under the authority of UNTAC electoral workers based at the district level. The UNTAC electoral unit hired Cambodians to undertake the first mass education campaign in the country on the meaning and practice of free and fair elections. Almost every Cambodian village was reached. As villagers gathered in front of a generator-powered television, UNTAC produced programs that explained in Khmer what UNTAC was and what the elections were about. A weekly UNTAC soap serial became extremely popular around the country, and it was common to hear people in Phnom Penh discussing an episode the day after its showing. UNTAC radio and television were the only sources that "spoke the truth," Cambodians often said. They were also the only source of neutral information about activities such as voter registration, the voting process, the election law, or the code of conduct for political parties and their followers. In an effort to redress the balance of the CPP-dominated airwaves, UNTAC radio and television also produced an equal-time-equal-access program to allow the registered political parties to present their ideas and platforms in five- and ten-minute programs using UNTAC facilities.

Under UNTAC's umbrella, hundreds of new political networks fanned out across the country, many stemming from the Thai border, where the resistance factions had been based for more than a decade. Dozens of new parties sprang to life after their leaders returned from France, the United States, and Canada, where they had emigrated as refugees. With money from overseas members, a trickle of local contributors, and willing landlords, hundred of party offices, bedecked with flags and banners, were opened.

The CPP's reaction to this competition was swift and uncompromising. Using its advantages as the incumbent, the SoC rallied its administrative structures and civil servants, including teachers, soldiers, and police, to work for the CPP. Those who refused were told they would lose their jobs. Mass CPP membership drives descended into factories, schools, and even people's homes, offering voters little choice but to register with the party. CPP leaders boasted that the party with the most members would win the election, a claim rejected on the UNTAC soap opera with the message that party members did not have to vote for their own party. There was no separation between the party and the state, though the Paris agreements specifically stated that separation was important for the fairness of the elections.

More menacing was the CPP's organized thuggery, whose protagonists, known as reaction forces (*kamlang protegam*), worked secretly with SoC police to thwart legal political opposition to the CPP. The party used its networks throughout the country, down to the village level. One early attempt to poll support by the CPP involved the confiscation of hundreds of thousands of voter registration cards by local party officials in Battambang, Kompong Cham, Kandal, Takeo, Prey Veng, and Siem Reap. Voters' names and registration card serial numbers were recorded and entered onto a CPP database, inspiring the fear that the party would monitor their votes. So many people were without voter cards that UNTAC's electoral unit designed a tendered vote system at polling stations whereby voters reregistered, voted, and had their votes counted separately in Phnom Penh after their registration was corroborated on the central voters' list in the capital.

The often devious and violent campaign tactics of the CPP—grenade attacks on opposition party offices, beatings, abductions, harassment, and threats—contrasted to the timid, by-the-book campaign styles of most of the political parties that ran in the election. These were unarmed, unprotected, and too small to counter the CPP. For its part, the CPP viewed opposition parties as the enemy, which made accepting the political opposition a traitorous act. Villagers complained that CPP cadres were bullying, but the cadres explained their actions as dutiful and patriotic. UNTAC investigators concluded that the pattern of attacks pointed to a coordinated plan ordered from the top echelons of the SoC/CPP. Political violence peaked in December but continued throughout the official campaign period, leading to more than 200 politically motivated killings between January and May 1993.

In the meantime, UNTAC continued its programs to prepare the electorate. Close to half a million radios were distributed, and even in remote areas groups of villagers listened to broadcasts by UNTAC, the Voice of America, Funcinpec, Khmer Rouge, or SoC radio. The SoC-controlled media gave favored access to the CPP, which attacked both Funcinpec and the BLDP. The CPP slogan that "Funcinpec is Khmer Rouge" was heard so often that gullible people repeated it. The opening up of alternative sources of information let people know what the opposition was thinking, and this was widely welcomed, probably to the detriment of the SoC/CPP message.

ELECTION ISSUES, PATRONAGE, AND VOTER AUTONOMY

Villagers' thoughts about the election in the provinces of Battambang, Takeo, Kandal, and Siem Reap appear to reflect a larger pattern per-

ceived across Cambodia. I concluded, on the basis of a number of interviews, that villagers were not generally prevented from attending
political rallies held by the opposition parties; they easily regurgitated
the CPP line that the Khmer Rouge was the major threat to their security
and therefore the main issue in the election; and they were sufficiently
skeptical of the CPP claim that Funcinpec and "Grandpa Son Sann"
were the Khmer Rouge to seek alternative views on the opposition parties.

By the middle of the campaign period, when the four major parties
lost some of their timidity and dared to hold political rallies at the village, district, and provincial levels (the smaller parties were able to do
less), these six election issues, in descending order of importance, were
articulated by the voters: (1) the return of the Khmer Rouge, (2) continuation of the civil war, (3) the corruption of state officials, (4) widespread lawlessness and banditry, (5) crushing poverty, and (6) the return
of the Vietnamese.

Cambodians of all classes and political persuasions expressed fear of
the return of the Khmer Rouge. This fear was voiced often and vigorously even in areas such as Takeo, which were long under SoC control
and far from the areas of Khmer Rouge attack, as well as in territory
under Funcinpec and BLDP control nearer the Khmer Rouge base areas.
The continuation of the civil war was a related concern. Older people
despaired at having had their children forcibly drafted into the SoC national army (Cambodian People's Armed Forces) over the past fourteen
years. Younger men and women complained that all they have known
is war. Children are steeped in this view. "Cambodia is full of misery,
always at war," was an often-repeated refrain.

The voters wanted to determine which party would bring peace to the
country with the least conflict. The CPP made clear that its solution was
to expand the army and defeat the Khmer Rouge. After twenty-two years
of warfare, and with the arrival of alternative solutions, this option
was no longer favored. This was especially the case after the arrival of
UNTAC and its promise of peace via the cantonment of soldiers, dis-
armament, and national elections.

The challenge for Funcinpec, the BLDP, and the LDP was to combat
the CPP's message that only it could resolve the issue of the Khmer
Rouge. CPP banners carried slogans such as "a vote for the CPP is a
vote for the party that saved us from Pol Pot." CPP officials warned
voters that "other parties were cooperating with the Khmer Rouge."

Funcinpec and the BLDP countered these allegations by reminding voters that they had been aligned with the Khmer Rouge up to 1991 in order to fight the CPP and Vietnamese hegemony. They also reminded voters that Hun Sen and Chea Sim were themselves former Khmer Rouge.

Perhaps the most persuasive counter to the CPP were appeals that only national reconciliation and an end to bitter back-stabbing by political opponents could establish peace and political stability. Funcinpec campaigned most vigorously on this platform. The party's call for negotiated peace with the Khmer Rouge after the elections had a wide appeal.

Along with peace, the notion that a vote for Funcinpec was a vote for Sihanouk brought support to that party. Sihanouk, as the big man (*neak tom*) of Cambodian politics for five decades, was the most important figure in Cambodia, even though he did not stand in the elections. His political style emphasized his natural right to rule as heir to a lineage that he claimed could be traced back to Angkor. His return to Cambodia in 1991 was interpreted by many Cambodians as having a religious significance, as only a king has the powers necessary to officiate over the Buddhist ceremonies marking the beginning and end of the planting seasons, the day of the dead, New Year, and other Buddhist festivals and ceremonies that have defined the Cambodian universe for centuries. His return seemed to promise the end of all of Cambodia's troubles as witnessed by the Phnom Penh gold sellers, who linked the event with increased land prices, a stable currency, and greater economic confidence.

The reverence and duty that many older Cambodians have toward Sihanouk clearly increased the support received by Funcinpec. As one old woman explained, "Sihanouk is our father, and wouldn't a good daughter vote for her father?" Funcinpec made clear its own close support for Sihanouk. As its July 15, 1992, *Bulletin* put it:

FUNCINPEC favours royalism more than any other party. . . . FUNCINPEC is a child which follows the Khmer tradition of listening to its father. . . . Our nation's father says the Khmer are having problems and not to add to these [the question of] royalism, which could bring further disruption. . . . The king also says wait until Khmers have independence, peace and territorial integrity then it will be up to him to decide.

This style of politics had been forbidden since the 1970s, and its references to royalism and the use of kin terms had enormous appeal. Support for Funcinpec began to increase when dozens of its offices around the country bearing pictures of Sihanouk were attacked with grenades by angry SoC supporters. The victims of the attacks were seen as heroes for bravely speaking out on long-forbidden topics such as corruption, human rights, political prisoners, the sale of public lands, and the like.

The split among voters over the pull of Sihanouk was reflected in a visit to the home of some elderly women. Taking Funcinpec leaflets from their pockets, they said, "We have chosen our party now," and laughed nervously as if to test my reaction. When one said, "We are afraid of the Yuon [Vietnamese] taking over, and this is the party that can solve that problem," a neighbor on the stairs shouted, "They [Funcinpec] said they would solve all the problems, but they don't say how." A few men in their thirties said that only the old women would vote for Funcinpec because of the lure of Sihanouk. "As for us," they countered, "we don't want the Khmer Rouge to come back, so we'll stick with Hun Sen." This one-room conversation seemed to reflect the countrywide pattern of support split between Funcinpec and the CPP.

The third issue that shaped voters' views was that of corruption. SoC abuses of power and excessive corruption among civil servants, police, soldiers, and other state officials had become a bitter issue, even among those involved in the government. School teachers had not been paid in months and begged UNTAC to intervene. Soldiers turned to banditry in several provinces to feed themselves. Civil servants in Phnom Penh stopped showing up for work. The government appeared on the verge of collapse. But Hun Sen, Chea Sim, Prince Chakrapong, and other CPP candidates continued to campaign across the country, distributing rice, cloth, salt, and money. Concern for the return of the Khmer Rouge, however, balanced against many of these complaints.

As both the Pol Pot and Hun Sen regimes were identified with communism, their opposition in the election often posed the issue of the vote as one between communism and freedom. SoC and the CPP were identified with communism, whereas Funcinpec and the other parties founded in Thailand, France, and the United States represented freedom. This simple dichotomy found a resonance with many. I was often told that the power of the communist cadres over the little people had no precedent in Cambodian history. "During the Sihanouk era," they explained, "we were left alone to grow rice, bring up our children, practice Buddhism, and do what we liked." In contrast, under Pol Pot and Hun Sen, "We had no freedom to move about, farm as we wished, and pray to Buddha." It became apparent weeks before the election that in spite of the CPP media campaign to convince the electorate that it was the only party that could protect the electorate from the return of the Khmer Rouge, there were grave reservations on the part of many voters about the continuation of Hun Sen's rule.

Of all the election issues, the fear of the Vietnamese, while seemingly least pressing, was a concern nonetheless. The CPP was blamed for allowing the Vietnamese to "take all our fish to Vietnam and log our forest bare." But most Cambodians conceded that, with the exception of Phnom Penh, the Vietnamese population was small and powerless. But for Funcinpec and the BLDP, Vietnamese immigrants represented an ominous threat to Cambodian sovereignty, and their campaign platforms repeatedly called for the repatriation of all Vietnamese not born in Cambodia.

By the end of the campaign, millions of voters had attended meetings of the CPP, the BLDP, the LDP, and Funcinpec. In the districts and subdistricts, CPP meetings were far more numerous than those of the other political parties because of the advantage the party enjoyed as the incumbent. As was explained to me at a CPP rally in Kandal province, the numbers attending the rallies for Hun Sen's party were higher than for the others "because the party has cadres in every place, and they tell the people to go to the meetings." Villagers often said that crowd numbers did not necessarily correspond to support for the parties. In some cases, villagers were prevented by CPP cadres from attending BLDP and Funcinpec rallies. The smaller parties were less able to organize rallies, not only because of their more meager resources, but also in some cases because of intimidation.

Calls to suspend, call off, or postpone the election were widely heard within the electoral component of UNTAC. Attacks on UNTAC personnel led to the demoralization of Cambodians and UN personnel in the months prior to the balloting. No one was sure whether the elections could even be held in such circumstances. In Phnom Penh, home owners locked their gates before sunset, and only the very brave ventured out into the abandoned streets. Armed bandits shot motorcycle drivers and stole their machines. People began to hoard rice and other dry goods a week before the election, fearing that the polls would spark violence and renewed warfare. In the sleepy district town where I was based on the eve of the election, the mood was tense. Villagers spoke in whispers around their small fires. The town's bulletin board had only the remains of political party leaflets with defaced and torn images. SoC soldiers rode past on motorcycles with AK–47 rifles at their sides. No one in UNTAC knew for certain whether the Cambodians would vote.

Yet, on the first day of polling the turnout was impressive, with crowds pressing into the polling stations at dawn. By the third day of polling, more than 90 percent of registered voters had turned out despite threats from the Khmer Rouge that it would attack polling stations, as well as widespread fears that SoC had special eyes and ears in the polling booths recording people's votes. UNTAC's campaign promising the secrecy of the ballot was, in the end, a more persuasive message. The Khmer Rouge, for reasons still not entirely clear, decided against attacking the polling stations.[14] Indeed, the Cambodian election went ahead with remarkably few incidents of violence.

The CPP appeared confident it would win. But after the second day of polling, the party became more circumspect. Deputy Minister Sok An told reporters, "under the democratic process whether we win or whether we lose, it's a normal affair."[15] At that time, the CPP was leading in the densely populated provinces of Prey Veng and Takeo and in the smaller provinces of Kompong Speu, Koh Kong, Pursat, and Stung Treng, with a total of thirty-one seats. However, when Funcinpec started to gain in the polls in Phnom Penh, Battambang, and Kompong Chom, the CPP did an abrupt about-face. When UNTAC radio broadcast preliminary voting results on May 29 showing a strong lead for Funcinpec, SoC Foreign Minister Hor Namhong complained to UNTAC chief Yashushi Akashi about misleading the population, saying that "Radio UNTAC was not impartial at all, as it gave public opinion the very wrong impression that Funcinpec had a big lead vis-à-vis the CPP." Deputy Minister Uch Kiman went further and announced that "there are people who felt UNTAC might have been rigging the elections. A lot of people doubt the impartiality of UNTAC, and there are a lot of complaints that UNTAC has not been very impartial."[16] Voters were outraged by these suggestions, complaining that the CPP was looking for excuses to stay in power. It was because of its reputation for thuggery that many people braved the consequences and voted the party out of office.

Patronage, as a social and economic system of relationships between

[14]One possible explanation was that the Khmer Rouge believed that Funcinpec would win and wished to maintain the option of negotiating a political future for themselves in the new government.
[15]*The Nation* (Bangkok), May 31, 1993.
[16]Ibid.

patrons and clients, is an ever-changing power relationship that is continually being renegotiated, and its usefulness to clients decreases when the terms are increasingly dictated by the patrons. A process such as this appears to have begun during the Pol Pot regime and continued to a lesser degree under Hun Sen. Likewise, popular disaffection with rulers rises when they extract more from their clients than they are willing to give or when better alternatives appear. Both of these developments help explain why Hun Sen and his party lost the election. Cambodians complained that their avowed patrons for the past fourteen years had prescribed their relationships, rather than negotiating them; that their power was inflexible and harshly enforced; and that the party was philosophically meaningless to them. Arguably, if the CPP's intimidation of the voters had not been so effective, the proportion of the vote the CPP received would have been lower than the 37.75 percent it got.

THE MEANING OF THE 1993 ELECTIONS

The 1993 elections were an important turning point in Cambodian history and politics. The elections promised the end of two decades of civil war, the dismantling of a one-party state, the isolation and eventual demise of the Khmer Rouge, the reintegration of Cambodia into the international community, and the return of the monarchy in revised form overseeing the development of a multiparty political system with strong powers for the prime minister.

Despite death threats from the Khmer Rouge and intimidation from the CPP, 90 percent of the electorate turned out to vote. The Khmer Rouge strategy of boycotting the election failed. The movement is now isolated and may never recover its former strength. The message of the voters was clear: the majority do not want to fight any more, even if this meant bringing Khmer Rouge leaders such as Khieu Samphan to Phnom Penh to take up titular positions in a new government.

Popular attitudes toward and expectations of Sihanouk are harder to gauge. There is a strong tendency among rural voters, at least, to want the restoration of a strong and powerful monarchy. But as Cambodia's reintegration into the world community brings new ideas to its youth, it is doubtful that younger men and women will be content with an authoritarian monarch. Whether Funcinpec can maintain its popular support in the face of parties espousing other ideologies remains to be seen.

One of the more profound meanings of the election is its lesson in the power of the vote. This can have both positive and negative results. One positive result is that the weight of authoritarian power structures was sufficiently lifted by UNTAC's activities to allow Cambodians to conduct politics in ways new for them. In the months preceding the election, twenty political parties were formed, dozens of newspapers appeared on the street, and human rights associations were formed across the country. And when it came time to vote, UNTAC's promise of a secret ballot allowed the electorate to oust those they wanted out of power. If the election results continue to be respected, Cambodians may develop different attitudes toward authority and power, rejecting deference for accountability, and replacing fear with confidence in relations with officials.

A negative appraisal may arise if the elected government is unable to budge the CPP from its entrenched positions in the military, police, and provincial offices, where officials have created lucrative fiefdoms. It also remains to be seen whether Funcinpec has the resolve to build institutions, such as an independent judiciary, that can protect the political liberties spelled out in the new constitution. In either case, it may not be too optimistic to predict that Cambodia can never return to the worst practices of the past. This is not to say that political intimidation will cease, politics will be free of corruption, and the problem of the Khmer Rouge will be solved without bloodshed. But the fact that Cambodians have so courageously embraced a new kind of politics, which made popular rules of fair play and allowed voters a measure of autonomy and a spectrum of choice, was a promising beginning. The elections were held during a time when new forms of social and political organization energized the polity, creating a gap between state and society. Even if the 1993 election is the last of this century, it has created a desire for political rights and legal channels to express political ideas. If the reality begins to match the desire, this can only be the beginning of a better Cambodia.

Afterword

DANIEL S. LEV

The chapters in this volume, along with the discussions provoked at the Woodrow Wilson, constitute a landmark of sorts in the study of Southeast-Asian politics, but partly because of something they generally ignore. What is missing is any mention of culture as a starting point for analysis. This remarkable silence passes over one of the primary a priori assumptions of post–World War II research in the region. The explanatory perspectives that have taken its place imply, in an interesting U-turn, that politics in Southeast Asia is not extraordinary.

One would have thought that a conference on the meaning of elections in Southeast Asia would promptly set the flywheels of cultural analysis spinning. After all, it has long been a standard source for understanding politics just about everywhere except in the European and North American heartlands of what is called Western culture, where political thought seems to count for more. In Southeast Asia, cultural studies have an established, though not exclusive, pedigree that stretches back a couple of centuries. Colonial research followed two divergent paths. One began early in European efforts to unravel the mysteries of the Orient, producing a heritage of popular mythology and philological and ethnological research. The second, well represented by the late colonial work of Furnivall, was that of exploring social and economic organization under the influence of colonial policy.[1] Both lines of research continued after World War II, but while most scholars tended to follow the second, for a mix of reasons that included a widespread appreciation of the significance of local world-views, cultural interpretations had wider influence. Since the 1950s, social

---

[1] J. S. Furnivall, *An Introduction to the Political Economy of Burma* (Rangoon: Burma Book Club, 1931), *Colonial Policy and Practice: A Comparative Study of Burma and the Netherlands India* (Cambridge: Cambridge University Press, 1948), and *Netherlands India* (Cambridge: Cambridge University Press, 1944).

243

244 Daniel S. Lev

scientists have habitually paid obeisance, at least, to the cultural determinants that apparently explain politics, social movements, economic behavior, international engagement, and much else in the region.

Cultural interpretations sort out along a range from the highly sophisticated to the inane, from enlightening analysis of local values to numbing boilerplate generalizations about bents to sacral authority, social harmony, conflict avoidance, the influence of mysticism, and more. The best studies represent some of the most refined, subtle, and provocative work in modern social science, framing new perspectives on political behavior that have informed generations of researchers. Even the richest work, however—Geertz and Anderson on Indonesia, for example—has had sapping side effects.[2] For one thing, as cultural analysis tends to isolate the local, it promotes sui generis conceptions of Southeast Asian societies, discouraging wider comparisons. For another, despite the availability of alternative interpretations, the persuasiveness of cultural explanations and the receptivity to them of area specialists have lent them remarkable purchase. Absent challenging questions in search of new data, interesting hypotheses that deserved debate turned instead into simplistic shibboleths repeated endlessly de rigueur by local and foreign scholars alike. In Southeast Asia, unlike Europe and North America, too little knowledge and too few scholars have been available to brake these tendencies. The compulsion to find a cultural matrix to explain political, social, and economic behavior in the countries of the region has only recently begun to fade slightly.[3]

In the chapters of this book, culture is barely mentioned except in

[2]The cultural analyses of Clifford Geertz and Benedict Anderson have had profound influence on modern Indonesian studies. For a sampling, see Geertz's *The Religion of Java* (New York: Free Press, 1960) and *The Interpretation of Cultures* (New York: Basic Books, 1973); and Anderson's essay, "The Idea of Power in Javanese Culture," in Claire Holt, ed., *Culture and Politics in Indonesia* (Ithaca: Cornell University Press, 1972). Anderson is one of only a few scholars who have, with equal skill, moved back and forth between explorations of culture on the one hand and social and political change on the other; his reach, moreover, has thus far extended to Thailand and the Philippines as well as Indonesia.
[3]It has not faded all that much, however. A telling example is the current effort to find the cultural-religious base of Asian capitalism. The religions that Weber thought unlikely to support capitalism as neatly as European Protestantism have been found, after the fact, to have analogously appropriate values after all. Confucianism having explained Japan, Korea, Hong Kong, Taiwan, and Singapore, Thai (but not Burmese) Theravada, and no doubt Islam will soon reveal their true selves. The counterargument that Weber might have got it wrong and that the matter, on new evidence, may be rather more complex, has been paid relatively little attention.

passing. During the conference from which they derive, the subject was brought up explicitly only once by a participant who wondered out loud whether we might not be missing an important cultural dimension of elections in the region. He may have been right—if we can agree on what exactly we mean by culture—but no one bothered to follow up. Emphases had changed. A shift in direction was signaled a decade or more ago by a revival of interest in Furnivall's studies in the political economy of social pluralism in colonial Burma and Indonesia but also by new studies that either ignored or challenged cultural approaches to Southeast Asian politics.

Why political analysis should have taken this turn deserves more attention than it can get here as a problem in intellectual history. More knowledge and a growing sensitivity to complexity are one answer, but another may be located in the same social and ideological transformations that have made elections a central issue. During the 1950s, when parliamentary systems were actually in place in most of the region—Burma, Indonesia, Malaysia, the Philippines, Singapore, and sporadically Thailand—elections were paid little research attention. Such studies as there were focused narrowly on who won and who lost, reasonably for election studies, or didactically on how to do elections right, but not on the systemic implications of the electoral process in new political systems.[4]

Two contradictory assumptions may account for this neglect. One was the lingering view that as democracy was surely the wave of the future everywhere, elections were no great surprise that required special attention. The other took just the opposite, nonuniversalist position that because democratic values were absent in Southeast Asian countries, with the possible exception of the Philippines, elections would not survive or anyway did not mean the same as in the "West"; historical deviations out of line with dominant local mentalities, they could be ignored as basically irrelevant. This second view was apparently confirmed by the uncertain experience or collapse of parliamentary systems in Thailand, Burma, Indonesia, and the Philippines, and the revision of

[4]A search through the on-line catalogs—books only—of the Universities of Michigan and Washington came up with fewer than a half-dozen more or less serious election studies in Southeast Asia before 1970, in any language. With the decline of serious elections, however, the number of studies increases, which may have to do in part with the demography of political scientists but also with a rising interest in political reform in the region.

them in Singapore and Malaysia. Whatever the proximate causes of Phibun's and Sarit's coups, or Ne Win's, or Sukarno's Guided Democracy, or Suharto's New Order, or Marcos's martial law, or Lee's autocracy, or Mahathir's tight reins, culture seemed to offer a solid base of interpretation.

Both arguments are still around but crumbling fast, along with their epistemological and ideological foundations, vitiated by upheavals in Southeast Asian political economies and, less certainly, in the imaginations (and maybe the political temperaments) of social scientists in and out of the region. Scholars are growing doubtful about the explanatory power of culture because our notions of it do not easily accommodate change, and also, under the influence of postmodernist raids on historical givens, because we have become increasingly sensitive to the manipulability of what is called tradition.[5] In addition, probably for related reasons, scholars seem to have become less self-consciously disengaged politically, less reticent about their ideological commitments. It is no longer at all unusual for younger Southeast Asian social scientists to be active on the side of reform, usually liberal reform. Similarly, many of their Southeast Asianist colleagues abroad have become less respectful than they used to be of local political authority and its habits, once deferred to by reference to local tradition or culture, and rather more unabashedly interventionist by way of human-rights nongovernmental organizations (NGOs) and the like, often in collaboration with colleagues in the region. Reading Southeast Asia in the 1990s is different than in the 1950s, but not only because of accumulated knowledge.

What makes the subject of elections significant is the threat they pose to existing distributions of power and systems of authority and the promise they imply of wholly new political structures. Two or three decades ago neither challenge nor promise seemed quite so serious as it does now, which may explain why elections mean so much more now than before. Between then and now some of the essential supports of electorally based parliamentary systems have taken shape: expanding commercial, professional, and intellectual middle-class groups above all,

[5]Doubts about cultural explanations of politics had begun to emerge even before Edward Said's *Orientalism* (New York: Vintage, 1978), which had a receptive audience. Skepticism has deepened with the proliferation of postmodernist literature over the last decade. See, among others, Timothy Mitchell, *Colonising Egypt* (Cambridge: Cambridge University Press, 1988); Nicholas B. Dirks, ed., *Colonialism and Culture* (Ann Arbor: University of Michigan Press, 1992); and John Pemberton's *On the Subject of "Java"* (Ithaca: Cornell University Press, 1994).

whose circumstantial independence, economic power, intellectual influence, and disaffection in themselves erode the confidence of existing regimes in their own authority. Historically these same social strata have everywhere produced similar political complaints, demands, and visions. Increasingly, during the last twenty years or so, monumental tensions, conflicts, debates, and occasional violence have occurred over relations between state and society, or between ruling elites and new groups no longer impressed by them. The NGO movement now solidly imbedded in the region embodies the conception of a self-motivated society distinct from the state and with rights against its power. It is strongest precisely in those countries with fast-growing economies, slow-changing political orders, and outmoded administrative structures incapable of serving the demands made on them.

Not surprisingly, then, scholarly interest in elections has a political and ideological edge, one more apparent among Southeast Asian than foreign social scientists but hardly absent among any. The essays in this volume are analytically detached, by and large, yet also not devoid of political concern. There is more skepticism and worry than cynicism, and most of the authors see in elections either the reality of change or the prospect of it. Again, the emphasis on change, and perhaps the commitment to change, makes it hard to rely on cultural analysis, whose bias is toward continuity and stasis. Loosed from the intellectual compulsions and strictures of cultural analysis, with its enchanting capacity to explain just about anything post hoc, researchers can roam freely through political, economic, and social regions to examine the potential, consequences, and implications of elections.

If not culture, what then? A great deal, but what becomes especially clear, once the obscuring drape of culture is drawn back, is that the political systems of Southeast Asia are not unique, as they once seemed. Given a question about the meaning of elections, it turns out that one of the least certain and effective things they do is designate leaders and representatives, which may be true everywhere. For the rest, however, the study of elections may reveal just how political systems work and change in a jumble of demographic, social, economic, and ideological constraints.

Elections are most intricately complex in those countries where political change is unstoppable because of the transformation of economic and social structures, and elections themselves figure in the process of change. What is involved, generally, is a challenge to strong state elites—

whether bureaucratic, military, military-bureaucratic, or dominant single-party—in favor of political participation, institutional reform and control, and policy influence by nonstate actors. To describe such change, journalists, scholars, and assorted other observers have too easily adopted the rhetoric of democratization, much in vogue now. If our understanding of democracy is in any way Rousseauian, it is unlikely in the modern state. At most one can hope for a politically engaged society and such limited, indirect, and formal participatory features as elections. Promising far more than any state is inclined to deliver, democracy certainly is not achieved via elections alone. For those who take the idea of it seriously, whether as analytical construct or political tenet, it is probably best referred to as a standard by which to measure political participation, but for the rest it is neither realistic nor necessarily even preferable.[6]

To be exact, the objective of reform (not alone in Southeast Asia) is less democracy than the republic, which is rare enough and hard to make work, but more practicable and even, if we worry about restraints on popular will, more humanly sensible than democracy. The issue is neither pedantic nor caviling, but a matter of analytical precision, political realism, and honesty. Particularly is this so in the study of elections, which have become an icon of democracy and tend to deflect attention from serious problems of institutional reform that often count as much or more in the everyday lives of citizens.

Elections are a principal instrument of the republic, but to be dealt with realistically they need to be pulled from their democratic pedestal. Otherwise they almost inevitably disappoint. For in the modern republic elections are variably useful to contradictory interests, few of them oriented to the good of the whole of society. On the one hand, as Anderson suggests, the electoral process, to the extent that it legitimates a political system and its ruling class, may serve mainly to domesticate citizens more effectively by making them complicit in their own domination. Voters may do little more than rotate members of an established elite, as Mosca and Michels figured out a century ago. On the other hand, as Rodan argues here with respect to Singapore, if it is too much to cast

---

[6]The argument I am making here, on analogy with the Javanese habit of replacing personal names of unsuitable weight for their bearers, is that democracy is too heavy a description for modern political systems, in none of which is there all that much interest in relying consistently on plebiscitarian procedures. Public opinion polls are hardly an adequate substitute.

elections as the basis of democracy, neither are they meaningless. The studies of Malaysia by Jomo and Crouch and the Philippines by Kerkvliet confirm the proposition that although elections may not do everything expected of them, they undoubtedly have political effect. Secure elites may not worry much about elections but are well advised to heed them as an impressive sample of public opinion—and, as often as not, they do.

Bringing elections down to earth allows us to view them in the naked messiness and elusiveness that they actually incur everywhere. Rodan's insistence on recognizing their political effect beyond a predictable outcome of winners and losers is the starting point of most of the essays here, which compels an examination of the problems made manifest by the electoral process. A few such problems stand out in Thailand, where economic growth and social change have generated more complex and farther-reaching political conflicts over reform than elsewhere in Southeast Asia. The implications of such reform have come into question, as the chapters by Suchit Bunbongkarn and Anek Laothomatas acutely demonstrate. Elections in Thailand have, in effect, posed a challenge to democratic thought by highlighting existing social and economic cleavages. It is not only political elites for whom elections set a few traps, but also reformers whose vision is stymied by voter behavior. Elections, after all, do not unify but divide, emphasizing differences of interests, organization, and political style between, among others, economically and politically dominant urban centers and rural areas inherently disadvantaged in any competition for influence. Thai farmers have played the electoral game to redress some balances, frustrating urban interests and disappointing those for whom reform meant not merely popular participation but bureaucratic efficiency, political honesty, an Aristotelian respect for the interests of all, and a sophisticated appreciation of political, social, and economic issues. But who can define the interests of a whole country anywhere, and whose interests are served by what kind of efficiency, and is it true that corruption and coercion are the preserve of only rural constituencies? Elections may bring out the best in political systems and the worst in people—an argument for a well-conceived republic and the kinds of political education on which most of the essays in this collection agree.

If the chapters on Thailand represent the problem particularly well, the same issues are evident elsewhere in Southeast Asia, wherever state/society relations are complicated by the absence of serviceable state institutions and by growing tensions among divergent interests within society itself. On the one hand, a point raised by Anderson, unless an electorally based political system is founded on state institutional capacities adequate to the claims generated by change, elections are likely to create more problems than they solve. Thailand may actually have some advantages in this connection that are lacking in both Indonesia and the Philippines, as they have been, among other available examples, in Italy. On the other hand, precisely because elections may deepen social cleavages by giving them concrete expression, the same groups that supported elections as a means of asserting control over the state may turn away from them in order to restrict access to state largesse.

The consequent tension between parliamentary and bureaucratic political modes is a common feature of modern states. A constant tug-of-war goes on between various groups that see a distinct advantage in, and develop ideological commitments to, one or the other. Swings of an erratic pendulum are recorded in the history of constitutions, legal systems, party ideologies, electoral systems, regulatory principles, institutional structures, and political theories. The situation is particularly volatile where politically dominant military establishments have a proven stake on the bureaucratic side, as in Thailand, Indonesia, and Burma. In these cases, officer corps, even after they have lost legitimacy or retreated from direct political command, as in Thailand, are tempting as potential allies for those who wish to avoid parliamentary controls or have been disappointed by the results of democratic experiments.

Elections, then, as the essays in this book demonstrate, provide no simple, neat, definitive solutions to most fundamental questions and are, moreover, a source of many intractable problems. If they fall short of democracy, they are essential but not enough for an effective republic. What is at issue over elections in Southeast Asia is the redefinition of political systems to allot, in various contestable proportions, space to the exercise of popular will, or at least public opinion. Elections symbolically reconstitute the relationship between state and society, separating the one from the other, establishing new rules of legitimacy to go with new elites arisen from new sources of wealth, power, and influence. But how much influence the electoral process is allowed to have, what it actually does and means within a political system, is a partially negotiated, partially coerced product, fully comprehensible only in the circumstances of local history.

Only in local proportions are resources of institutional capacity, legitimacy, influential status and power, and popular support mixed and brought to bear in shaping the functions of elections within a political system. Consequently, the study of elections must take into account whose chances are improved or weakened by them, for the advantages of elections to many groups may not be all that great. It is this reality that renders electoral corruption and manipulation complicated subjects, for if such abuse usually favors the powerful, it may also allow weaker groups to adapt to new rules of the game.

Elections, then, are only an introduction to a bewildering set of associated issues in Southeast Asian politics that require attention of a sort, now, that assumes not so much cultural stability, institutional continuity, or social structural solidity but, rather, change in most of the fundamentals one can imagine. The electoral republic, wherever it happens to be taking form, naturally generates new problems in an endless struggle between social classes and organized groups to sculpt political systems favorable to their own ends. Thinking about elections inevitably suggests further research on political parties, party systems, and the fashioning of appropriate electoral systems, but also the organization of economic and social interests, the formation of new political elites, the reformation of state institutions, and the working out of ideologically conceived virtues and pathologies to suit everything else. Reading this book about elections in Southeast Asia makes it hard to stop at elections.

It is also hard to miss something else that bears methodological, theoretical, and maybe even ideological significance. These essays make it clear that Southeast Asian politics and political systems are not a genre apart. The issues that arise from studies of elections in Southeast Asia are not in principle different from similar issues anywhere else; and these essays suggest ideas that might usefully be applied elsewhere. Yet there is a worrisome question that probably ought still to torture all comparatists. For all the similarities, are there also differences that can be accounted for only by some better-defined notion of culture?

Index

254 *Index*

Index